# Bureaucratic Behavior
## in the
## Executive Branch

# Bureaucratic Behavior in the Executive Branch

## An Analysis of Organizational Change

LOUIS C. GAWTHROP

ASSOCIATE PROFESSOR OF POLITICAL SCIENCE
STATE UNIVERSITY OF NEW YORK AT BINGHAMTON

THE FREE PRESS, NEW YORK
COLLIER-MACMILLAN LIMITED, LONDON

To V. B. G.

# Preface

The interpretation and explanation of behavior in any organization—public or private—is basically a study of change. How do organizations respond to internal and external environmental change? How do they attempt to affect change within their own structures? And how do organization members, in turn, respond to changes fostered by their superiors?

Many organizations expend considerable amounts of their available resources simply to be able to forecast change long before it actually occurs. Other organizations, however, respond to change less actively. Still others attempt to ignore the forces of change, usually only to fade into obscurity because, as change is inevitable, neither man nor organizations can ignore it and hope to survive for long. Viewed in this context, organizational change can provide an excellent focal point to analyze bureaucratic behavior within a given organizational setting.

To advance this proposition, however, is simply to indicate that the concept of change is itself meaningless; it has no substantive content *per se*. One does not study "change"; instead one examines change by observing the way specific organizational phenomenon varies over specified periods of time. Thus, change simply provides a conceptual framework which can be utilized to develop meaningful relationships among substantive organizational aspects. The description and evaluation of the patterns of variation in the substantive content of organizational behavior is what is meant by "change."

For instance, to understand how and why an organization responds to internal and external change the way it does, the question of organizational loyalty must be considered. The intensity of a sense of loyalty which an individual feels toward his organization will, to a great extent, influence his willingness to alter his behavioral patterns in accordance with organizational directives. In other words, it can be suggested that the extent to which any organization is capable (or incapable) of developing a strong sense of allegiance among its members will significantly affect the manner in which it is able to respond (either positively or negatively) to change. But as some wags have occasionally noted, man has all the characteristics of a dog, except loyalty—which simply suggests that organizational loyalty is a learned trait. How the organization may proceed to develop this subjective feeling among its membership is one of the major areas of inquiry that should be explored if organizational change is to be viewed in its proper perspective. However, a strong impression reflected here is that little insight can be gained into this complex question unless two other facets of administrative behavior are given prior consideration.

First, some attention must be directed to how decisions are made within an organization, and, on an entirely different level, how any given administrative structure is organized to make decisions. Second, attention must also be directed to how conflict is resolved within organizational settings. Making decisions and resolving conflict are two functions required of every organization, not to mention every human being. A major premise assumed here is that both are integrally related to each other; both are directly related to the concept of organizational loyalty; and both are indirectly related to the problems of organizational change. The primary purpose of the chapters that follow is to develop a systematic analysis of this premise as it relates specifically to the executive branch of the United States government.

Thus, the manner in which the executive branch of the federal government resolves internal conflict, makes decisions, develops a sense of loyalty within its ranks, and responds to the internal and external forces of change will be examined. Hopefully, this sequence will permit a smooth transition from the basic to the more complex levels of bureaucratic behavior.

In addition, a basis for comparative analysis has been included. Because the concepts to be explored can be discussed only in relative—and, hence, relational—terms, the analysis of each concept, as it applies to the executive bureaucracy, is paired with a similar treatment directed at private, nongovernmental organizations. In this fashion, a broader perspective of administrative behavior generally can be gained, and the conclusions and propositions advanced concerning bureaucratic behavior in the executive branch specifically can be made more meaningful. Furthermore, by applying some of the more well-established and generally accepted propositions and theories that have developed in the literature of private organizations to governmental situations, similar and dissimilar behavioral patterns may be disclosed. In those instances where similarities in administrative behavior do emerge, an easy means of identification can be established; and in instances of dissimilar behavioral patterns, the differences can be meaningfully explored.

The overall focus of this study is on the development of an analytical model which can be used to explain the functioning of bureaucratic systems. The descriptive propositions are advanced as hypotheses to be tested. Without theory, empirical research becomes purposeless, and without synthesis, the advancement of knowledge ceases. The type of synthesis which has been attempted here includes not only combining relevant data and theory from the private and public spheres of organizations, but also combining a positivist and normative approach to organizational behavior in political bureaucracies. Indeed, given the wide range of normative considerations which enter into virtually every aspect of public bureaucracy, it is unrealistic to ignore this aspect of organizational behavior. The primary purpose of combining these two approaches is to offer a revision of the traditional normative debate, which, for years, has dominated the "politics of administration" dialogue, in terms of the analytical model which is developed.

Only one brief clarifying note seems necessary at this point: The term "private organization" as used repeatedly in the subsequent chapters should be specifically interpreted to refer to the large, complex, private industrial and business corporations in our society. This, of course, eliminates many other types of private organizations, just as there are many public governmental organizations other than those located in the executive branch of the federal government. Be this as it may, the purpose here is not to write a miniature "handbook of organizations." The present inquiry, to repeat, is limited to how bureaucratic behavior in the executive branch of the federal government is conditioned to respond to the inevitable demands for change. This inquiry is developed within a context of some well-established propositions borrowed from the literature on large, complex, profit-motivated, product-producing, private corporations. Hopefully, the comparison will prove to be enlightening as well as valuable in focusing on some of the most salient characteristics of governmental bureaucracy.

In the preparation of this inquiry Richard Fenno, Frank Rourke, Tom Davy, and Sid Wise were, as usual, generous in their willingness to read substantial portions of the manuscript. They are absolved, of course, from any deficiencies which may remain. I was especially fortunate to obtain the excellent secretarial skills of a true professional, Miss Alice Buck, in the preparation of the final draft. Furthermore, I am deeply indebted to my colleagues at the State University of New York at Binghamton for providing the indirect and frequently intangible types of support so vital to the success of any research effort. Finally, it is hardly necessary to add that my primary source of support and confidence was derived from my wife. Her aid and assistance are reflected throughout these pages in innumerable ways.

*Louis C. Gawthrop*

# Acknowledgements

Permission for the use of passages of copyrighted material from the following publishers and authors is gratefully acknowledged:

Center for the Study of Democratic Institutions for John Wilkinson's article "Possible Futures," contained in *Center Diary: 17* (1967).

McGraw-Hill Book Company for *Changing Organizations* by Warren Bennis, copyright 1966.

John Wiley and Sons, Inc., for *Administrative Decision-Making* by William J. Gore, copyright 1964.

William Capron for his panel paper, "The Impact of Analysis on Bargaining in Government," delivered before The American Political Science Association in New York, September, 1966.

Houghton-Mifflin Company and William Heinemann, Ltd., London, for *The Coming of the New Deal* by Arthur M. Schlesinger, Jr., copyright 1958.

American Management Association and Whirlpool Corporation for quotations contained in AMA Research Study No. 32, *Management Creeds and Philosophies*, copyright 1958.

Prentice-Hall, Inc., for *Organizational Decision Making* by Marcus Alexis and Charles Z. Wilson, copyright 1967.

The Macmillan Company for *The Economics of Political Parties* by Seymour Harris, copyright 1962.

UNESCO for "Ends and Means in Planning" by Edward C. Banfield, contained in *International Social Science Journal*, Vol. 11, No. 3, 1959.

Harper and Row, Publishers, for abridgment of pages 249, 250, 256, 274–75 from *Conduct of the New Diplomacy* by James L. McCamy, copyright 1964.

# CONTENTS

PREFACE V

ACKNOWLEDGEMENTS ix

1. The Meaning of Bureaucracy 1

2. Controlling Conflict—Nongovernmental
Organizations 21

3. Controlling Conflict—The Federal Executive
Structure 47

4. Decision Making—Theoretical Considerations 82

5. Executive Branch Decision Making 105

6. Organizational Loyalty 131

7. Organizational Change—A Conceptual Model 172

8. Executive Branch Consolidation 189

9. Executive Branch Innovation 214

10. Conclusion 239

INDEX 269

# 1

# The Meaning of Bureaucracy

Bureaucracy is a term which lends itself to emotional responses. The Bureaucrat is no great hero in our folklore of the rugged individual. Furthermore, one gets the impression that for the average citizen, bureaucracy and the bureaucrat are terms that normally are associated with governmental functions. Thus, an assistant to the head of the U. S. Treasury Department is a bureaucrat, while the assistant to the head of the "treasury department" of U. S. Steel is an administrator. The comptroller function in the U. S. Government is carried out by the Comptroller General, and his office is part of the bureaucracy; the same function within Du Pont is carried out by an administrative subunit within the corporation.

The truth of the matter is that bureaucracy is a generic characterization of all large-scale, complex organizations, public and private. It is not an exclusive property of governmental units. This, of course, does not mean that there are no differences between governmental and nongovernmental organizations.

The executive structures of the federal government and General Motors are different in many important respects, even though both reveal highly developed bureaucratic characteristics. However, before these differences and similarities are examined, a clear understanding of the particular characteristics of bureaucratic organizations, and how these differ from nonbureaucratic organizations, is essential. The purpose of this chapter, then, is to establish at the outset a bureaucratic model that can be used in subsequent chapters to explore the nature of the federal executive structure.

## Distinguishing Characteristics of Bureaucracy

The classic model of bureaucracy, of course, stems from the writings of the German sociologist, Max Weber (1864–1920).[1] As seen by Weber, the principal characteristics of bureaucracy can be reduced to the following specific functions: (1) bureaucratic jurisdiction is precisely fixed by operating rules and regulations, (2) bureaucratic structures are hierarchially organized on the basis of a firmly established pattern of superior-subordinate relationships, (3) the formal internal operation, or management, of the bureaucracy is accomplished through the transmission of intraorganizational communications, decisions, directives, and so on, in the form of written documents, which are preserved as permanent records of the organization, and (4) bureaucratic officials must reflect a high degree of administrative specialization and expertise, not only concerning their specific functional responsibilities, but also concerning the operating rules, regulations, and procedures of the bureaucratic organization itself.

[1] "Bureaucracy," *From Max Weber*, Hans Gerth and C. Wright Mills (eds.) (New York: Oxford University Press, 1946), and Max Weber, *Theory of Social and Economic Organization*, trans. by A. M. Henderson and T. Parsons (New York: Oxford University Press, 1947).

Weber's purpose was to formulate an ideal-type definition of a particular form of social organization, viz., a bureaucracy. These characteristics are not to be found in actual bureaucratic structures in their ultimate degree. Rather, they must be viewed as relative and not absolute tendencies. For instance, it should be apparent that not all organizations are bureaucratic structures. The first and second characteristics cited above are frequently evidenced in innumerable small groups that are technically classified simply as organizations. However, an important difference between bureaucratic and nonbureaucratic tendencies is suggested by the last two characteristics. If both of these factors exist, then it is fair to assume the existence of a bureaucratic operation. Therefore, the conditions which may be necessary for the third and fourth characteristics to develop need to be considered.

### Size

Although it is impossible to specify the precise point in the development of an organization when bureaucratic characteristics emerge, it is reasonable to suggest that the size of the organization represents an important factor. Simply stated, when intraorganizational communications can no longer be effectively transmitted on the basis of interpersonal, "face-to-face" verbal exchanges, Weber's third characteristic must be adopted if operating effectiveness is to be maintained.

In more precise terms, the size of the organization directly affects the role patterns of its members. In the growth of an organization, when that point is reached where top-level organization officials, who are responsible for the formulation of policy decisions, are no longer able to participate in, or supervise directly, the actual implementation of these policy decisions, a basic role dichotomy must develop within the organization that clearly separates—physically as well as psychologically—the positions of authority from the specialized positions of function,[2] or, the policy makers from the administrators. When this state is reached, and roles become dichotomized, bureaucratic procedures normally result.

For instance, the organization's top-level policy makers become almost totally dependent upon information collected and prepared by others who are completely removed from the formal policy-making process. Consequently, intricately involved reporting procedures are usually devised to insure that such information will be received in reliable and accurate form. Furthermore, since verbal communications must be replaced by written transmittals, standardized formats and routing procedures must be developed in an effort to maximize transmittal speed and accuracy. Finally, the organization's system of graded authority will, in all probability, become increasingly structured in order to insure (at least, theoretically) that at any point within the organization, at any given time, individual responsibility and accountability can be precisely pinpointed.

### Time

Another aspect that contributes to the development of bureaucratic procedures in any organization is the passage of time. Time, like change, has no substantive content. It is an important factor, nonetheless, in the study of bureaucratic behavior, generally, and organizational change, specifically. And in considering the conditions needed to satisfy Weber's bureaucratic model, the passage of time along with size are basic.

Consider the proposition that any group could duplicate Weber's four main bureaucratic characteristics with deliberate efforts. Almost everyone is familiar with the antics of aspiring bureaucratic marionettes who head small social or fraternal

[2] Robert Presthus, *The Organizational Society* (New York: Alfred Knopf, 1962), pp. 27–36.

associations, or who are in charge of small work groups. To these individuals, in-group relationships are regulated by the most formalistic procedures. The result, of course, is a gross caricature of the bureaucratic model despite the fact that every tangible characteristic of a bureaucracy may be present. It is evident, therefore, that some other factor must be present before a true bureaucratic organization can emerge.

With one exception, each of Weber's bureaucratic characteristics can easily be verified empirically. The lone exception involves the fourth condition, which requires that bureaucratic officials must become experts in their functional specialities, *as well as experts in the nature of bureaucracy itself.* This latter point is essentially an intangible quality that actually involves the personal development of a particular set of organizational attitudes and values. In other words, bureaucracies can *only* be made to operate efficiently by individuals who reflect a bureaucratic orientation—e.g., the bureaucrats—and it is only with the passage of time that such an orientation can be expected to develop.

If an organization prematurely adopts bureaucratic procedures, the previously existing, informal, and interpersonal behavioral patterns may continue to function as effectively as ever. In this case, only the empty shell of a bureaucratic structure exists. On the other hand, if the size and scope of the organization destroy the efficacy of these informal behavioral patterns, bureaucratic operating procedures must, of necessity, be substituted, and a bureaucratic orientation will eventually evolve in the minds of the operating personnel. Such a process, of course, involves the passage of time and, for this reason, time itself must be viewed as an important contributory factor in the development of a bureaucratic orientation. Furthermore, it is through the passage of time that various bureaucratic factors are able to manifest themselves in a manner that yields organizational continuity, builds up an organization "memory bank," establishes effective operating procedures, and develops a sense of organizational loyalty that transcends any personal commitment to the leader or top executive.

The growth of an organization from infancy to bureaucratic adulthood is well illustrated by the administrative development associated with the United States foreign aid program. The initial efforts at formulating organizational structures and procedures for this program have been described by Herbert Simon. As he noted, by April 13, 1948, approximately thirty people were associated with the first agency established to administer the foreign aid program, the Economic Cooperation Administration. Nine days later, ECA personnel had "mushroomed" to 138, and by July 26, 741 individuals were employed by the agency. Also on July 26 the first official organizational chart of the ECA was reproduced. "From the beginning of August on, it provided a set of historic boundaries in terms of which new claims for territory had to be argued."[3] The foundations for a bureaucratic *structure* were laid in the early months of the program's development. However, for a number of reasons, the development of a bureaucratic *orientation* lagged behind the structural and procedural developments for nearly two years. Not until the ECA was phased out and replaced by a new agency, the Mutual Security Administration, did the gap begin to close. As a result of the Korean War the concept of mutual security replaced the theme of European recovery as the dominant operating focal point of the aid program. The scope of the operations of the MSA was expanded to include Asia, as well as Europe, and military, as well as economic assistance. In the process the agency and the program became more complex; the compactness and relative simplicity of the administrative operations of the ECA were gradually lost. In addition, the glamour, excitement, and strong sense of personal dedication that had characterized

[3] "Birth of an Organization: The Economic Cooperation Administration," *Public Administration Review,* vol. 13 (December, 1953), p. 235.

the initial period of the ECA were slowly replaced by a more orthodox set of bureaucratic attitudes on the part of MSA personnel. In short, it was only through the passage of time that the bony frame of the bureaucratic adolescent began to fill out and develop as a fully mature bureaucratic organization.

Each of these points will be examined in greater detail in subsequent chapters. For our present purposes, however, having discussed the characteristics of bureaucracy, and the two major factors which contribute to the development of these characteristics, the major advantages and disadvantages which are normally associated with bureaucratic organizations can now be examined.

## Advantages of Bureaucratic Organizations

A basic prerequisite for a realistic understanding of the executive branch of government is an objective recognition of the fact that bureaucracy itself is neither good nor bad. It is a neutral term which connotes a particular type of organization without imputing any value judgment. Applying ethical or moral norms to organization goals, one may assume that "good" and "bad" *organizations* do exist. Various complex gambling syndicates have revealed a highly refined and sophisticated application of bureaucratic methods. On the other hand, so, also, do many of our major church groups. Condemnation of one and approval of the other does not—or at least should not—stem from the nature of their bureaucratic structure. Bureaucracy is simply an administrative device that can be employed to accomplish an effective means-ends relationship. Any assessment of the means must be accomplished in terms of the extent to which they positively or negatively affect the attainment of goals.

Insofar as the positive aspects of bureaucracy—i.e., its advantages—are concerned, the simplification of complex tasks ranks high. Complex organizations are constantly confronted with complex problems which require complex solutions. As a result of human limitations—physical and mental—these solutions can only be found if the problems are successively subdivided into a series of related simple problems. A bureaucratic organization satisfies this requirement by segmenting the overall organization into a set of highly specialized subunits, each assigned responsibility for a single phase of the overall operation. Although a modern industrial assembly line can hardly be considered a bureaucracy, the principle is the same. By subdividing a complex problem into simple and manageable proportions, ideally a set of simplified solutions will emerge that can be unified into a single complex solution to the previously unmanageable complex problem.

A second major advantage of bureaucracy logically follows from the first. Because tasks must be simplified, functional specialization results, and it is the process of specialization which produces what Weber referred to as the "technical superiority" of bureaucracy. Thus, every complex problem, having been broken down into small, manageable proportions, is then examined, analyzed, and "solved" by a group of trained specialists or experts who, in their respective capacities, are capable of responding with precision, speed, and maximum efficiency. Viewing the subunits within the bureaucratic structure collectively, the operating efficiency and goal attainment functions of the organization are enhanced significantly by the utilization of expert knowledge which focuses on narrow segments of a total problem.

A third major advantage of bureaucracy also follows logically from the previously stated propositions. If the simplification of complex tasks yields a set of subunit specializations and a correspondingly high degree of individual expertise in each area, then expertise should—theoretically, at any rate—encourage an increase in objective, impersonal decision making at the subunit level. For example, the decision-making process in a nonbureaucratic, small-group setting may be conducted on the basis of very informal and even personal considerations. Under these circumstances, all members of the organization either participate in, or perceive that they are capable of participating in, the actual decision-making process. Consequently, subjective values can be applied to operating procedures without necessarily diminishing the overall efficiency of the organization. Indeed, in this type of organizational setting the "human" or personal factor of administration becomes the most distinguishing characteristic of the nonbureaucratic model. The corner grocery store obviously has a much greater degree of flexibility to deal with its customers on a personal or "humanistic" basis than does the branch store of one of the major food chains. Consequently, it seems reasonable to conclude that subjective-type decisions, based on personal considerations, need not necessarily be "bad" or disruptive if this personal bias can be standardized throughout the entire organization. But within large, complex organizations, where the interpersonal, informal, face-to-face relationships cannot be maintained, the standardization of personal bias can no longer be assured. Under these circumstances, as Weber noted, the continued application of an individual's own subjective values to policy or operating decisions can seriously disrupt the operating effectiveness of the organization.

To avoid the dysfunctions associated with the utilization of personal biases by organizational members, bureaucracies generally have two alternative devices which can be employed—specialization and socialization. In the first instance, the subjective values of the individual are, in effect, *eliminated* by thoroughly routinizing work tasks. In the second instance, personal biases are *replaced* by a set of subjective values and attitudes approved by the organization. In both instances, the techniques of bureaucracy have been employed to minimize the internal personal conflict which may develop between organizational procedures and individual values. On the assembly line, a mechanical or physiological solution can frequently be applied to maximize the occurrence of purely objective responses on the part of the employees.[4] In the executive levels of the modern corporation, a standardized set of organizational values is superimposed on one's personal values. In both instances, the end result to be achieved is the same—individual ambiguity is minimized and organizationally approved behavior is standardized.

## Disadvantages of Bureaucratic Organizations

Despite the obvious advantages of a bureaucratic approach to the *solution* of broad, complex problems, bureaucracies can also *create* problems, or problem situations, which, for the most part, nonbureaucratic organizations can avoid. This is not to suggest that each of these problems is, in fact, evidenced in every bureaucratic organization, or that none of them are ever evidenced in nonbureaucratic settings. However, given the basic characteristics that differentiate bureaucratic and nonbureaucratic organizations, it does seem reasonable to suggest that it is easier for the latter groups to avoid and/or resolve these problems.

The two basic internal problems that are evidenced within every bureaucratic organization are: (1) the manner in which organizational behavior is controlled and (2) the effectiveness of the internal decision-making process. In both instances, the greater the size, scope, and complexity of the bureaucratic structure, the more serious both problems become, and, conse-

---

[4] For a good summary statement of the literature on physiological organizational theory (also referred to as scientific management) as it has evolved from the concepts of its founder, Frederick W. Taylor, see James G. March and Herbert A. Simon, *Organizations* (New York: John Wiley and Sons, Inc., 1965), Ch. 2.

quently, the greater the share of organizational resources which must be utilized to maintain maximum operating effectiveness in both areas.

### The Control of Organizational Behavior

The problem of control is central to *any* organization, and is really quite simply stated: How does an organization get its members to act the way it wants them to act? Used in this context the term *organization* is not to be viewed as an organic entity in the philosophical sense. An organization is actually a composite image of the attitudes, values, and beliefs of its members, and especially its top-level officials. Admittedly, the effects of operating continuity tend to blur the past, the present, and the future into one conglomerate image which frequently gives rise to the romantic notion of *The Organization*. Nevertheless, it must be recognized that organization decisions are made by individuals—by fallible human beings—and they must be examined in this perspective.

In order to maximize individual effectiveness, the bureaucratic organization must insure that actual performance of its administrators closely coincides with the established expectations. However, this is only possible if the individual is aware of the full range of expectations that are placed on his performance. In other words, the individual should be fully informed as to how he is expected to carry out his assigned tasks, how his specific role relates to the roles of the other individuals assigned to his immediate subunit, and how the function of his specific subunit relates to the overall goals, policies, and programs of the bureaucratic organization. The extent to which these conditions are satisfied depends almost exclusively on the speed, accuracy, and clarity with which the organization's policies and procedures, its demands and expectations, and its rules and regulations are communicated to the individual member through the hierarchal structure.

This relates directly to Weber's "dehumanizing" tendency of bureaucracy. In practical terms, the goal of any complex organization should be to minimize—indeed, eliminate—individual behavior that is contrary to the responses desired by the organization. As noted above, one way to achieve this goal is to limit as narrowly as possible the discretionary range of alternative courses of action at the disposal of the individual, or, more simply, to limit the number of alternatives that are available to him. The assembly line operator who tightens the bolts on the right front and rear wheels of the new automobiles as they pass by is really not confronted with too many decision-making dilemmas which could affect his operating performance. However, as individual responsibility increases, administrative discretion must also increase, and the range of the individual's behavioral responses becomes more complex. Under these circumstances, the bureaucratic organization cannot literally control every decision and every action of the subordinate. It cannot limit his alternatives simply because it cannot anticipate all of the possible alternatives that might occur. Thus, a second way in which the bureaucratic structure may attempt to eliminate individual behavior contrary to the responses desired by the organization is to proceed on the assumption that the subordinate official will always gauge his decisions and his actions in terms of the best interests of the organization.

Normally, this assumption will be operationally valid if (1) the individual has a clear conception of what is expected of him in terms of preferred behavior, (2) he has a clear conception of the resources at the disposal of the organization which can be used to reward approved behavior (and which can be denied in the absence of such behavior), and (3) he is convinced that the risks involved in deviating from his expected behavioral pattern outweigh any advantage that may be incurred.

In actual practice, however, very few large, complex organizations ever attain this ideal state. Despite the frequently stated administrative principle that the loyalty of the individual member should be directed exclusively to the overall bureaucratic structure, the fact remains that for many individuals the specific subunit to which they are assigned becomes, for all practical purposes, their Organization. Frequently, bureaucratic loyalty is perceived in terms of subunit loyalty; organizational rewards and satisfactions are seen as being obtained through the subunit, or not at all; and operating values and norms are imposed directly on the individual by his subunit and only indirectly on him by The Organization.

Furthermore, in any large, complex bureaucratic structure, organizational goals can rarely be stated in clear and precise terms. Goals, as such, are not designed to provide objective and rational definitions of purpose but, rather, are geared to supply the basic ingredient needed to gain an emotional, ethical, or normative commitment from the individual administrator. For the most part, goals of bureaucratic organizations represent broad generalizations which are quite ambiguous in content, but which are easily adaptable throughout the entire organization. That is to say, because of their ambiguous nature, such statements must be given specific content if purposeful behavior is to result. In effect, this means that the goals have to be translated into many different "languages" or programs that can be meaningfully adapted by each of the specialized subunits within the overall organization. But, in the process of translating general policy goals into specific programmatic actions, the organization loses a certain degree of control over its component subunits.

Given a specific program to implement, each subunit is on its own, so to speak, to carry out its responsibilities in a manner consistent with the overall policy goals of the organization. However, since these goals are ambiguous to begin with, they are subject to diverse interpretations by the various subunits which have a tendency to view these generalized policy goals in

terms of their own specialized interests. Thus, conflicting interpretations of organizational goals are a consistently present
problem in any large bureaucratic setting.

In small, nonbureaucratic organizations the likelihood of
this type of conflict developing, although not extinct, is significantly lessened. Daily, face-to-face, interpersonal relationships
diminish the possibility of misunderstanding and increase the
degree of organizational consensus, at least insofar as what the
goals of the organization mean to imply. The sales manager of a
small, nonbureaucratic-type organization may walk downstairs
to discuss a problem with the production manager, and the two
may walk over to the warehouse to get the views of the distribution manager. But an entirely different situation prevails when
divisions rather than offices are separated by hundreds of miles
rather than hundreds of feet. In both cases conflict may develop
in the specialized units. The major distinction between the two
is that in the nonbureaucratic setting, conflicting subunit pre-
ceptions of organizational goals are frequently more easily
reconciled with the overall goal objectives than is the case within
a bureaucratic structure, although it must be recognized that
basic disagreement over the choice of goals can result in both
settings. In this regard, nonbureaucratic organizations enjoy no
apparent advantage or suffer no disadvantage vis-à-vis their
bureaucratic counterparts.

One conclusion which emerges from this bureaucratic
problem situation is that the image of the large, complex organization as being "monocratically organized"[5] leaves something
to be desired insofar as a realistic description of bureaucracy is
concerned. Instead, a composite image of bureaucracy emerges
in which subunit goals, loyalties, norms, sanctions, and rewards
blend together to form the composite. To a very real extent, the
organization is controlled by its subunits, just as much as it is able

---

[5] Max Weber, *From Max Weber, op. cit.,* p. 197.

to control them. Unless the organization is prepared to expend a disproportionate share of its resources to achieve and maintain a monocratically controlled internal order, the composite image referred to will have to be accepted as a reasonable substitute. This represents a serious problem for bureaucratic organizations, and one which will be examined in greater detail in the next two chapters.

### Effective Decision Making

The second basic problem capable of causing decreased operating efficiency within any organization involves the procedural devices that are employed to insure an effective decision-making process. In bureaucracies, especially, this represents a continuing dilemma that can seriously disrupt operating effectiveness.

One of the most widely accepted theories of public administration which dominated the literature in this field for nearly fifty years was the policy-administration dichotomy.[6] Although it has become increasingly less persuasive in its appeal in recent years, at the height of its recognition this theory served as the definitive guide to proper organization decision-making procedures. Within the context of this theory, a clear and precise

6 Some of the early scholars of public administration who shared this view were: Woodrow Wilson, "The Study of Public Administration," *Political Science Quarterly*, vol. 2, 1887, pp. 197–222; Frank Goodnow, *Politics and Administration* (New York: Macmillan, 1900); Leonard D. White, *Introduction to the Study of Public Administration* (New York: Macmillan, 1926); and W. F. Willoughby, *Principles of Public Administration* (Baltimore: Johns Hopkins Press, 1927). For examples of the literature which marks the demise of this theory see: Fritz Morstein Marx (ed.), *The Elements of Public Administration* (Englewood Cliffs: Prentice-Hall, 1946); Paul H. Appleby, *Policy and Administration* (University: University of Alabama Press, 1949); Herbert A. Simon, Donald W. Smithburg, and Victor A. Thompson, *Public Administration* (New York: Alfred A. Knopf, 1950); and Dwight Waldo, *The Administrative State* (New York: The Ronald Press, 1948).

distinction could be applied to all bureaucratic organizations between the policy-making functions and all other functions which were purely administrative in character. Decision making was the exclusive responsibility of top-level executive officials, who were expected to be sensitive to the relevant social, economic, and political considerations of the moment. However, once these decisions were made, they were then to be implemented by the value-free administrative specialist whose major contribution to the system was his impersonal, expert objectivity. The theoretical dichotomy was clear, precise, and, unfortunately, unrealistic.

Top-level executive officials—the policy makers—have become, in this age of advanced complexity, extensively dependent upon their bureaucratic subordinates in several important respects. Conversely, of course, this implies that the bureaucratic subordinates—the administrative officials—have become extensively involved in the policy-making process. The extent to which this is the case may vary among different organizations, but certainly one can conclude that the clear dichotomy which was said to exist between these two functions does not provide a very meaningful insight into the true nature of organizational decision making.

In the first place, it is all too obvious that within any bureaucratic organization—governmental or nongovernmental—the best devised plans of top-level policy makers can be seriously impaired—either deliberately or otherwise—by the actions of administrative officials who are assigned the responsibility for implementing the basic policy decisions. Legitimate miscalculations, oversights, poor judgment, and so on, by administrators can decrease the effectiveness of any policy decision. In a more deliberate sense, subordinate administrative officials can directly affect the outcome of policy decisions through the manner in which they *choose* to implement these decisions. One of the most effective means administrative subordinates can employ to alter top-level policy decisions is through over-compliance or literal implementation. Law enforcement officials have the potential power to halt the judicial machinery of virtu-ally any local community simply by literally enforcing their respective municipal codes.

In the second place it can be said that policy makers have become increasingly dependent upon administrators to supply them with a constant source of relevant, accurate, and meaning-ful (i.e., easily comprehensible) information. Ideally, of course, the bureaucratic organization should be structured to insure that all relevant information affecting present or future policies will be made readily available to the top-level executive officials. However, as desirable as this may appear, it cannot be applied literally. In most instances it is not even known what raw data are relevant; but, even if this limitation could be overcome, consider the effort that would be required to review and analyze all of the raw data which was directly relevant to the existing or future policies of an organization.

Therefore, in the third place, policy makers in large-scale, complex bureaucracies have become increasingly dependent upon administrators to carry out the function of information consolidation. Decisions are made from the bottom to the top of the hierarchal structure as the relevant data is passed from one level to the next. Because the organization "funnel" is in-verted, the administrative "law of gravity" does not insure that every bit of raw data or information fed into the base of the structure will eventually reach the apex. Indeed, in this respect the administrative process is very similar to a chemical process in which the end product may bear little resemblance to any of the individual raw materials that were originally introduced.

Every administrative subordinate acts as a data filter for his immediate superior, who, in turn, must also serve as a filter for the man to whom he is accountable. Each of these individuals makes certain decisions as to what information is to be passed on to higher echelons, and, although they are by no means completely "free agents," the important element of discretion is introduced at every level. By the time the process culminates at the apex, the top-level policy officials are, more often than not, confronted with the task of deciding which set of decisions to accept. These official policy makers, in many respects, become policy ratifiers who grant organizational legitimacy to certain suggested courses of action.

The delegation of real decision-making power is inevitable in the large bureaucratic structure. The risks involved, however, are high and constant. The most trusted and competent subordinate will make some poor judgments in the screening process. Potentially vital information may be viewed as trivial, and not passed on. Or, even when importance may be recognized, information may be refined to the point where its true value is lost or distorted. How to keep the information channels open to the top of the organization is a fundamental problem facing every complex structure, and it certainly must be considered as one of the major "disadvantages" of bureaucratic organizations.

In contrast, the decision-making procedures in the small, nonbureaucratic setting are much less prone to the dilemmas discussed above. As noted before, the twin organizational functions of policy making and administration are frequently merged rather than split in the nonbureaucratic structure. Because of the limited size and scope of such organizations, the policy makers, who also may serve in an active capacity at the operating levels, are able either to collect their own information, or to evaluate the information collected by others on the basis of directly acquired experience at the operating level. Consequently, although problems may still develop in the communications systems in nonbureaucratic structures, it is much easier to maintain an effective system in the smaller environment.

## Summary

On the basis of the preceding discussion it is reasonable to suggest that large-scale, bureaucratic organizations do have a decided advantage over other nonbureaucratic types in that programs of tremendous magnitude and complexity can be undertaken. The reduction from the complex to the manageable through the division of labor and specialization, results in greater expert knowledge and, theoretically at any rate, a greater sense of professional detachment or dispassion. But if a bureaucratic setting encourages the development of each of these factors, it also—mainly as a result of its size—creates certain internal problems which can adversely affect the operating efficiency of the organization. The two major problems involve the manner in which organizational behavior is controlled and the manner in which decisions are made.

The purpose of this chapter has been to examine a few of the basic characteristics which tend to distinguish bureaucratic from nonbureaucratic organizations. Having established the major boundaries which incorporate the bureaucratic setting, the discussion can now be directed to the differences between governmental and nongovernmental bureaucracies, with particular attention being focused on the organizational structure of the executive branch of our federal government. In this connection the two basic problems which consistently plague all bureaucratic organizations to a much greater extent than nonbureaucratic structures—the control of organizational behavior and the decision-making process—are also the same functions which can be used to demonstrate the most significant differences between governmental and nongovernmental bureaucracies.

Of the two, the problem of internal control, or the manner in which conflict is resolved, shall be considered first in view of the fact that the allocation of decision-making authority within bureaucratic structures is an integral part of the control function.

Furthermore, unless bureaucratic conflict can be resolved satis-factorily, the effectiveness of every other function within the organization, including decision making, will be seriously jeopardized. Because nongovernmental bureaucracies differ significantly from their governmental counterparts in the manner in which the control problem is approached and resolved, the focus of the next two chapters will be directed to this central organizational function.

# 2

# Controlling Conflict—Nongovernmental Organizations

## The Inevitability of Conflict

As noted in the previous chapter, when dealing with large-scale, complex organizations, intraorganizational conflict is inevitably bound to develop. In this respect there is no difference between governmental and nongovernmental bureaucracies. The validity of this proposition as it specifically relates to private, nongovernmental bureaucracies results from three basic factors.

### Delegation of Authority

Bureaucratic organizations mean specialization, and specialization means not only the division of labor, but also the division of responsibility. Thus, each specialized subunit within the organization is assigned specific responsibilities to accomplish certain tasks. However, the degree of effectiveness with which the various subunits will be able to meet their assigned responsibilities will, to a great extent, depend on the authority they possess to accomplish their goals. Since authority, like responsibility, is also delegated from superior officials to their subordinates, this creates a potential conflict situation in any bureaucratic setting simply because it is much more difficult to delegate authority than responsibility.

Certainly this represents no great insight into the internal behavior of organizations; indeed, it is a simple observation concerning the behavior of the individual. The best of us would, in many instances, be quite willing to divest ourselves of many of our personal responsibilities if we could nevertheless retain whatever degree of authority or power may be associated with our daily tasks. Similarly, in organizations, a superior is frequently reluctant to delegate an equal balance of responsibility and authority to a subordinate, since, to a very real extent, such delegation represents a decrease in the superior's ability to be able to control his subordinate. The potential conflict inherent in this situation is that a reversed dependency relationship may develop, in which case the subordinate may be able to control quite effectively the actions and/or decisions of his superior. The manner in which Warden, the First Sergeant of "B" Company in James Jones' *From Here to Eternity*, is able to influence the actions and decisions of his company commander, Captain Holmes, is an excellent example of how a reversed dependency relationship can develop within a military setting. Several years ago, an eyeball-to-eyeball confrontation took place between the then-Assistant Attorney General, Nicholas Katzenbach, and the former Governor of Alabama, George Wallace, over the integration of the University of Alabama. One of the national television networks subsequently presented a special account of the top-level decision-making process within the executive branch which preceded that dramatic moment on the front steps of the University's Administration Building. President John F.

Kennedy and his brother Robert, who was then the Attorney General, were shown conferring with advisers in Washington with regard to the range of alternatives at the government's disposal. Finally, only two possible courses of action were seriously considered by top-level executive officials: the government could attempt to force compliance through the use of either the federal courts or federal troops. In either case, substantial risks were involved, but, particularly in connection with the latter alternative, grave consequences might result if Alabama's Governor Wallace chose to use his state's military forces to resist any efforts by federal troops to enforce the federal government's integration order. The ultimate decision by the President to use the federal troops was influenced by an evaluation of the anticipated reactions of the Governor made by the Assistant Attorney General. Katzenbach obviously was subject to control by both his immediate superior, the Attorney General, and the President; but it was equally obvious that, under the circumstances, the ultimate decision of the President was effectively controlled by the information he received from a subordinate executive official. In this instance the President was almost totally dependent upon the judgments he received from Katzenbach. To avoid the emergence of this type of relationship, delegated responsibility need not be balanced with a commensurate degree of authority. Under these circumstances, however, the operating effectiveness of any organization will be seriously hampered. In either event, therefore, conflict may develop.

### Dysfunctions of Specialization

The second source of intraorganizational conflict stems from the first. Increased specialization results in a corresponding increase of expertise. The more an individual directs his time and effort toward a specialized area, the greater competency he normally will develop. As already noted, expertise is one of the basic advantages large-scale bureaucratic organizations enjoy over nonbureaucratic structures. However, the emergence of the expert is not without its disadvantages insofar as potential sources of intraorganizational conflict are concerned. First, experts are, by definition, information monopolists; that is, they frequently enjoy monopolistic control over highly specialized, technical, *and* valuable data on which their superiors must rely in order to make the necessary and appropriate decisions. This situation merely tends to reinforce the "reversed dependency" relationship mentioned above. Second, experts frequently are susceptible to the most basic of all organizational maladies: myopia and an inflated concept of self-importance.

The myopic expert is a fairly common feature of the bureaucratic structure. This should cause neither surprise nor disappointment; it generally has to be recognized as one of the occupational characteristics of the bureaucratic environment. Specialization—by the very nature of the type of demands it places on the individual—imposes a severe limitation on one's organizational responsibilities. One extreme effort to avoid this type of bureaucratic situation was employed by the president of the Arkansas-Louisiana Gas Co., who assigned one of his top executive subordinates the dual responsibility of buying *and* selling gas, "so he'll know just what the gas he's selling costs."[1] In another instance, a wearing apparel manufacturing company turned a problem of lagging production over to its line operators completely and made its staff engineers available on a "consulting" basis only. The result was not only an increase in quality and production but also dramatic decreases in employee turnover and absenteeism. Some companies feel so strongly about the disadvantages associated with specialization that limited experiments have been conducted to end it completely. One oil company completely erased the organization chart of one of its most inefficiently operated refineries in Ontario. It then pro-

[1] "Arkansas-Louisiana Gas' Wit Stephens," *Wall Street Journal,* January 17, 1962.

ceeded to staff the refinery with an operating crew that worked as a unit or, more precisely, as a totally integrated team. With the exception of the accountants and lab technicians, every man on the team was trained to do everybody else's job. The refinery is now reported to be operating on a profit, with maximum efficiency and high employee morale. Another example can be found with an electronic equipment company which has abandoned its assembly lines and returned to the old concept of individual craftsmanship. An individual worker is now assigned the responsibility of assembling a particular item—e.g., a voltmeter—from start to finish. Total responsibility for the quality of that item rests exclusively with the worker, and any customer complaints are directed to the individual who "made" the product. One rather fantastic result of this experience is a reported 50 per cent decrease in man-hours devoted to building the instrument.[2]

In addition to the problem of "technical myopia," specialization may also give rise to another organizational dysfunction that can be referred to as "technical omniscience." In other words, expertise stemming from specialization frequently produces a strong conviction on the part of the expert that his judgments—i.e., his decisions, actions, recommendations, and so on —are not only logically sound but also "objectively" superior. A consequence of this situation, as suggested by one top-level corporate official, is that frequently, "Staff men who must work across divisional lines often feel that their work is handicapped unless they report to the highest possible level—preferably to the president."[3]

[2] Each of these examples have been selected from Chris Argyris' excellent article, "We Must Make Work Worthwhile," *Life* magazine, vol. 62 (May 5, 1967), pp. 56–68.

[3] Quoted in Budd Shils, "The Need for Top Level Administration of Office or Clerical Operations," AMA Management Report No. 56, *Shaping a New Concept of Administrative Management*, American Management Association (New York, 1961), p. 18.

This attitude is especially evidenced when other, nonexpert opinions are involved. Therefore, a potential conflict situation is present whenever top-level organizational officials either ignore or reject the judgments of their subordinate experts. Individuals with authority but without expert knowledge are required to review the judgments of individuals with expert knowledge who are without top-level authority. In short, the individuals in positions of authority—top-level executives—are often confronted with a "no-win" situation when they are forced to review the judgments of their expert subordinates. The reputation of the leader is not likely to be significantly enhanced by accepting the recommendations of the specialist since, in all likelihood, the expert will view the decision of his nonexpert superiors as the only possible correct decision that could have been made. On the other hand, if his expert judgments are vetoed or amended, he inevitably will feel the decision of his superiors was wrong.[4] Whether open conflict develops under these circumstances will vary according to other factors present within the organization. Nevertheless, it is true, as Presthus notes, that within organizations, "There is an inherent tension . . . between those in hierarchal positions of authority and those who play specialized roles."[5]

## Limitations of Resources

One may legitimately question the nature of a supposedly rational organization if specialized subunits are established only to have their recommendations ignored or rejected by a group of nonexperts. Assuming top-level organizational officials have confidence in the reliability of the judgments of their specialized subunits, why should their recommendations not be accepted?

---

[4] Herbert A. Shepard, "Responses to Competition and Conflict," in *Power and Conflict in Organizations*, Robert L. Kahn and Elise Boulding (eds.) (New York: Basic Books, 1964), pp. 130–33.

[5] Presthus, *op. cit.*, pp. 29–30.

One of the most important reasons lies simply in the fact that the resources at the disposal of the organization are limited. The aggregate "demands" of all subunits within the organization invariably exceed the supply of available resources. In this sense, "demands" can be considered as requests for more money, additional personnel, more space, machinery or equipment, authorization to embark on new programs, to engage in new research, and so forth. Viewed in this context, therefore, the task of top-level executive officials is to rank subunit demands in order of preference or importance as those terms are defined by the non-expert policy makers of the organization.

As far as the subunit is concerned, the importance of having its requests or "demands" granted should be considered in terms of both manifest and latent rewards. The manifest rewards are obvious; new personnel can be added, new equipment can be obtained, a new program can be initiated, and so on. Latent rewards, while not as obvious, may be just as significant. "Winning" in the competition over available resources represents, in effect, a gain in recognition, status, and prestige. Conversely "losing" is frequently interpreted as the withdrawal or reduction of recognition, status, and prestige. In terms of operating effectiveness at the subunit level, these are important considerations. Faced with a gain or loss of latent rewards, intraorganizational competition can become keen, and competition can quite frequently turn into out-and-out conflict.

As a result of these three factors, bureaucratic conflict must be viewed as inevitable. Consequently, the appropriate question to be considered by any large nongovernmental bureaucratic structure is not how to *avoid* conflict but, rather, how to *control* it.

## Unilateral Control Patterns

The most elementary form of control is the simple superior-subordinate relationship in which the latter consistently responds correctly to the commands of the former. In this context, the formal rules and regulations of the organization endow the superior with legitimate authority, and the subordinate with a clear set of obligations. Failure to meet one's obligations usually results in the imposition of organizational sanctions or punishment, whereas correct responses are generally rewarded.

This concept of a quasi-conditioned reflex found its way into the literature of bureaucracy under the heading now often referred to as classical administrative management theory. The main characteristic of this theory was its scientific approach, as revealed in the efforts of its adherents to develop a science of administration. The initial efforts in this direction were supplied by Frederick W. Taylor in 1911 with the publication of his book, *The Principles of Scientific Management*. March and Simon have referred to the work of Taylor and his followers as physiological organizational theory since the central concern of this group was the relationship between men and machines.[6] The most efficient utilization of the human body as related to a particular machine in the performance of an assigned task was the focal point of investigation for Taylor.

The attempt to apply Taylor's scientific approaches to the management levels of organizations was initiated by Luther Gulick and Lyndall Urwick in 1937 when they put together a now-classic set of essays entitled, *Papers on the Science of Administration*.[7] Concerned primarily with management functions, the writers of this period[8] stressed the highly formalized nature of administration. Organizational economy and efficiency were the established goals to be achieved in dealing with the relationships

[6] March and Simon, *op. cit.*, pp. 12–22.

[7] (New York: Columbia University, Institute of Public Administration, 1937.)

[8] For an excellent bibliographical essay on the scientific management literature of this period see John H. Massie, "Management Theory," in *Handbook of Organizations*, James G. March (ed.) (Chicago: Rand McNally, 1965), pp. 387–422.

between individuals. The dominant characteristics of this theory can best be symbolized by Gulick's cryptic administrative code-word, POSDCORB, and the organizational chart.

As seen by Gulick every bureaucratic organization had to concern itself with seven basic elements of administration—planning, organizing, staffing, directing, coordinating, reporting and budgeting (P-O-S-D-CO-R-B). Given this administrative profile, Gulick felt all bureaucratic activity could be assigned to one of these seven general management functions. The goal to be achieved was operating efficiency, and the POSDCORB formula, which was just one of Gulick's many management concepts, was one means to that end. It symbolized the formalistic nature of the theoretical concepts that developed during this period. More importantly, however, it symbolized the almost exclusive attention that was given by these scholars to the development of prescriptive propositions which, for the most part, were value-laden, and really quite unscientific.[9]

In connection with the role the individual bureaucrat was assigned by these theorists, a good argument could be made that beneath the veneer of scientific objectivity lay a very definite bias which revealed a Hobbesean view of man in an administrative environment. In a very real sense, an administrative Leviathan was created in which the individual's role was made stable, secure, predictable, and rewarding as long as he responded as directed and as expected by his superiors. The administrative symbol which best reflected this Hobbesean attitude was the organizational chart.

The organizational chart reflected the major emphasis placed by scientific management theory on formal structure. Viewed in this perspective hierarchal organizations were simply an extended series of superior-subordinate relationships —a system of graded authority. Every member of every organi-

[9] One of the best critiques of the classical period is presented in Dwight Waldo's *The Administrative State* (New York: The Ronald Press, 1948).

zation had a role; that is, in the organization's formal chain of command, every member was assigned specific authority and responsibilities. If every member of the organization was made aware of his proper role, then uncertainty and ambiguity were decreased, and operating efficiency was correspondingly increased. Clarity of individual authority and responsibility was insured (it was felt) by schematically diagraming every superior-subordinate relationship. Thus, the now familiar organization chart became the essential "road map" to the understanding of

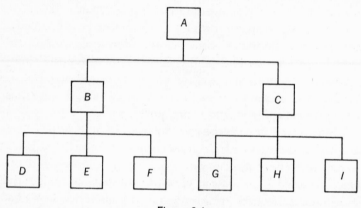

Figure 2-1

any bureaucratic structure. Typically, it appears as a neatly arranged series of cells or boxes, although the symmetry of the oversimplified example given in Figure 2-1 is not always found in complex structures.

Within this framework, authority flowed down, responsibility flowed up. The superior-subordinate relationships were viewed as unilateral, and the implicit, but nevertheless dominant characteristic of this theory was its punitive quality. As Shepard has stated, "An organizational chart can be viewed as a suppression chart; in the case of conflict the chart tells who can suppress whom."[10] A similar impression is revealed by Massie in his discussion of the scientific management theories of James D. Mooney as they appeared during the 1930's. Mooney developed an involved theoretical concept of organizational structure which included four basic principles (coordinative, scalar, functional, and staff). He then applied his theory to four institutional settings: The Roman Catholic Church, the military, the national government, and industry. As Massie observes, "It is interesting to note that the two most autocratic forms of institutions, the church and the military, were considered by Mooney to be the best examples of good applications of his principles."[11]

The above comments concerning administrative management theory must not be taken to mean that the theory is passé. Although it is now generally recognized that the classical theories represent significant limitations to the understanding of organizational behavior, many of the concepts and propositions of this period can be used as valuable tools in the analysis of organizations. The pattern of any organization's formal structure is essential knowledge. In this connection, classical administrative management theory provides a convenient starting point for a student of organizations. But it is *only* a starting point; it is hardly the type of theory that can be used to examine or to understand the internal behavior of an organization in any degree of depth. Contemporary or "modern" organization theory attempts to correct this inadequacy; in this context, a definite correlation between administrative functions and intra/interpersonal complexities is recognized. Consequently, the literature of the present period, which has been variously referred to as the socio-psychological approach, the administrative *process* approach, the administrative behavioral approach, and so on, examines the organization in an altogether different context.[12]

[10] Shepard, *op. cit.*, p. 128.       [11] Massie, *op. cit.*, p. 392.

[12] Abraham Zalesnik's extended essay on "Interpersonal Relations in Organizations," in *Handbook of Organizations, op. cit.*, is a good starting

## Reciprocal Control Patterns

The fundamental distinction between classical and "modern" administrative theory is that the former views all interpersonal control relationships as following a unidirectional or a unilateral course—*from* superior *to* subordinate—whereas the latter views these relationships in terms of multidirectional and reciprocal forces. This basic difference generally results from the different approaches to organizations taken by the two groups.

The classical theorists analyzed hierarchal control patterns almost exclusively in terms of the organization's formal, explicit, and officially stated role structure.[13] By contrast, most contemporary students of administration place greater importance on the value of the informal, unofficial, and implicit role structure as a means of obtaining a more realistic understanding of organizational behavior.[14] Obviously, these approaches are not mutually exclusive; the basic difference between the two is one of emphasis. Profitable insights can still be gained by examining a complex bureaucratic structure in terms of its formal, highly structured control patterns in which it is assumed that such concepts as "obedience" and "willing subordination" will serve as

point for a review of the research that has been conducted in this area. March and Simon, in their book, *Organizations, op. cit.*, examine the individual and his behavioral patterns within the organization in terms of motivation, conflict, and cognition. The social and psychological integration of the individual into the organization is given exhaustive treatment in the writings of Chris Argyris; see especially his *Integrating The Individual In The Organization* (New York: John Wiley and Sons, 1964).

[13] The writings of Taylor, Gulick, Urwick, and Mooney characterize this approach. See Massie, *op. cit.*

[14] Peter Blau and Richard Scott, *Formal Organizations* (San Francisco: Chandler Press, 1962); March and Simon, *op. cit.*; Robert Golembiewski, "Small Groups and Large Organizations," and William Starbuck, "Organizational Growth and Development," both in *Handbook of Organizations, op. cit.*

effective behavioral determinants. However, a meaningful understanding of organizations cannot be obtained unless the intra- and interpersonal relationships which prevail within every organization are examined in terms of an interweaving set of sociological, psychological, and political considerations.

For instance, an understanding of how a given individual adapts to a particular bureaucratic setting involves an examination of various sociological propositions. Likewise, the values, attitudes, and beliefs that the individual brings with him to the organization—and the extent to which they blend together,with the values and attitudes of the organization—are, in effect, a psychological inquiry. And, finally, the various tactics employed by the individual to maximize his rewards and to minimize his costs or "punishments" frequently involve the use of "politics" or political stratagems. In each instance, the resulting effect may indeed be quite informal, unofficial, and/or implicit, but it is nonetheless important to recognize the efficacy of these factors as a means of understanding organizational behavior.

The organization chart, by formally designating B as a subordinate to A, explicitly suggests that A is able to control B, whereas a close study of the sociological, psychological, and/or political relationships which prevail between A, B, and other members of the organization may demonstrate that, in fact, A is just as much controlled by B as he is able to control him. The nature of this type of reciprocal relationship, plus the more complex type of multilateral control pattern will be examined in greater detail in connection with how organizations can attempt to control conflict.

## Control Techniques

Generally, there are four methods nongovernmental organizations can utilize to deal with internal conflict: problem solving, persuasion, direct control, and bargaining.[15] For the

¹⁵ March and Simon, *op. cit.*, pp. 129–31.

first two of these to be effective there must be common agreement among all parties involved in the conflict as to the basic goal objectives to be achieved. Furthermore, the success of both the problem-solving and persuasion techniques depends on the extent to which a strong feeling of mutual identification can be realized among everyone involved in the conflict.[16]

### Problem Solving

Problem solving, observes Herbert Shepard, depends on the acceptance of the assumption that the ultimate solution must be mutually satisfactory to all parties involved.[17] The same condition may be applied to the techniques of persuasion. The basic difference between these two control methods, however, is significant. Problem solving is most effectively employed where there exists a high sharing of organizational goals, subunit goals, and individual values and attitudes. In this instance, conflict usually stems from the absence of available objective data that needs to be applied to a given situation. The assumption in this case is that through concerted search efforts, the most appropriate data can be found and the proper solution can be obtained.

For instance, disagreement may arise among the personnel of a company's shipping department over the fastest means of transporting the company's products to another city. The problem can be solved by simply conducting an extensive search of all available objective data—i.e., bus, rail, air, and trucking schedules. From this search, the correct solution will emerge. The main point to stress in connection with problem solving is that only one correct solution can be allowed. The ultimate solution cannot rationally be questioned or rejected; it is purely factual.

### Pure Persuasion

Problem solving, therefore, is not effective when more than one correct "objective" solution is allowed. If, in the search for

[16] Shepard, *op. cit.,* p. 134.    [17] *Idem.*

an acceptable solution, two sets of equally valid data are uncovered, which provide equally relevant solutions to the problem at hand, persuasion must be employed to have one party accept the solution of the other as more satisfactory than his own. Or, to put it another way, persuasion is the attempt to convince the other party to the conflict that the advantages of your solution are greater than, and/or the disadvantages are less than, those offered by his proposal.

Because conflict of this nature usually develops over the choice of two or more equally defensible sets of data, the ideal situation involving persuasion would be one in which one alternative is *logically preferable* to all others. For instance, if the same shipping department mentioned is directed to find the fastest *and* the cheapest means of transporting the company's products to another city, an entirely different solution is presented. Two variables are now involved which, in all probability, will reflect a negative correlation. Therefore, provisions have to be made to allow for the emergence of more than one ultimate answer. An extensive search of all available objective data—e.g., the same schedules—may reveal two or more equally acceptable choices. Under these circumstances, the final choice has to be made on a preferential basis; however, in order to make this type of determination, other variables must be considered. For example, proximity to the various transportation terminals may be considered an important factor, or the care given to the freight in transit may also be taken into consideration. In any event, for a logically preferred choice to emerge, a high degree of consensus must develop around a single *set* of interrelated variables.

### Manipulated Persuasion

The instances of pure persuasion at work within an organization when conflict involves subunits rather than individuals are less frequent. When conflict does develop between subunits within nongovernmental organizations, the attempt to resolve the conflict within the context of persuasion may more accurately be referred to as manipulated persuasion.

Pure persuasion, in one sense, can be viewed in qualitative terms—one party attempts to persuade another of the inherently superior quality of the former's proposal. However, if one cannot persuade another in this manner, the tactics of persuasion may shift from a qualitative to a quantitative approach, which is to say that one party of a conflict may attempt to gain additional support and approval for his own position from other individuals or groups from within the organization.

In a one-to-one conflict situation both groups may adamantly refuse to concede to the other's position. In this case, one subunit may seek to strengthen its position by expanding the scope of the conflict in an effort to gain the support of other subunits. Unless the other group originally involved in the conflict reacts similarly, thus maintaining a balance of conflict, it may very well find itself cast as the isolated group pitted against the rest of the organization. Under these circumstances, persuasion —which has been manipulated—is usually readily obtainable. As one corporate vice president has noted:

> When (staff personnel are) trying to sell a change in method, system or procedure to a line executive, there is no substitute for casting the president's shadow if logic and persuasiveness have failed. And besides, staff men, like most of us, tend to value themselves in terms of the organization level to which they report. The higher the status, the less vigorous the opposition from the proponents of the status quo.[18]

This method of resolving conflict is probably the most important control strategy available to large-scale, nongovernmental bureaucracies. Manipulated persuasion is a subtle

[18] Quoted in Budd Shils, "The Need for Top Level Administration of Office and Clerical Operations," *op. cit.*; p. 18.

modification of coercion which attempts to maintain the illusion of objective and rational discussion. It is, in effect, an attempt to legitimize a pseudo-majoritarian principle which correlates the "right" solution with a quantitative measure of support. Responsible opposition and criticism may be permitted—indeed, encouraged—in complex nongovernmental bureaucracies to serve as an indicator of a "rich and healthy" diversification of opinion. But, every organization must place certain limits on the extent and scope of internal opposition. Consequently, if the scope of conflict between two subunits is expanded, and support from other subunits within the organization begins to cluster around one position, the opponent group is generally expected to become "persuaded" that its position is not the logically preferred alternative. The acceptance of this "preferred position" concept is a desired, as well as a desirable, action on the part of the opponent group. It is an action, in fact, that can be viewed from within the organization as commendable, and possibly even worthy of some reward.[19] However, to refuse to adopt this course of action—i.e., to maintain an intransigent position— is usually interpreted unfavorably within the organization.

## Direct Control

Depending, of course, on the intensity of the opposition, the organization may respond mildly or severely, and this demonstrates the real source of success which many private organizations claim for their problem-solving and persuasion techniques. Top-level executive officials, in effect, hold the "trump card" of direct control, i.e., ultimate unilateral authority. This ever-present threat effectively sets the limits of debate and defines acceptable criticism. It also represents the risks that may be incurred by subordinate executive officials for violating these

[19] For a perfect illustration of this point, see "The Frustrating Warfare of Business," *Life* magazine, vol. 62 (May 5, 1967), pp. 40–52.

limits of behavioral tolerance. The nature of these risks vary, of course, from company to company. To cite one example, the Whirlpool Corporation makes it quite clear that for those who cannot conform to the company's attitudes and policies, separation is the only alternative. A Whirlpool public relations statement specified:

> We have one direction in which we are going. Any person who is not in agreement with this does not belong in this company. Sooner or later, he will be in conflict and he will be unhappy and ineffective. He will either be invited to leave or will leave voluntarily. Occasionally, precisely this situation develops. It happens rarely, but it does happen—even within our management group. We have had people who came in from the outside and were not made aware of or did not find out our attitude, or who just assumed that we didn't mean all the things we said; they have been "hard-nosed" in their managerial function and have alienated themselves from the rest of the management group.[20]

In a 1954 General Electric Company management manual, all G.E. executives were given a chart headed "Management as a Profession" in which they were informed that management was, among other things, the practice of leading by persuasion rather than by command. A footnote appended to this latter statement directed the reader's attention to the small print at the bottom of the page which stated:

> It is recognized that there may be emergency conditions where persuasion has failed and results of continued efforts at persuasion . . . would be worse than temporary use of "Command"

[20] Quoted in Stewart Thompson, "The Management Creed and Philosophy of Whirlpool Corporation," AMA Research Study No. 32, *Management Creeds and Philosophies*, American Management Association (New York: 1958), p. 71.

. . . In so doing, the manager is acknowledging temporary failure as a "Professional Manager," and hence, resorts to (command) as an expedient only and takes requisite steps to identify and correct the root causes of the failure in order to prevent subsequent similar failures.[21]

In the final analysis, problem solving and persuasion can be "made" to work in those organizations which are potentially capable of imposing a full set of sanctions on the deviant individual or subunit, including the ultimate sanction of dismissal. Problem solving and persuasion cannot be "made" to work in organizations which cannot monopolize the power of dismissal. If this power must be shared with other external organizations, then problem solving and persuasion may be desirable means of resolving conflict from the point of view of the organization, but they may not be viewed as the most desired methods by organizational subunits or individual members. Under these circumstances, if problem solving and/or persuasion prove ineffective—if the organization is not able to monopolize direct unilateral control—then organizational conflict can only be resolved through bargaining.

*Bargaining*

To revise Dahl's definition of power slightly,[22] if A *is not* able to force B to do something that B would not otherwise do (but that A wants done) then the only alternative left open to A is to negotiate—bargain—with B. Compromise becomes the primary tactic in bargaining, and the ultimate form that bargaining takes is a negotiated settlement. For bargaining to be

[21] Quoted in Harold Smiddy, "Management as a Profession," *50 Years Progress in Management: 1910–1960*, The American Society of Mechanical Engineers (New York, 1960), pp. 29–30.

[22] Robert Dahl, "The Concept of Power," *Behavioral Science*, vol. 2, No. 3 (July, 1957), pp. 202–203.

successfully employed, all parties must be satisfied that the final outcome does not jeopardize their individual self-interests. In short, everybody must "win" at least more than they "lose" in a successful bargaining situation. If the reverse is the case, then one can only conclude that the bargaining process was characterized by miscalculation, irrationality, or coercion, in which case the definition of bargaining no longer applies.

Bargaining assumes the existence of a near-balance of power among all parties involved. A parity of power does not mean parity of formal authority, however. Within large, complex bureaucracies, bargaining relationships may develop among individuals of equal status and authority as well as among individuals of unequal status and authority, i.e., bargaining between superiors and subordinates. In nongovernmental organizations the bargaining situations which may develop deserve close examination.

## Bargaining in Private Organizations

To begin with, it might seem incongruous to associate bargaining with nongovernmental bureaucratic organizations as an effective internal control technique. As noted above, bargaining emerges when organizations cannot unilaterally apply the ultimate sanction of dismissal. And yet, for most private business and industrial organizations this basic power is ever-present; there are relatively few private business or industrial firms which cannot summarily dismiss subordinate executive officials.

Most corporations, however, shun this tactic whenever possible and rely, instead, on lateral transfers or demotions with a corresponding decrease in salary. This approach is frequently more effective than outright dismissal since the individual who is being shifted is likely to respond or react in one of two ways: either he refuses to accept the sanction, which is implicit in the transfer, and resigns from the organization—in which case the effect of dismissal is realized—or the individual accepts the sanction as a challenge to restore his now-somewhat tarnished image within the corporate structure to its former luster—in which case the organization has "gained," in all probability, a much more effective executive. IBM, particularly, has enjoyed considerable success in this regard.[23]

Under certain circumstances, however, even such direct, unilaterally imposed sanctions and commands as transfer, demotion, and so on, may be deliberately avoided by top-level executive officials, even at the cost of accepting a bargained or negotiated settlement to an intraorganizational conflict.[24] In connection with the type of interpersonal relationships which do develop in these nongovernmental bureaucracies between top-level and subordinate executive officials, the organization is the ultimate monopolist insofar as direct sanctions are concerned. But the direct and unilateral imposition of these sanctions frequently can have severe adverse consequences on the state of organizational morale, loyalty, operating effectiveness, and goal attainment. Therefore, efforts are generally made to avoid the costs which may be incurred through the use of direct "force" or control. One possible solution which is being suggested here is that deliberate efforts may be exerted to create the impression of equality between superiors and subordinates. In other words, a manipulated bargaining situation may be created in which subordinate executive officials are granted participating status in the control process.

Thus, a distinction should be made between a *pure bargaining* situation, which prevails when no one party enjoys an absolute power advantage over any of the other parties involved, and a

---

[23] "Can IBM Keep Up The Pace?," *Business Week* (February 2, 1963), pp. 92–98.

[24] On the limited effectiveness of direct control see Robert Dahl and Charles Lindblom, *Politics, Economics, and Welfare* (New York: Harper Torchbook, 1963), pp. 106–109.

*manipulated bargaining* situation, which exists when one party in a conflict (a top-level executive official) does enjoy an absolute power advantage over the other parties involved (subordinate executive officials) but, for various reasons, prefers either to avoid using this power or to avoid creating the *impression* that direct control was used.

Horwitz, in his studies involving organizational hostility, observes, ". . . the evidence is clear that hostility depends less on how strongly the person feels about the issue than on whether he has received the weight [degree of deference] he expects for his point of view." Consequently, ". . . hostility is a function, not of the weight [degree of influence] a person has in joint decision-making . . . but of the reduction of his expected weight [degree of subject matter authority] in decision-making."[25] The main thought that emerges from the Horwitz study is that as long as the individual is satisfied that a proper degree of deference has been granted to his point of view by organizational superiors, his hostility reaction will, in all probability be minimal if his superiors do not accept his judgment.

Although manipulated bargaining situations may develop, few private, nongovernmental organizations are ever forced to deal with conflict at the managerial or executive levels on the basis of a pure bargaining relationship. For reasons that will be discussed in the next chapter, the emergence of a pure bargaining relationship in any bureaucratic situation depends on factors which are essentially absent in private business and industrial organizational settings.

[25] Murray Horwitz, "Managing Hostility in the Laboratory and The Refinery," in Kahn and Boulding, *op. cit.*, pp. 79–82. The bracketed phrases have been inserted by me to replace Horwitz's term "weight". If his entire article is read there is no difficulty in understanding his use of the term "weight." However, in isolating two sentences in which the term "weight" appears three times, some confusion may result as to his intended meaning. For this reason I have inserted three phrases which I feel will clarify the meaning which the statement is intended to convey in the above context.

## Summary

Within any large-scale bureaucratic operation conflict is bound to develop; one of the major problems confronting all top-level executive officials, therefore, is how intraorganizational conflict can be effectively controlled. The purpose of this chapter has been to examine how this problem is approached by top-level executive officials in private, nongovernmental (i.e., business and industrial) organizations. On the basis of the preceding discussion, certain generalizations can be offered.

It seems reasonable to suggest that in nongovernmental bureaucratic environments, direct or unilateral control methods still represent a significant determinant of organizational behavior. In this respect, there is no difference between the current and classical analyses of organizations. What is different, however, is the manner in which nongovernmental organizations now utilize their sanction and reward systems. In most progressive management circles today, direct control has become an implicit factor rather than an explicit force. Effective bureaucratic management is presently committed to the assumption that operating performance will be improved by reducing anxiety rather than by instilling "fear" in the minds of subordinate administrative officials.

This shift in attitude can also be explained in terms of a general recognition and acceptance by top-level executive officials of the informal, unofficial, and implicit patterns of interpersonal relationships which inevitably develop throughout the middle and lower administrative echelons. This attitude represents a recognition and acceptance of the fact that multilateral and reciprocal interpersonal relationships can effectively complement the formal and official unilateral superior-subordinate patterns which exist within every organization. However, when these informal relationships contradict rather than complement the formal control patterns, the organization must be prepared to resolve the conflict, which means that it must be prepared to act directly or unilaterally, if necessary.

On the other hand, the high costs frequently incurred as a result of the use of direct control methods may very well cause top-level executive officials to seek other, "less expensive" means of control. Problem solving, pure persuasion, manipulated persuasion, and manipulated bargaining are four control techniques which minimize the degree of formal and direct intervention of the organization in the resolution of conflict. Amending the March and Simon definitions slightly,[26] one can say that problem solving and pure persuasion represent the resolution of conflict through objective analysis, whereas manipulated persuasion and manipulated bargaining represent the resolution of conflict through psychological manipulation.

The distinction between pure and manipulated persuasion should be clear, as should the distinction between pure and manipulated bargaining. Less clear, however, may be the distinction between manipulated persuasion and manipulated bargaining. The differences which do separate these two approaches to conflict are, as conceived here, admittedly subtle, highly speculative, and somewhat tentative. Consequently, for our present purposes it should be sufficient to group both together under the single heading, manipulated agreement. Thus, conflict within private, nongovernmental organizations is resolved either through *objective analysis*, *manipulated agreement*, or *pure bargaining*. This arrangement can be represented as shown in Figure 2-2.

When objective analysis cannot be applied, manipulative techniques must be utilized by the organization or by its component subunits to resolve internal conflict. However, for manipulation to act as an effective control technique, organiza-

---

[26] March and Simon, *op. cit.*, p. 131.

tional sanctions and rewards must be monopolized by the top-level executive official or officials, including the ultimate sanction of dismissal. If this latter condition cannot be satisfied, i.e if the allocation of sanctions and rewards must be shared with other external organizations or groups, then the organization

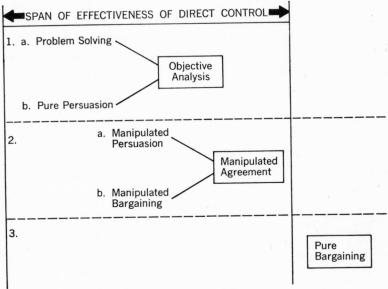

Figure 2-2

must engage in pure bargaining techniques as a means to control conflict.

But—for reasons which will become readily apparent in the following chapter—the conditions which dictate the use of pure bargaining as a control device are basically nonexistent in the bureaucratic environments of business and industrial organizations. Or, to reverse this proposition, one of the basic characteristics of private, nongovernmental bureaucratic organizations is the centralization and monopolization of *de facto* authority at the apex of these hierarchal structures. Consequently, the existence of a pure bargaining situation in any private business or industrial organization is to be viewed as an aberration, which means, in effect, that *objective analysis* and *manipulated agreement* are the two basic control techniques utilized by nongovernmental organizations.

Having established the control patterns which prevail within private organizational settings, we can now direct our attention to an examination of the characteristics of control techniques as applied within a governmental organizational environment—the executive branch of our federal government.

# 3

## Controlling Conflict—
## The Federal Executive
## Structure

To begin with, it should be noted that there is virtually no difference between the hierarchal *structure* of the executive branch and the organizational pattern of any large-scale, non-governmental bureaucracy. The President, situated at the apex of the executive hierarchy, is directly responsible for the operations of the twelve major departments, each headed by a cabinet-ranked Secretary, which comprise the core of the executive structure. (Obviously, the President's responsibilities extend well beyond the boundaries of these twelve departments; however, for the present we will limit our discussion to these executive subunits.)

Each of the twelve Departmental Secretaries, while directly accountable to the President, is, in turn, responsible for the over-all operations of his respective department. Thus, each Secretary becomes the top executive official of a major hierarchal subunit within the executive branch. In fact, if size in terms of full-time

# The Government of the United States

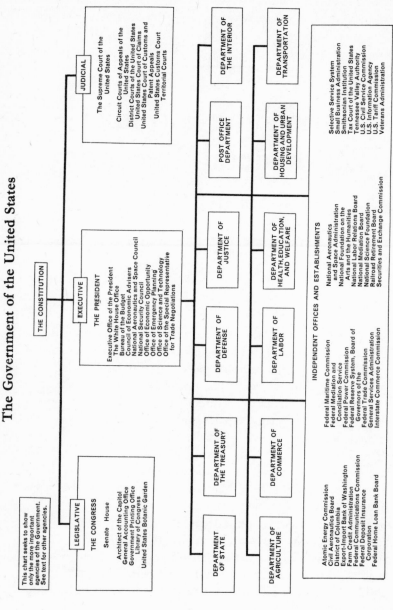

This chart seeks to show only the more important agencies of the Government. See text for other agencies.

THE CONSTITUTION

**LEGISLATIVE**

THE CONGRESS
Senate    House

Architect of the Capitol
General Accounting Office
Government Printing Office
Library of Congress
United States Botanic Garden

**EXECUTIVE**

THE PRESIDENT

Executive Office of the President
The White House Office
Bureau of the Budget
Council of Economic Advisers
National Aeronautics and Space Council
National Security Council
Office of Economic Opportunity
Office of Emergency Planning
Office of Science and Technology
Office of the Special Representative for Trade Negotiations

**JUDICIAL**

The Supreme Court of the United States

Circuit Courts of Appeals of the United States
District Courts of the United States
United States Court of Claims
United States Court of Customs and Patent Appeals
United States Customs Court
Territorial Courts

DEPARTMENT OF STATE

DEPARTMENT OF THE TREASURY

DEPARTMENT OF DEFENSE

DEPARTMENT OF JUSTICE

POST OFFICE DEPARTMENT

DEPARTMENT OF THE INTERIOR

DEPARTMENT OF AGRICULTURE

DEPARTMENT OF COMMERCE

DEPARTMENT OF LABOR

DEPARTMENT OF HEALTH, EDUCATION, AND WELFARE

DEPARTMENT OF HOUSING AND URBAN DEVELOPMENT

DEPARTMENT OF TRANSPORTATION

INDEPENDENT OFFICES AND ESTABLISHMENTS

Atomic Energy Commission
Civil Aeronautics Board
District of Columbia
Export-Import Bank of Washington
Farm Credit Administration
Federal Communications Commission
Federal Deposit Insurance Corporation
Federal Home Loan Bank Board

Federal Maritime Commission
Federal Mediation and Conciliation Service
Federal Power Commission
Federal Reserve System, Board of Governors of the
Federal Trade Commission
General Services Administration
Interstate Commerce Commission

National Aeronautics and Space Administration
National Foundation on the Arts and the Humanities
National Labor Relations Board
National Mediation Board
National Science Foundation
Railroad Retirement Board
Securities and Exchange Commission

Selective Service System
Small Business Administration
Smithsonian Institution
Tax Court of the United States
Tennessee Valley Authority
U.S. Civil Service Commission
U.S. Information Agency
U.S. Tariff Commission
Veterans Administration

Figure 3-1

Source: *U.S. Government Organization Manual, 1967–68*, p618.

48

employees (excluding military personnel) is used as a comparative gauge, then the direction of the various executive departments imposes certain responsibilities on Department Secretaries which are certainly comparable to the demands made of many of the top executives of our nations' leading private corporations. Viewed in this context, General Motors is only slightly larger than the Post Office Department. Similarly, the Department of Agriculture and Du Pont are virtually identical in size, as are the General Dynamics Corporation and the Department of Health, Education, and Welfare. As many individuals are employed by RCA as are on the payroll of the Treasury Department, and B. F. Goodrich has as many employees as the State Department. The Justice Department utilizes as many individuals to carry out its functions as the Dow Chemical Company employs to maintain its operations, and the Labor Department has approximately the same number of personnel as "Gussie" Busch hires to keep the barrels rolling in St. Louis and to maintain the other related activities of the Anheuser-Busch Corp.[1] In short, to head an executive department of the federal government is to direct a major enterprise, at least insofar as size is concerned. As a result, each department can be viewed as a bureaucratic entity in itself. For example, the organizational structure of the Department of State is essentially similar to the basic hierarchal patterns found in virtually every major nongovernmental organization.[2]

Within each department the Secretary has one or, in some instances, two immediate subordinates who are ranked as either Deputy or Under Secretaries. The next lower level in all departments is filled with a varying number of Assistant Secretaries

[1] Personnel figures obtained from *Statistical Abstract of the United States*, U. S. Department of Commerce, Bureau of the Census (1965), p. 411, and *Fortune* magazine, vol. 72 (July, 1965), pp. 150–157.

[2] *The United States Government Organization Manual*, published annually by the Government Printing Office, provides organizational charts for every executive department and agency.

# Department of State

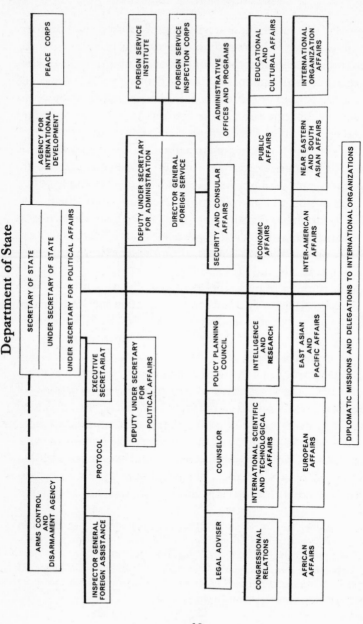

**Figure 3-2**
Source: *U.S. Government Organization Manual, 1967–68,* p622.

who may be responsible for the operations of a major departmental subunit, or who may have overall departmental responsibilities. Departments are generally subdivided into divisions, offices, and/or bureaus. The precise hierarchal order of these intradepartmental subunits may vary, but in most departments each of these subunits is directed by a senior career official.

Within this context, therefore, the executive branch, if viewed solely in terms of the classical administrative management theory, reflects a tight, hierarchal pattern of well-defined role structures and positions of authority and responsibility. In actual operation, however, this pyramidal pattern exists within an extremely decentralized and flexible system. The extent to which organizational decentralization prevails in the executive branch can best be demonstrated by examining the manner in which conflict develops and is resolved.

## Executive Branch Conflict

For internal control to be effectively applied in any organization, ideally several conditions must be satisfied: superior-subordinate relationships must be clear and precise; if responsibility is delegated (as inevitably it is), commensurate grants of authority must also be allocated; actual power and formal authority should coincide; organizational rewards and sanctions must also be made clear and precise; organizational goals must be stable, consistent, clear, and operationally feasible and meaningful; and finally, the organization must be able to monopolize the ultimate sanction of dismissal. If each of these conditions is met, it can then be assumed that the organization should have little difficulty in maintaining internal control.

Of course, an absolutist position could be that by employing direct, unilateral control the only one of the above-mentioned conditions that must be satisfied in order to insure effective internal control would be the last. However, as we mentioned in connection with nongovernmental organizations, direct unilateral control is seldom viewed as a desirable means to control conflict; in fact, in numerous instances, direct control is not even considered as a feasible solution simply because of the extensive complexity which is associated with many intraorganizational conflicts. Furthermore, conflict within the executive branch can become much more complex and involved than in any nongovernmental organization, thus making direct control all the less effective.

Like its nongovernmental counterpart, the organizational bureaucracy of the executive branch is composed of a wide variety of subunits which must compete for their share of the overall limited resources. Under these circumstances, competition frequently becomes conflict. In addition, as the degree of public policy complexity increases, bureaucratic specialization and expertise also increase. This situation lends itself to the generation of conflict between organizational subunits which frequently cannot be resolved unilaterally. Also, as a result of the broad scope of the many executive programs currently being implemented, administrative responsibilities of various subunits inevitably overlap and jurisdictional conflicts frequently emerge. This latter point probably represents a greater source of conflict in the executive branch than it does in nongovernmental organizations.

Thus, while it is apparent that many of the major causes of conflict in nongovernmental organizations are also present in the governmental hierarchy, conflict within the executive branch is additionally aggravated by a set of considerations which, for the most part, are either absent or only minimally present within private bureaucracies. Specifically, conflict within the executive branch frequently results from the fact that overall organizational goals are (1) generally vague, frequently inconsistent, seldom operationally meaningful, and/or (2) (except in their broadest, most abstract form) subject to frequent shifts in emphasis, if not changes in substance, as a result of changing Administrations.

### Absence of Tangible Goals

The point made in Chapter 1 that organizational goals in *any* large-scale bureaucratic structure can seldom be stated in clear and precise terms is reasserted here. The goals of large, private industrial and business organizations are frequently broad generalizations which are quite ambiguous in content. For instance, the Whirlpool Corporation was forced to confront this problem directly in 1958 after it had mushroomed from 970 to approximately 19,000 employees in seven years. What had previously served satisfactorily as an unwritten, implicitly accepted "creed," had to be translated into an explicitly stated, formally written document. In discussing the problem of organizational goals, one Whirlpool executive official provided—unknowingly—a good example of a man in a quandary.

Until recently the company was small enough so that everyone within the organization had a "feel" of what the company wants to be. They all knew that *quality* ranks first in all our decisions, that *integrity* is unquestionable. . . . I believe that our rapid expansion makes it necessary for us to sit down and spell out our creed. It will only express in writing those things that, prior to our sudden growth, we were able to understand almost without conscious thought . . . a creed can only be effective if it is written to express the kind of spirit that has always prevailed within the company. In documenting our creed we will merely put into words what has actually been the spirit and the unwritten attitude of us all . . . we believe that we have a company that has *earned the right to exist*, we feel we can *do the impossible*. Without this spirit our company. . . . could not have experienced the growth that has come about within the last few years. I suppose that "spirit" means the *basic energy* behind our firm. Certainly it should be expressed in our creed.[3]

The key terms emphasized in this statement were undoubtedly meaningful to the speaker, and perhaps to a handful of other Whirlpool executives, but the fact remains that any company creed or philosophy which attempted to extend these terms to 19,000 employees was bound to reflect a highly ambiguous—one might even say esoteric—tone.

Nongovernment organizations, however, have no monopoly on ambiguous goal objectives. Note, for instance, a statement by Sumner Whittier who was the head of the Veterans Administration during the Eisenhower Administration. Whittier probably was quite satisfied that he had clarified the precise mission of his organization when he stated:

> The vaster and more complex an organization becomes, the greater the need for clarity and simplicity.... Abraham Lincoln . . . described the Veterans Administration's mission in words now widely quoted throughout the Agency: "To care for him who shall have borne the battle, and for his widow and his orphan." We have worked out a more specific statement of mission and of overall policy to describe our goals: "The Veterans Administration is dedicated to administer veterans laws *effectively, expeditiously*, and with *sympathetic understanding*, and to exercise *constructive leadership* in the field of veterans affairs."[4]

As we have all known for some time, it is hard to improve on Lincoln; thus, the VA and the Whirlpool Corporation are not

[3] Thompson, "The Management Creed and Philosophy of Whirlpool Corporation," *op. cit.*, p. 71, emphasis added.

[4] Sumner Whittier, "Administrative Management in the Veterans Administration," AMA Management Report No. 56, *Shaping a New Concept of Administrative Management*, American Management Association (New York: 1961), p. 97, emphasis added.

too far apart insofar as the degree of ambiguity which is perpetuated throughout both organizations by their respective policy statements. But, the point that is being developed here involves differences, not similarities, between governmental and nongovernmental organizations. In connection with organizational goals significant differences do exist.

Traditionally, the profit motive has been cited as the key characteristic which distinguishes private industrial and business organizations from governmental bureaucracies. In many respects, the term has become an overworked cliché.[5] Nevertheless, despite the point made in Chapter 1 that organizational goals, stated in a profit context, may lend themselves to diverse and often conflicting interpretations by various subunits within the organization, it is true that within the sphere of business and industrial enterprise, all organizational activity can be measured in terms of a calculated unit cost system.

Actually, the stated goals of any private organization may be quite incidental to its implicit goals. Viewed in one perspective there is absolute clarity and precision in the fundamental goal of an organization like the Ford Motor Company, for example. Every member of this organization's automotive divisions, from the highest to the lowest levels, is inevitably aware of the fact that his particular function within the organization contributes either directly or indirectly to one basic organizational goal—the production of cars. The final products of any private organization, therefore, represent the most tangible goal that can be devised. But in addition, the final products also represent a composite cost figure which can be broken down and analyzed in precise detail. If operating losses are incurred, cost reductions must be effected and/or prices must be increased. If

---

[5] Julian Feldman and Herschel E. Kanter offer a nice summary of the various ways in which profits can be used in the analysis of private business and industrial organizations in their article, "Organizational Decision-Making," *Handbook of Organizations, op. cit.*, pp. 629–31.

neither one of these alternatives can bring about a shift from a deficit to a profit situation, then the organization is in financial difficulty. For this reason, therefore, every member of the organization should have a precise twofold commitment to contribute directly or indirectly (1) to the production of tangible products and (2) to the continued solvency of his organization.

However, insofar as the federal bureaucracy is concerned, it should be apparent that neither one of these commitments can be translated into specific individual behavioral guides. No tangible product is involved; instead, the executive bureaucracy is geared to provide numerous services, to meet basic needs, to satisfy various desires, to assume certain responsibilities, to apply certain regulations, and to maintain various standards— all with little regard being directed to the question of the financial solvency of the organization, i.e., the federal government. The proliferation of these diversified functions precludes any single end product from emerging, unless one cites such abstract concepts as "the public interest," "the national welfare," or simply "the democratic way of life" as constituting that final "product." But the point is, how can one analyze the public interest or the national welfare in terms of a calculated unit cost system? With some exceptions, it has generally been considered impossible.

The Department of Defense is perhaps the most prominent exception in that it has been able to demonstrate rather dramatically how cost analysis techniques can be successfully applied in a governmental environment. To a certain extent, the Department is dealing with tangible "products"—military hardware. In this regard, decisions concerning design, performance specifications, and quantity can directly affect the cost factor. In the domestic area, the Post Office Department is probably best suited for this type of cost accounting approach. It, too, deals with tangible "products" in a sense. How much does it cost to deliver a letter? What is the margin of profit or loss in stamp sales? What costs can be reduced? In addition to cost analysis, various indices of productivity have been devised and applied to other executive subunits whose activities lend themselves to this type of measurement.[6] In all of these subunits reliable data can be collected, and rationally sound, *economic* decisions can be made in terms of either increasing productivity or decreasing costs. However, although there are undoubtedly numerous government operations which could be (and are) analyzed on a cost-efficiency basis, the fact remains that the conclusions which emerge from such an analysis—however sound—frequently have to be subordinated to other, *noneconomic* considerations. (A more detailed discussion of this point is developed in later chapters.)

For instance, one of the perennial dilemmas of the U. S. foreign aid program concerns the proper utilization of the appropriated funds. As viewed by some, requests for project grants from various nations should be judged solely on the basis of sound business criteria. In this regard, no money should be earmarked for any project unless it can be conclusively demonstrated that the project represents an economically sound and technically feasible undertaking. On the other hand, the State Department has on numerous occasions in the past viewed foreign aid primarily in terms of American foreign policy considerations, and, consequently, economic and technical considerations have been subordinated to military and political factors insofar as the use of foreign aid funds have been concerned.

Domestically, the complex problems associated with water resources, flood control, irrigation, and erosion control suggest the need for coordinated governmental planning, and yet the continued division of responsibilities in this area between the Bureau of Reclamation in the Department of the Interior, and the Corps of Engineers in the Department of Defense can only

[6] *Measuring Productivity of Federal Government Organizations*, Executive Office of the President, Bureau of the Budget, 1964.

be understood in terms other than sound economic principles. The creation of the latest cabinet Departments of Housing and Urban Development, and Transportation are ostensibly two attempts to consolidate functions in an effort to reduce costs, increase productivity, and/or increase governmental efficiency in these two vitally important areas.

However, despite these efforts, government is "politics," and as such, basic economic criteria frequently have to be subordinated to other, noneconomic considerations. It is this type of multifaceted environment in which governmental bureaucrats have to operate, and, for the most part, it presents a dramatic contrast to the environment of their nongovernmental counterparts. Consequently, the type of conflict which emerges from within the governmental organization as a result of the absence of tangible goals is virtually nonexistent within the organizational structures of private industry and business.

### Administrative Discontinuity

A second basic cause of conflict in the executive branch, also rarely evidenced in most private organizations, results from the frequent change of administrations. Operating effectiveness within any organization is directly related to the degree of stability evidenced within the bureaucratic structure, particularly as stability relates to the tenure of key administrative officials. Stability, experience, and cohesiveness are important concepts which can significantly affect the functioning of any organizational structure. To a very real extent, however, the key factor is continuity. It is continuity, for instance, which permits one to entertain the romantic notion that while individuals may come and go, *The Organization* lives on. In more precise terms this notion actually means that organizational change is effected on a gradual and incremental basis to avoid a major disruption of existing organizational goals, values, and operating patterns. On the other hand, continuity—and, hence, stability, experience, and cohesiveness—is extremely difficult to achieve or maintain in the face of frequent and extensive changes in key administrative officials and organizational goals and values. In the absence of continuity—or to use Garceau's delightful term, with the development of a discontinuous continuum[7]—there is a very high probability that one or several organizational maladies will appear among operating personnel: apathy, alienation, demoralization, or aggression. In any event, as the degree of continuity increases, intraorganizational conflict will be easier to manage, and, conversely, conflict will become increasingly difficult to control as the degree of continuity decreases. One way to approach the question of continuity is to examine the rate of turnover of top executive officials. Viewed in this perspective, similarities can be demonstrated between governmental and nongovernmental organizations; once again, however, the differences between the two are much more significant.

For instance, there is not too much difference between the tenure of the President of the United States and the average tenure of the presidents of some of our major corporations. A random selection of twenty-five of the top five hundred industrial corporations in America suggests that the top executive officials of these firms have been serving in their present capacity as president for an average of six years.[8] Therefore, the differences between public and private organizations, insofar as continuity is concerned, cannot be explained simply in terms of tenure. Two other factors do exist, however, which directly relate to the problem of continuity. First, our political Chief Executives are, for the most part, selected from outside the executive branch, whereas corporation presidents are, for the

[7] The term, used by Garceau in a totally different context, conveniently projects the connotation desired here. Oliver Garceau, "Research in the Political Process," *American Political Science Review*, vol. 45 (March 1951), pp. 69–85.

[8] *Fortune* magazine, *op. cit.*

most part, coopted from within the existing organization. Second, the process of selecting a corporation president is usually followed by an interrelated series of individual promotions at the upper management level. In the executive branch, however, when a new President assumes office, an entirely new administrative team of top-level executive officials normally accompanies him.[9] The net result of both factors is that private organizations are in a much better position to maintain a fairly high degree of operating continuity than is the executive branch.

The presidents of the twenty-five corporations mentioned served an average "apprenticeship" of nineteen years in their respective companies before they were elevated to the top executive position, and each of the twenty-five served in an average of three upper management positions before assuming their current responsibilities. A good example of the type of intra-organizational top-level executive shifting which takes place in many private corporations can be found in the set of management changes announced by the Ford Motor Company in 1965. Charted in Table 3-1 are the various upper management positions which five of these individuals have held prior to 1965. Also indicated is the year each joined the company. Collectively, these five Ford executives reflect a total of 106 years of company experience, with an average of 21.2 years each. Under these circumstances, organizational stability, experience, and cohesiveness—continuity—are virtually assured of being maintained at a high level.

This is not to suggest, of course, that every time a new President of the United States assumes office, a dramatic and abrupt 180 degree policy change will result. Campaign rhetoric to the contrary, the fact remains that every new President inherits a wide range of prior commitments and established programs which cannot be stricken aside. Because of the permanent

[9] For a competent study of political changeover see Laurin Henry's *Presidential Transitions* (Washington: The Brookings Institution, 1960).

nature of many governmental programs and the staggered terminal dates of others, the probability of drastic public policy change being effected by a new President is slight. Nevertheless, there are other subtle ways in which the operational continuity of existing governmental programs can be disrupted. For

### Table 3-1. Top Level Career Patterns of Five Selected Ford Motor Co. Executives[10]

| Names | Entered | Sequence of Recent Positions | | | |
|---|---|---|---|---|---|
| Lee A. Iacocca | 1946 | VP & Gen. Mgr., Ford Division, 1960. | VP-Car & Trk. Grp., 1965. | | Member, Bd. of Directors, 1965. |
| W. D. Innes | 1940 | Gen. Mgr. Eng. & Foundry Div., 1963. | VP-Eng., Trans., & Pts. Grp., 1965. | | |
| Elgar F. Laux | 1953 | Gen. Mktg. Mgr., Ford Division 1960. | Exec. Dir., Mktg., Staff 1964. | VP-Marketing, 1965. | |
| J. Edward Lundy | 1946 | Treasurer, 1957. | VP-Cntlr., 1961. | VP-Finance 1962. | Member, Bd. of Directors, 1965. |
| Robert Stevenson | 1934 | Gen. Mgr., Trans. & Chassis Div. 1961. | VP-Eng, Trans. & Pts. Grp., 1964. | VP-Overseas Automotive Oprns. 1965. | |

[10] *1965 Annual Report*, Ford Motor Co., Dearborn, Michigan. I am grateful to Mr. J. B. Dunkel, Jr., of Ford Motor Co. for suggesting this format of the career pattern chart.

instance, one effective approach is to bring into the executive organization individuals who are philosophically opposed to the objectives of the public policies they are expected to achieve. As Seymour Harris has noted in this regard:

> . . . it is not always easy to repeal laws that the Republic has already accepted and that in general it favors. . . .

The [Eisenhower] Administration surmounted the last difficulty to some extent through repeal by appointment. . . .

For example, Albert M. Cole was made an administrator of the Housing and Home Finance Agency even though he voted as a Congressman against most of the important public housing programs. John B. Hollister, while a member of Congress, voted against the Reciprocal Trade Agreement and was known to share Senator Taft's economic isolationist viewpoints. Nevertheless he became head of the agency for administering foreign aid, the ICA.

As Assistant Secretary of Agriculture, James J. McConnell was in charge of the Price Support Programs he had referred to a few months earlier as "a perfect example of modern socialism."

As Congressman from North Dakota, Fred Aandahl voted five out of seven times against public power programs. Naturally he became Assistant Secretary of the Interior in charge of power. As Congressman from Montana, Wesley D'Ewart was a leading advocate of a bill to turn public grazing lands over to private interests. He became the Assistant Secretary of the Interior in charge of lands and reclamation.[11]

Another example of administrative discontinuity can be found by examining the organizational development of the U. S. Foreign Aid program. From the beginning of the Marshall Plan in 1948, the longest period of time this program has operated *without* a major organizational disruption has been approximately three years. As of 1967, four Presidents have, over the years, assigned the responsibilities of this program to six different agencies, which have been directed by eleven different administrators. Under these circumstances, operating effectiveness has, to say the least, been less than impressive, and, on various occasions in the past, several of the "organizational

[11] Seymour Harris, *The Economics of the Political Parties* (New York: Macmillan, 1962), p. 15.

maladies" referred to above were clearly manifested within the various aid agencies.

Thus, the governmental setting gives rise to several "unique" conflict situations which, for the most part, are not present in nonpolitical administrative environments. Therefore, it is reasonable to ask to what extent the control techniques generally applied in private business organizations can be effectively utilized within the executive branch?

## Characteristics of Executive Branch Control

Problem solving and pure persuasion (objective analysis), as noted previously, are control techniques which are most effective in resolving intragroup, interpersonal, low-level conflict. Where a single, objectively right answer is sought, or a single, logically preferred conclusion is allowed, the former can be determined by problem solving; the latter, by pure persuasion. These techniques are certainly just as applicable in governmental organizations. For this reason, nothing more will be added to what has already been said concerning these two control methods. Instead, the problem of organizational control in the executive branch will be examined solely in terms of the other two aforementioned techniques—manipulated agreement and bargaining.

### Manipulated Agreement

As noted previously, manipulated agreement is characterized by two basic considerations if it is applied effectively. First, a subtle and indirect form of organizational coercion is involved in which the scope of conflict is enlarged to the point where one party to the conflict finds itself in an isolated position against a substantial portion of the rest of the organization. This situation then gives rise to the second factor which reinforces the effectiveness of manipulated agreement; namely, the concept of collective responsibility. Once "consensus" appears to exist on any given point, opposition is expected to end, and collective responsibility becomes the guiding organizational principle. Failure to recognize or to accept this principle is simply to invite the imposition of any of the full range of sanctions at the disposal of the organization, up to, and including, the ultimate sanction of dismissal. On the basis of these two major considerations, it seems reasonable to suggest that manipulated agreement, as applied in the executive branch, is, at best, a semieffective control technique, and that conflict, in most instances, must be resolved (if it is resolved at all) through negotiation, accommodation, compromise—in short, through bargaining. The semieffectiveness of manipulated agreement as a control technique in the executive branch is due to several factors: the limitations imposed on the President, the semiautonomous nature of the various executive subunits, and the wide latitude permitted for the expansion of conflict.

LIMITATIONS ON PRESIDENTIAL CONTROL. Manipulated agreement was earlier identified as a "pseudo-democratic" form of direct, unilateral control. Manipulated agreement can be made to work effectively only if the ultimate sanctions of control are monopolized by top-level executive officials. Thus if agreement cannot be obtained through the tactful manipulation of coercion and consensus, direct control must be applied, including, of course, the ultimate sanction of dismissal. The President, technically, can at any time demand the resignation of any member of his Cabinet. But, to a very real extent, this option is limited, if not negated, by various other political and administrative considerations. Every executive control action involving the President and any member of his Cabinet—from a mild contradiction or rebuff to outright dismissal—must always be viewed as a potential political liability to be publicly avoided if at all possible. For this reason, the President of the United States, unlike the president of a major corporation, is much more restricted by the "law of anticipated reactions," as Friedrich calls it.[12] The President must—or, at least, he should—be aware of the possible political effects that any positive control action aimed at his subordinates will have in terms of his own reputation, status, and prestige. These factors, as Neustadt contends,[13] are what the President *must* protect at all costs, and in many instances the President is confronted with the stark reality that a Cabinet dismissal may severely damage his own "power" base.

The administrative considerations which may limit the President are equally important. Administrative operations within a particular department may be seriously impaired if the dismissal of the department head touches off a series of protest resignations among the department's subordinate executive officials. As has already been noted, administrative continuity is, under normal circumstances, difficult enough to develop and maintain; forced resignations or dismissals of Cabinet officials merely tend to aggravate an already existing organizational problem. Moreover, the President is limited administratively as a result of his extremely broad span of control, i.e., the number of executive subordinates who report directly to the President. By even the most conservative count, the activities of *at least* fifteen individuals must be subject to the direct supervision of, and consultation with, every President. (Twelve Cabinet Secretaries, the head of the White House Staff, the Director of the Bureau of the Budget, and, of course, the Vice President.) Depending on the temperament and personal interests of the President, this figure could very easily increase; but even if his span of control is limited to this absolute minimum of fifteen (and one observer has noted, "No President has ever gotten

[12] Carl J. Friedrich, "Public Policy and the Nature of Administrative Responsibility," *Public Policy*, Vol. 1 (Cambridge: Harvard University Press, 1940), pp. 3–24.

[13] Richard E. Neustadt, *Presidential Power* (New York: John Wiley and Sons, 1960).

down to fifteen"), this almost inevitably assures the sacrifice of effective control to superficial control. By comparison, the median number of subordinates reporting directly to the presidents of 100 large, private companies in 1966 was just less than nine. Of the 100 private companies examined by Dale, only eleven had spans of control incorporating fifteen or more executive subordinates.[14]

For these reasons the President is limited by very practical considerations in the extent to which his implicit use of force can be effectively translated into actual power insofar as his relationships with his executive subordinates are concerned. Much the same can be said of the relationship between Departmental Secretaries and their subordinates. Consequently, manipulated agreement, without the extreme sanction of dismissal to back it up, must depend on voluntary compliance, or else give way to bargaining. This is not to suggest that the President and his Department Secretaries do not enjoy the formal authority to impose many severe sanctions; however, the costs incurred in imposing severe punishments on executive subordinates normally exceed any gains that may be derived from attempting to exert positive control. For this reason, top-level officials within the executive branch are limited to a policy of moderation in the resolution of conflict. Manipulated agreement must be replaced by pure persuasion; if this tactic proves unsuccessful, a pure bargaining situation must result.

THE SEMIAUTONOMOUS SUBSYSTEM. To a very real extent, any examination of the executive bureaucracy is a study of the use of pure bargaining control techniques simply because of the many firmly entrenched, semiautonomous individuals and subunits that fill the executive structure.[15] The Corps of Engineers of the

[14] Ernest Dale, *Organization* (New York: American Management Association, 1967), p. 95.

[15] Dahl and Lindblom, *op. cit.*, Ch. 12; Robert Presthus, "Authority in Organizations," in *Concepts and Issues in Administrative Behavior*, Sidney

U. S. Army and its jurisdiction over the nation's rivers and harbors has been well publicized as the virtually untouchable bureau within the Department of Defense.[16] Likewise, the Federal Bureau of Investigation enjoys a somewhat similar reputation within the Justice Department.[17] Furthermore, some of the most important administrative positions within the executive branch are held by individuals who are covered by the Civil Service Classification Act. This means, in effect, that they can be removed from their positions only as a result of gross insubordination, undesirable personal habits, negligence, criminal acts, or as a result of having their jobs abolished.

Included in this category of civil service employees is the cadre of senior career, civil service professionals, including most bureau chiefs. The bureau chiefs are, for the most part, thoroughly competent and proficient specialists who direct the vital subunits of the various executive departments. However, because of their civil service status and their extensive seniority, they must be viewed in the dual perspective as being both a part of, and apart from, the President's executive team. Describing them as political entrepreneurs is perhaps an overstatement;[18] nevertheless, even when conflict develops between them and their politically appointed superiors, the degree of security they enjoy is frequently considerable.

For instance, in March, 1966, a long, smoldering feud between the Administrator of the State Department's Bureau of

Mailick and Edward H. Van Ness (eds.) (Englewood Cliffs: Prentice-Hall, 1962), pp. 122–36; J. Leiper Freeman, *The Political Process* (New York: Random House, 1965 revised).

[16] Arthur A. Maass, "Congress and Water Resources," *American Political Science Review*, vol. 44 (September, 1950), pp. 576–93. See also his *Muddy Waters* (Cambridge: Harvard University Press, 1951).

[17] Joseph F. Marsh, Jr., "The FBI Retirement Bill," in *Public Administration and Policy Development*, Harold Stein (ed.) (New York: Harcourt Brace, 1952).

[18] Freeman, *op. cit.*, p. 13.

Security and Consular Affairs, Assistant Secretary of State Abba Schwartz, and the Director of the Bureau's Passport Office, Frances Knight, was fully publicized.[19] Basically, the differences which developed between these two individuals involved their conflicting interpretations of the Department's passport and visa policy. In this respect, Miss Knight opposed her superior's more liberal attitude. Realizing that Miss Knight could not be dismissed, Schwartz attempted to employ the time-honored administrative tactic of intradepartmental transfer. However, this attempt failed because Miss Knight was quite effective in rallying more support to her defense (ten U. S. Senators in a signed statement to the Secretary of State, and a close alliance with the chairman of the Senate Internal Security Subcommittee) than Schwartz was able to get to back his position. The situation was finally resolved by a departmental reorganization which was designed to eliminate the position held by *Schwartz*.

The problem of executive control is further compounded when one realizes that the President as the Chief Executive is additionally limited by the vast multitude of independent offices and agencies which only indirectly come under his control, although their actions and policies may have direct consequences on his national programs. Included in this grouping are all of the multimember Independent Regulatory Commissions, the various government corporations, and other administrative structures such as the Export-Import Bank, the Federal Reserve System, and the U. S. Tariff Commission. Semiautonomous by law as well as by custom, these agencies are guided by individuals who, although appointed by the President, serve prescribed terms in office which normally extend beyond the term of the President who appoints them. Their terms are also staggered so

[19] In this instance, although Schwartz headed a bureau, he was the political appointee of John F. Kennedy. Miss Knight, as head of the Passport Office, was a career civil servant.

that no single President can normally expect to "gain control" of these groups through the appointive process. In order to co-ordinate the actions of these agencies with those of the other executive departments, agreement has to rely mainly on volun-tary compliance or, once again, give way to a pure bargaining situation.

THE SCOPE OF CONFLICT. In other words, what is being sug-gested here is simply that certain Executive department subunits and individuals—if they are so disposed—can frequently mobi-lize a wide range of "power" factors to offset executive branch control techniques. Political considerations can frequently be exploited; senior civil servants can count on the Classification Act to provide a counterbalancing force; and similar legal restric-tions frequently render the various independent agencies immune to executive control. In short, one basic distinction be-tween governmental and nongovernmental organizations is that the definable limits placed on conflict in the latter are not neces-sarily applicable in the former setting. Or, to restate the premise, the executive branch official has many more potential alternate appeal routes at his disposal than does his nongovernmental counterpart in private business or industry.

The middle management executive of a major private con-cern, whose recommendations have been ignored or vetoed, whose duties are to be reorganized or even absorbed by another unit, or whose budget has been drastically curtailed, has pitifully few alternatives at his disposal other than to accept the decision or to resign in protest. When confronted with the same circum-stances, the executive branch administrator may, as a result of personal loyalty or a strong sense of personal obligation, volun-tarily comply with the decision. Or, if he is initially opposed to the decision he may be convinced by his superiors (through pure persuasion) that the final decision is actually in his own best interests. If this fails, the executive subordinate may have one other option available. He may attempt to expand the scope of conflict well beyond the limits of the executive structure in an effort to gain support for his position from various external groups. The inclusion of external groups in the manner in which executive branch conflict is resolved means that top-level executive officials, including the President, are forced to take into consideration the attitudes of groups over which they have no direct control. In other words, the decision-making and control powers of the executive organization must be shared, in many instances, with other, "outside" groups. This situation, it will be noted, coincides with the definition of pure bargaining established in the previous chapter. It is the control technique most frequently employed within the executive branch to resolve conflict.

### Bargaining—The Role of External Groups

The role assumed by various external groups in the planning and operating stages of most private corporations is—or, at least, should be—quite significant. Indeed, one of the most telling criticisms that can be aimed at many large-scale private organizations is their failure to grant sufficient consideration to the values and attitudes of many of these groups. Probably, the two best publicized groups external to any private corporation are the stockholders and the buying public, i.e., its customers. Both groups, on occasion, have been able to negate management decisions. The theory that ultimate corporate authority rests with the stockholders is not an empty platitude; recommendations and propositions by corporation officers are occasionally rejected by the stockholders. Likewise, the customer may not always be right, but he is never wrong—at least, if he refuses to buy a company's product. In many product fields, particularly where competition is intense, even slight downward shifts in sales may set off Pavlovian-type responses on the part of executive officials. The "public" callously disregarded the familial tribute paid to Edsel Ford, and the line was terminated after two production cycles. General Motors fared no better when Buick sales dropped sharply following the release of the 1958 barred rear window model. In this situation the division manager lost his job a year later.[20] In other words, it is reasonable to suggest that when demand is elastic and competition is high, the indirect influence of the customer over corporate policy and operating decision can be substantial.

However, a major difference exists between the amount and type of influence enjoyed by the primary groups external to the private corporation and those external to the federal bureaucracy. In the latter case, the primary external groups may actually become *directly* involved in the daily operating procedures of the organization. As a consequence, executive branch control techniques frequently take on the character of a bargained settlement in which the groups external to the executive branch become principal negotiators. The two most significant external forces which will be examined here are the congressional committees and the interest groups.

THE CONGRESSIONAL COMMITTEES. Within the context of the American Constitution, the public policy functions of the legislative and executive branches are stated quite explicitly: the Congress shall make the laws and the President shall insure that the laws are faithfully executed. But such terms as "Congress", "The Executive Branch," and "The President" are not very helpful if one is concerned with formulating a precise understanding of legislative-executive accountability and responsibility.

Technically, of course, the President as an individual is accountable to the collective entity referred to as Congress for any actions taken by his vast army of administrative subordinates. After all, he is situated at the apex of the executive hierarchy, and the operations of that structure are ultimately his responsibility. However, there are several reasons why this type

20 "General Motors Planning," *Business Week* (Oct. 5, 1963), p. 137.

of literal interpretation cannot be given to the division of powers which exists between the two branches.

Insofar as the President is concerned, the most obvious fact which emerges is that he is directly accountable *only* to a national electorate. He may be indirectly accountable to Congress, but the legislative branch—while it may harass, stymie, thwart, veto, negate, or ignore executive decisions and actions—cannot positively exert direct unilateral control over the President (except in the instance of impeachment proceedings). Secondly, the President cannot literally be held accountable for all of the actions that take place within the federal bureaucracy since, as we have discussed before, he personally does not enjoy direct unilateral control over the entire executive structure. And finally, the President, situated as he is atop the organizational pyramid, inevitably is forced to view the direction of the public policy process in the broadest, most all-inclusive terms.

For Congress, the basic point that must be made at the outset is that the term itself is simply a composite expression for a cluster of smaller operational groups—the congressional committees. Thus, executive-legislative relationships actually have to be examined in terms of executive-congressional committee relationships. But this only balances one half of the equation. The next step is to give a more precise meaning to the term "executive branch."

Since the congressional committee system is established on the basis of functional specialization, every executive function falls within the purview of some legislative subgroup. Consequently, for the individual congressional committees, the problem of defining the "executive branch" has been effectively simplified; the "executive branch," is viewed primarily in terms of the particular executive departments or agencies which fall within a particular committee's sphere or jurisdiction. Likewise, "Congress," as seen by executive administrators, actually means the particular congressional subgroups to whom they are accountable. However, the relationship between these executive and legislative subunits can become complex. Every executive subunit is accountable to at least two, usually four, and possibly even more congressional committees and/or subcommittees. Every request for statutory authority originating from within the executive bureaucracy must be considered by a House and Senate subject-matter committee; if the proposal involves the expenditure of public funds, additional authorization must be received from the House and Senate Appropriations Committees; and finally, every executive subunit is subject to review by the House and Senate Government Operations Committees which are given wide latitude to insure the most efficient and economical expenditure of appropriated funds by the executive branch.

Thus, the relationship which actually develops between the two branches involves specific congressional subgroups which are related to specific executive subgroups by a common functional interest. Viewed in this context, the role of the congressional committees as related to organizational control and conflict within the executive branch can be studied more meaningfully.

Moreover, it should be noted that Congress is organized to deal with public policy questions in terms of specifics, not in terms of abstract principles.[21] The committee system is designed to encourage legislative specialization, and the reward systems in the House and Senate place legislative expertise in a decidedly preferential position. Time is another factor—or, more precisely, the lack of it—which causes congressmen and their committees to concentrate almost exclusively on the specific aspects of executive programs. Given the tremendous range of demands that are made of our legislators, few can enjoy the luxury of

[21] Richard E. Neustadt, "Presidency and Legislation: Planning the President's Program," *American Political Science Review*, vol. 49 (December, 1955), pp. 980–1021.

evaluating executive actions and decisions in terms of abstract policy justifications. But, probably most important of all, congressional committee preoccupation with program specifics is primarily an exercise in self-defense. In other words, the congressional subgroups are significantly limited in the extent to which they can influence basic policy decisions made in the executive branch. The burden of proof, so to speak, rests with the various committees to demonstrate that these policy decisions are ill-advised, and this is not always a simple task. For instance, it is frequently difficult to reject, or even to question the basic premises which underlie most major policy decisions made by the executive branch. Consequently, committee members are inevitably forced to limit their evaluations of such decisions to the specific means which shall be employed to achieve a certain end or goal. And in this regard, the annual review sessions conducted by the committees provide a convenient means whereby executive programs can be periodically monitored.

*Annual review sessions*, figuratively speaking, are annual meetings between executive administrators and congressional committees which culminate in a "contractual agreement." In return for certain considerations to be supplied by the committee—statutory authority, funds, and so on—the officials of the executive bureaucracy "promise" to achieve certain goals, or to accomplish certain results. In granting initial requests for a totally new program, the committees must, for the most part, act on faith alone.[22] However, in all subsequent sessions, prior promises can be evaluated on the basis of actual administrative performance, and the attitudes of congressional committee

---

[22] Congressional decision-making in the absence of objective data accumulated from prior experience is best evidenced in the various congressional hearings during the 80th Cong., 2nd sess. (1948) on the European Recovery Program (the Marshall Plan); the hearings on the establishment of the Peace Corps (88th Cong., 1st sess. 1963); and the hearings on the Poverty Program (88th Cong., 2nd sess. 1964).

members toward the particular program will be affected to the extent that their expectations do or do not coincide with their evaluation of executive performance.

On the basis of this approach to public policy evaluations, it should be apparent that congressional committees—if they are to make a reasonably accurate assessment of the correlation between expectations and performance—must concentrate their efforts and resources on the analysis of specific details. That is, they must concern themselves primarily with the administrative implementation of public laws. Viewed within this context, therefore, the most important and significant relationship which develops is between the congressional committees and the specific executive officials who are responsible for making actual operating decisions.

Such a person is obviously not the President; nor is he likely to be a Departmental Secretary or Under Secretary since both of these individuals are primarily concerned with problems involving policy formulation and coordination. It is not until one reaches the middle management level—occasionally the Assistant Secretaries, but more frequently the senior career employees—that this relationships becomes meaningful. Generally speaking, these are the individuals who possess the type of information needed by congressional committees to solve the "promise-performance" equation. Below this middle management level, any information received lacks the necessary authority to be of real use to the committees; above this level, although the degree of authority increases significantly, the information received tends to become increasingly diffuse.

Since a significant number of Assistant Secretaries are selected from the ranks of senior career employees[23] attention should be directed to the relationship between senior civil service bureaucrats and the congressional committees in an

[23] Dean E. Mann with Jameson W. Doig, *The Assistant Secretaries* (Washington: The Brookings Institution, 1965), pp. 27–30, 112–114, 271.

effort to explain how these committees may influence the control and conflict situations which may develop within the executive branch.

*The senior career Executive official* is distinguished from top-level executive officials by one characteristic: permanence. The civil service specialists who function at the operational level provide a degree of continuity and stability which is essentially absent at the upper levels of the executive organization. The most enduring relationship which the senior careerists (bureau chiefs and the "supergrades"—G.S.-16, 17 and 18) develop over their extended years of service is not with the President or their Department Secretaries, but, rather with the chairmen and the ranking members of the particular set of congressional committees which have jurisdiction over their daily operations. For both the career federal employees and the ranking congressional committee members, Presidents and their administrations simply represent a four- or eight-year portion of a total career which may span twenty, thirty, or forty years. As a result, the frame of reference utilized by these individuals—which is so important in providing an environmental orientation and in organizing one's occupational behavior around this orientation —cannot, except in the case of the Assistant Secretaries, focus on the President. Instead, the enduring frame of reference for the federal careerists and the senior committee members is generally stated as simply "public service," as defined in terms of a particular and rather narrowly specialized functional activity. The common bond which develops between these two groups is simply the sharing of the same functional interests. The House and Senate Committees on Agriculture are collectively concerned with basic agricultural policy as devised by the Department of Agriculture, but even more specifically the House Agricultural Subcommittee on Forests is clearly concerned with the specific operating decisions made by the Department's Forest Service. Likewise, for those congressmen who are assigned to the various commodity subcommittees, the actions taken by the Agricultural Stabilization and Conservation Service in connection with acreage allotments, marketing quotas, and price support levels, represent the most tangible and enduring bond that could be developed. Every legislative subunit has a tie-in with some executive subunit; this alliance is continuous, it is operationally meaningful, and, if the career executive employee is at all astute, it should be mutually beneficial.

The members of the congressional committee benefit from this relationship by (1) getting the type of information they need as legislators, and (2) getting the type of service they need as constituent representatives. The executive career employee benefits by gaining additional support from "his" committee. Top-level executive officials can benefit insofar as they are able to capitalize on the career bureaucrat-congressional committee relationship. However, in those instances where a compatible relationship exists between the career administrator and the legislative subgroup, any effort by politically appointed executive officials to alter or ignore this situation is likely to result in conflict.

On the basis of the above discussion it should be apparent that in the *formulation* of basic policy decisions, top-level executive officials are able to maintain a fairly high degree of internal control as a result of the relatively minimal interference or influence that external groups, such as the various congressional committees, are able to exert on the process. However, as the process shifts from policy *formulation* to program *implementation*, the executive responsibilities also shift to middle-level management officials who are primarily concerned with operating performance. Actual performance also becomes the primary focal point of interest for most legislative subgroups. Consequently, it is at this level that congressional influence becomes maximized, and the effectiveness of executive control techniques is significantly weakened. The middle-level executive official thus becomes a man divided in his loyalty, in part to the President or his Departmental Secretary whose policy decision he is expected to carry out, and in part to "his" legislative subgroup whose support and confidence he must maintain. As a result of this situation, conflict is potentially ever-present within the executive branch at the middle and lower operating levels of the hierarchy, and in those instances when the potential conflict becomes an actual reality, operating effectiveness can be seriously jeopardized simply because effective control techniques cannot be unilaterally imposed by top-level executive branch officials. In this regard, organizational authority is not monopolized, but is shared with an external group, and, as a consequence, the resolution of conflict frequently assumes the characteristics of a negotiated settlement between executive branch officials and the members of a particular legislative subunit; in short, a pure bargaining relationship develops.

THE INTEREST GROUPS. The other significant external force which is frequently able to assume the role of principal negotiator in the resolution of executive branch conflict is the interest groups. Interest groups, along with the congressional committees, become tied in with the operations of specific executive subunits as a result of shared interests. For example, the American Farm Bureau Federation or the National Rural Electric Cooperative Association, like the House and Senate Agricultural Committees, are very interested in the specific operational decisions made by the various component units within the Department of Agriculture. Although an interesting theory concerning the changing role of interest groups in our society has been advanced by Eldersveld,[24] they, like the congressional committees, have traditionally been concerned with the specific

[24] Samuel J. Eldersveld, "American Interest Groups: A Survey of Research and Some Implications for Theory and Method," in *Interest Groups on Four Continents*, Henry W. Ehrmann (ed.) (Pittsburgh: University of Pittsburgh Press, 1958), pp. 173–96.

implementation of public policy decisions. In this regard, the influence exerted by the interest groups within the executive branch at the operating level is frequently significant. For instance, they may be able to have one of "their men" appointed as an Assistant Secretary. In the Agriculture, Labor, Commerce, and Interior Departments particularly, the affected interest groups have been consistently successful in this regard. Furthermore, it is important to recognize that the flow of personnel between interest groups and the executive branch goes in both directions. That is, although interest groups seek to exert influence in the appointment of various executive branch officials, many middle-level operating officials in turn seek to establish close relationships with the interest groups which may prove beneficial whenever they leave the executive organization. Finally, in terms of communications, many executive subunits are absolutely dependent upon maintaining close cooperation with interest groups. It is the interest groups which provide the executive branch with lines of contact to select publics which can be mobilized for concerted political action when the occasion demands.

This latter point illustrates one aspect of the multipattern system which emerges when each of these three units—the executive branch, the interest groups, and the congressional committees—are viewed in terms of an interrelated triangular system, as shown in Figure 3-3.

Within this context, one tentative hypothesis suggests that the importance of this sytem—or, more correctly, subsystem, as Freeman refers to it[25]—lies in the fact that when the subsystem, involving a particular executive subunit, interest group, and legislative committee, reveals a high degree of cohesiveness, any efforts by top-level executive officials to alter the operating procedures of the executive subunit involved would be seriously limited unless concurrence, if only tacit, could be obtained from

[25] Freeman, *op. cit.*

the remaining "partners" of the subsystem. In order to maximize executive branch control, the ideal situation, of course, would be to gain the support of all three units. However, it could be hypothesized that conflict could probably be resolved if the support of at least two of the three "subunits" could be obtained. Ironically it would seem that the support of the two external

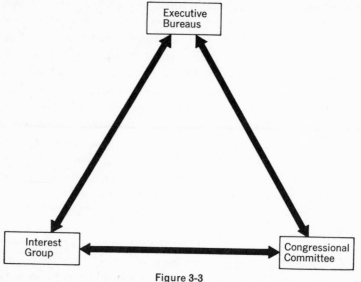

Figure 3-3

groups would be most valued by executive officials since they would then be in a fairly secure position to impose direct, unilateral control techniques on the executive subunit involved. Since support of the two external groups could not be obtained through manipulated agreement, pure bargaining would be the only context in which the conflict could be resolved.

It should be apparent, therefore, that the role of external groups must be considered in conjunction with any discussion of executive branch control techniques. Unlike their nongovernmental counterparts, governmental bureaucratic structures are extremely porous organizations, especially at the middle and lower levels. As a result, the "pressure" in the organization's chain of command—that system which circulates influence and authority throughout the entire structure—is weakened due to constant leakage. To maintain the "pressure" at an effective level despite the weaknesses in the structure requires extra effort on the part of top-level executive officials, including particularly, the President. If this extra effort cannot be, or is not exerted, then the overall operating effectiveness of the executive branch will diminish.

## Summary

The situation involving methods of control within the federal executive structure takes on, in many respects, a fundamentally different character than that which is evidenced within complex, nongovernmental bureaucracies. Obviously, the oligarchal model of bureaucratic organizations which fits neatly into most business and industrial hierarchies, does not apply to the executive branch. Within the governmental setting, actual— as opposed to formal—bureaucratic power is not necessarily inversely related to the degree of functional specialization. Nor is it stable, permanently fixed, and easily discernible as is generally the case in private organizations. In short, governmental bureaucratic power more closely resembles Dahl's analysis of community power—dispersed and unequal[26]—simply because the federal executive bureaucracy is a composite set of semi-autonomous subunits. Viewed in this context, therefore, it should be recognized that as the delegation of authority increases in the executive branch, the power to control organizational behavior becomes increasingly fragmented, dispersed, and unequal. It is this basic point which distinguishes governmental and nongovernmental organizations insofar as the internal control mechanisms are concerned.

[26] Robert Dahl, *Who Governs?* (New Haven: Yale University Press, 1961).

# 4

# Decision Making— Theoretical Considerations

The basic assumption reflected here is that both decision making and the control process are simply two sides of the same bureaucratic coin. This means that the twin processes represent the two most important problem areas confronting every major bureaucratic organization. As Simon has noted:

> The task of "deciding" pervades the entire administrative organization quite as much as does the task of "doing"— indeed, it is integrally tied up with the latter. A general theory of administration must include principles of organization that will insure correct decision-making just as it must include principles that will insure effective action.[1]

The purpose of this chapter, therefore, is to analyze several basic concepts of decision making within an essentially theoretical

[1] Simon, *Administrative Behavior*, p. 1.

framework. Decision making, as specifically related to the executive bureaucracy, will be examined in the following chapter. These two chapters, in conjunction with Chapters 2 and 3 should provide a balanced and integrated presentation of the twin organizational processes which inevitably must be dealt with by the executive bureaucratic structure if it is to respond to the inevitable demands for organizational change.

## Aspects of Decision Making

Decision making is popularly defined as the process that is associated with the choice among two or more possible courses of action. Many important variations of this simplistic definition are available. For instance, the Simon quotation above introduces the very significant term *"correct* decision-making." Viewed in this context, then, decision making involves the *correct* choice among two or more alternatives. In addition, the outstanding early contributions to our knowledge of administrative decision making by Chester Barnard present another important dimension—*logical choice*. Decision making, wrote Barnard, is the deliberate adapting of means to ends, and this in turn constitutes the essence of formal organization.[2] Thus, the concept of deliberate choice as suggested by Barnard actually must be interpreted as a concept of logical choice, in which case decision making then becomes the *rational* choice between two or more alternatives.

For Simon, the role of rationality enjoys a central focus in the decision-making scheme; "The theory of administration or organization," he wrote, "cannot exist without a theory of rational choice."[3] For this reason, therefore, a discussion of the decision-making process can logically begin with the aspect of rational choice.

[2] *The Functions of the Executive* (Cambridge: Harvard University Press, 1938), p. 186.

[3] H. A. Simon, *Models of Man* (New York: Wiley and Son, 1957), p. 196.

## Rationality

Decisions, in a sense, are individual responses to certain situations (stimuli) which require a response. Sitting on a bee and the subsequent response can hardly be examined as a decision-making situation simply because the time gap between the stimulus and the response is virtually zero. Therefore, one aspect of decision making which distinguishes it from a simple spontaneous reaction is that a sufficient period of time must transpire between the demand for a response and the response itself in order to allow the individual the opportunity to make a choice. But even this is not a completely satisfactory explanation since it implies that decision making must involve conscious and deliberate consideration to be viewed as rational; however, this definition fails to recognize two important types of decision responses: those classified as habits, and those which must be made almost instantaneously. In regard to the former, does the shifting of gears on an automobile constitute rational decision? Actually, is a conscious and deliberate decision always involved? As for the latter, how much time does a batter have to deliberate the advisibility of swinging at a pitch following the pitcher's delivery? In both instances, conscious deliberation plus frequent repetition of the same event gradually alters the decision maker's response to an automatic-type reaction. Under these circumstances, the key factor is constant repetition, or frequent recurrence of the same event, which leads to the semiconscious response that technically is still a decision. For the most part, the countless daily decisions we are forced to make involve familiar circumstances which require very little conscious deliberation. Set responses develop to similar decision demands which tend to recur frequently. Thus, the bulk of the decisions that most of us are forced to make during the course of an average day usually becomes firmly established, i.e., "programmed", as part of our daily routine. Under these circumstances, very little conscious deliberation or original decision-making activity is involved.

The level of intellectual activity changes significantly, however, when one is confronted with a situation for which no routine response exists. Under these circumstances a "nonprogrammed" situation could be one which is totally unique to the individual; or, if it has occurred previously, its recurrence is so infrequent that the previous responses are forgotten; or, even if it does occur frequently, certain variables associated with the situation may have changed significantly so as to render past responses obsolete. In short, just as there are many instances during the course of a single day for which we utilize rote responses to certain types of decision demands, there are also numerous instances when we are called upon to make a "real" decision.

When an individual is confronted with a nonprogrammed situation how does he proceed to arrive at a rational conclusion concerning the most appropriate response? A relatively simple and self-explanatory series of steps can be followed in this regard.

1. Establish goal or objective to be achieved.
2. Collect all relevant data.
3. Organize the data into a meaningful body of information.
4. Determine the range of available alternatives.
5. Determine the consequences associated with each alternative.
6. Select that alternative which represents the most preferred set of consequences in relation to the desired objective.

If each step of the above process could be applied perfectly, then a totally objective and rational choice should result. However, it should require little insight to discern the limitations inherent in the above scheme.

*Limitations of Rational Decision Making*

In the first place, since a nonprogrammed situation almost by definition involves a high degree of uncertainty and ambiguity, it is not realistic to expect that goals will be or even, in all cases, can be stated in clear, precise terms. Although this is not always the case, goals and objectives under nonprogrammed conditions are frequently stated in broad, abstract, and ambiguous terms in order to maximize decision-making flexibility when the ultimate choice has to be made. Second, one can never be certain that all relevant data have been collected; indeed, under nonprogrammed conditions, one might not even be certain as to what constitutes relevant or irrelevant data. Third, Simon notes the impossible dimensions imposed by any attempt to determine the range of all available alternatives: "Rationality requires a choice among all possible alternative behaviors. In actual behavior, only a very few of all these possible alternatives ever come to mind."[4] So what we actually must say insofar as the formulation of alternatives is concerned, is that rationality involves a choice *not* among all possible alternatives but, rather, among all *known* and *available* alternatives.

Having arranged the list of known and available alternatives, the final step is accomplished by selecting from this universe that alternative which presents the decision maker with the most favorable set of consequences as related to the objective which he seeks. This, of course, assumes that the consequences of each of the known and available alternatives have been thoroughly considered. However, consequences actually are only estimations of future occurrences, and the reliability of these "predictions" depends on the reliability of the data collected as well as the reliability of the methods used to analyze the data. In some instances, the consequences can be quite accurately stated; in other instances, particularly those involving complex problem situations, estimated consequences of various

[4] *Administrative Behavior*, p. 81.

alternative actions may represent nothing more than personal guesses. For these reasons, a theory of rational choice must be stated in such a way so as to account for these four limitations—goal ambiguity, imperfect search procedures in the collection of data, limited alternatives, and the imprecise prediction of consequences associated with each alternative.

As Alexis and Wilson note, the manner in which these decision-making dilemmas are resolved will depend, to a great extent, on the type of decision-making situation that is involved.

> The more complex the problem, the more extensive the search. Similarly, the more unique the problematic situation, the more random the search will be. Therefore, unique and highly complex problems are likely to involve extensive search and a good deal of randomness. At the other extreme, recurring and routine problems are likely to involve limited and well-structured search.[5]

Under these circumstances, unique and complex decision events, while demanding extensive and random search procedures, also impose the highest degree of uncertainty on the decision maker. Therefore, one might assume that rational behavior would dictate that the search for the most appropriate alternative would expand proportionately with the complexity and uniqueness of the problem situation. In fact, however, rational search for alternatives and their anticipated consequences is controlled by a modified "law of diminishing returns." In other words, at some point additional search becomes unprofitable, as gauged by the type of resources which happen to be utilized in the search process. Cyert and March formally present this idea in propositional terms:

> ... the assumption of infinite search has been replaced by a theory of search that recognizes certain costs to search, and thus

[5] Marcus Alexis and Charles Z. Wilson, *Organizational Decision-Making* (Englewood Cliffs: Prentice-Hall, 1967), p. 77.

makes the allocation of resources for securing information one of the investment decisions to be made. The modern entrepreneur does not scan all alternatives nor does he have all information about all alternatives. He invests in information only so long as the expected marginal return from the information gained exceeds the expected marginal cost.[6]

Very real limitations, therefore, are imposed on decision making in any complex bureaucratic environment, particularly in those instances involving nonprogrammed problem situations coupled with a wide range of variable factors. Thus, whether we use the term "bounded rationality" from Simon, or "adaptively rational" rather than "omnisciently rational" as proposed by Cyert and March, we are, nevertheless, referring to the very practical decision-making situation which develops within a less-than-perfect context as a result of certain limitations imposed on the system. These limitations include the limited capacities of both the system and the individual decision maker to gather, sort, and analyze information; the cost factor involved in extensive search procedures, and, possible of greatest significance, the limitations of available time that may be devoted to searching procedures.

The necessity for any decision implies some time limitation. In the absence of any deadline, no need for decision making exists. Therefore decision making imposes on the individual some obligation to act in a certain manner in some specified period of time. Of course, the extent of the time period may significantly affect the way in which the individual approaches the problem situation. The difference in which the individual proceeds to reach a decision to an important situation can be substantial if the decision is required in one day as opposed to one hour; or one year as opposed to one month. One of the most

[6] Richard M. Cyert and James G. March, *A Behavioral Theory of the Firm* (Englewood Cliffs; Prentice-Hall, 1963), p. 45.

common practices of virtually all responsible decision makers is to seek additional extensions of time in an effort to reduce the degree of uncertainty that is confronted in complex problem situations.

Of course, this is not always possible. The baseball player is working under the pressure of an extremely short time period; military commanders engaged in battle are frequently forced to make immediate decisions which may have momentous consequences; business executives, political officials, and government bureaucrats, all are frequently exposed to the rigors of rapid decision-making demands. Consequently, when all of the various limitations imposed on the decision-making process are taken into account, the best that can be said of any theory of objective rationality is that it represents an idealized myth. The time limitation, along with the others that have been discussed, creates an entirely different context in which the decision maker is forced to operate than that presented by the classical economic model in which the decision maker—"economic man"—seeks only to maximize his gains and minimize his losses. The distinction, presented by Simon, is between "economic man" and "administrative man." The former seeks to optimize or maximize his gains in the economic decision-making process, while the latter can only hope to "satisfice" or satisfy his goal objectives. In terms of bureaucratic decision making and, particularly, executive branch decision making, this distinction deserves more detailed analysis.

### Optimizing-Satisfying

As noted above, it is generally regarded that "administrative man" cannot maximize his goal objectives as can his purely economically motivated counterpart simply because he is forced to take into account a much wider range of considerations than solely cost-utility factors. Instead, the administrator seeks a *satisfactory* alternative; or, as Simon contends, he "satisfices—

looks for a course of action that is satisfactory or 'good enough.'"[7] In a more recent study Simon and his co-author James March present the same thoughts in slightly different terms.

Most human decision-making, whether individual or organizational, is concerned with the discovery and selection of satisfactory alternatives; only in exceptional cases is it concerned with the discovery and selection of optimal alternatives.[8]

The intricate distinctions between the optimizing and satisfying approaches are discussed fully in other sources.[9] For our purposes here it is sufficient to note that although an extensive and impressive body of literature supports the satisfying decision-making approach as applied to the administrative process, it would appear that this approach is more theoretical than practical, much more limited than its generalized tone would suggest, and, indeed, much more apt to raise serious theoretical questions than to answer them. Optimizing is certainly the exceptional pattern of decision-making behavior if by optimizing one means the selection of the best alternative from *all other possible* alternatives. Because of the limitations imposed on the human decision-making apparatus, "the best of all possible

[7] Simon, *Administrative Behavior*, p. xxv. The terms "satisfying" and "satisficing" are used synonymously here in much the same way as Simon himself seems to use them. As long as one bears in mind that both terms imply administration solutions that are "good enough," no difficulty should be encountered. The term "satisfying" does not imply the type of emotional stimulation or deep sense of satisfaction one may experience as a result of a need fulfilled or an objective achieved.

[8] March and Simon, *Organizations*, p. 141.

[9] Donald W. Taylor, "Decision-Making and Problem Solving," pp. 59ff; Julian Feldman and Herschel Kanter, "Organization Decision-Making," pp. 629ff, both in *Handbook of Organizations, op. cit.*; Roland N. McKean, "Sub-Optimization Criteria and Operations Research," in Alexis and Wilson, *Organizational Decision-Making, op. cit.*, pp. 164–73.

alternatives" will obviously never be known in complex de-cision-making situations. Consequently, to apply this definition to the term "optimal" is simply to place virtually every decision event in the category of satisfying by default. On the other hand, if optimal is defined as the best of all *known* and *available* alterna-tives, then it seems fair to suggest that executive decision makers optimize in many situations. Several factors should be considered in making this distinction.

In the search for alternatives and their associated conse-quences, Simon states that minimum standards of acceptability will be established prior to the search; as soon as the minimum standards are met, the search will halt, and that particular alter-native will be adopted as the preferred course of action. If alter-natives are presented to the decision maker as a series of discrete events which are noncumulative and nonrecoverable (that is, alternatives which cannot be accumulated and comparatively evaulated as a group, but, rather, evaluated singly, and accepted or rejected; except that, if rejected, they cannot be recalled or recovered), then all decisions *must be* of the satisfying type. The ball player (i.e., batter) must make a series of discrete, indepen-dent decisions concerning a varying number of pitches; he does not have the opportunity to view, for instance, six pitches col-lectively and select the most desirable. Instead, on the basis of extensive training and experience, he is expected to select, or "satisfice," on the basis of certain minimal standards. The pitcher, on the other hand, is faced with an entirely different situation. Every delivery represents a final decision selected from a wide variety of possible alternatives. Numerous variables must be calculated by the pitcher in reaching his final decision, but in any event, the goal of the pitcher, in most instances, is clearly to optimize—achieve maximum gains at minimum costs. Thus, the first point that needs to be emphasized is that if all known and available alternatives can be considered collectively, then the ultimate decision, assuming the presence of adaptively rational behavior, can be considered as an *optimum* choice. If, however, all known and available alternatives cannot be considered collectively, but, instead, are considered singly as discrete events, then the decision maker's most rational course to follow would appear to be the selection of that alternative which will yield satisfactory, though not necessarily maximum or optimum, results.

Another dimension that has to be considered in connection with the optimizing-satisfying dichotomy is that of the degree of risk associated with uncertainty. The evaluation of alternatives is actually the evaluation of the consequences associated with each alternative. As noted before, consequences are by definition estimates of future circumstances. Uncertainty is present in most complex decisions, although the degree of uncertainty may vary from 0 per cent to 100 per cent.[10] The consequences of jumping from the top of a ten-story building, or slapping a policeman in the face can be estimated with a fairly high degree of confidence. On the other hand, the consequences of the Peace Corps program, for instance, when it was initiated, could only be imagined; indeed, after the first year of the operation, probably no one was more pleasantly surprised than the top-level Peace Corps officials themselves with the success of the program during its early stages. Therefore, a degree of uncertainty is present in most complex decisions, but this is not to suggest that uncertainty alone becomes the crucial factor in determining whether the decision maker will seek an optimal or simply satisfactory solution. Instead, the manner in which the decision maker selects a particular alternative will be determined by the degree of uncertainty as it is related to the degree of risk involved. Used in this

[10] For an interesting monograph which presents a scheme for the measurement of uncertainty see David W. Conrath, *Organizational Decision-Making Behavior Under Varying Conditions of Uncertainty* (Philadelphia, Wharton School of Finance and Commerce, University of Pennsylvania, October 1965), mimeograph.

context, risk refers to (1) the probability that the decision alternative ultimately selected *may not* achieve the desired results, *and* (2) the probability that severe deprivations—psychological and/or material—will be incurred by the individual decision maker and/or the organization if the decision alternative selected does not, in fact, achieve the desired results.

The baseball analogy can be used also to illustrate this point. A varying degree of uncertainty applies to both pitcher and batter as each is required to estimate the consequences of his decision. The pitcher cannot be certain that his pitch will go where intended, or, even if it does, that the batter will not hit it safely. The batter cannot be certain that he will even hit the pitch, or, if he does, that he will get on base. However, as the degree of risk, as perceived by each man, changes, so also may their behavioral patterns insofar as the decision-making process is concerned. For example, there is a high probability that the "clean-up" batter, while perfectly content to achieve a "satisfactory" gain in the early innings of the game, will be intent on achieving maximum or optimal gains as he comes to bat in the last half of the ninth inning with bases loaded, two outs, and his team behind by three runs. Similarly, the pitcher who is confronted with this given situation could hardly be expected to seek anything less than an optimum gain—namely, retiring the batter. Of course, in this situation, the optimum gain also represents a satisfactory solution, but anything less than the optimum situation represents a highly unsatisfactory solution. Thus, as the degree of risk associated with the element of uncertainty mounts, the search for the "best" alternative gradually replaces the selection of merely a "good enough" choice. Conversely, as the degree of risk diminishes—as a team builds up a comfortable lead over its opponent in the early part of the game—the strategy may very well shift to finding simply comfortable, or satisfactory, solutions to the various problem situations.

By discussing decision making in terms of the degree of risk associated in conjunction with the element of uncertainty, certain hypotheses concerning the use of optimizing or satisficing techniques are suggested. For instance it might be reasonable to assume that as the degree of risk mounts along with the uncertainty associated with a particular course of action, the decision maker will be inclined to select that course of action which minimizes the risk and satisfies some degree of success. He might, in other words, simply seek any satisfactory solution which is good enough to minimize adverse effects. On the other hand, one could also view this situation in terms of the converse; namely, facing a high risk situation, the decision maker will continue his search for an "optimal" solution rather than for any satisfactory alternative that is presented. Likewise, it could be suggested that as the perceived degree of risk decreases, the decision maker will be more inclined to select a "satisfactory" solution rather than to extend the search for an optimal alternative.

Alexis and Wilson suggest that a problem situation becomes increasingly complex as the number of variables that need to be considered increase. In this instance, greater complexity results in a more extensive search process for the most appropriate solution, i.e., one attempts to do more than merely satisfy certain minimal requirements. Or, more precisely, as the element of risk increases, the minimal decision-making standards which might have provided "satisfactory" solutions under low-risk situations are no longer appropriate, but, instead, are replaced by other "minimal" standards which, under high-risk conditions, may very well represent near-maximum standards. As McKean notes, such standards or criteria are actually proximate indicators which are designed to direct the decision maker toward the maximization of whatever he seeks to maximize.[11]

The manner in which the individual chooses between the satisfying-optimizing approaches is determined to a great extent

[11] McKean, *op. cit.*, p. 165.

by the attitudes, values, and beliefs that have been inculcated into him by his organization. More will be said about this at a later point in this and subsequent chapters. However, it is necessary to note at this point that the satisfying approach is more appropriately applied to certain problem situations than others. It does seem to offer a sound decision-making approach in those instances involving low-level, low-risk, noncomplex, and routine decision events. It does not seem to offer a meaningful or helpful analytical concept which can be applied to top-level, high-risk, complex, and unique problem situations. As will be seen in later chapters, it is felt that a real advantage is to be gained by separating these two concepts insofar as the analysis of bureaucratic behavior is concerned. On the other hand, little appears to be gained by way of understanding behavioral differences which emerge within bureaucratic settings if all decision making is to be viewed on a sliding scale of "satisficing."

### Subjective Rationality

As previously indicated, decisions are frequently required despite the fact that sufficient data on which to base objective, rational conclusions are lacking. Under these circumstances, the decision maker is literally forced to rely heavily on various subjective preferences which are established and maintained, in part, by the accumulated knowledge of prior operating experience.

Ideally speaking, decision-making authority should be directly related to formal organization authority. As the individual progresses upward within the organization, more formal authority is acquired, and at the same time his decision-making responsibilities are increased. The extent to which these responsibilities increase is related to the increasing complexity of decision problems and the increasing range of variable factors that have to be taken into consideration when decisions are demanded. Thus, one of the fundamental differences between the office manager (O), the department head (D), the vice president (V), and the president (P) of a particular organization is, as diagrammed below, the range of variables that must be taken into account when each is required to assume his decision-making duties. Although the diagram is simply intended as a representational scheme, note that top-level executive officials (here represented by the president) are forced to take into account considerations which actually extend beyond the boundaries of the organization itself.

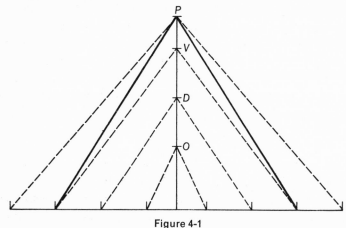

Figure 4-1

As the number of variables increase, the number of possible alternative solutions will also increase, and, at the same time, the ability of the decision maker to estimate the consequences of each possible alternative will become increasingly uncertain. Under these circumstances, the utilization of subjective preferences, approved by the organization, is frequently not only the necessary but the only means that can be employed to introduce a degree of confidence into the complexities of the decision-making process.

Organizationally approved subjective preferences may also be referred to as the organizational image as perceived by the individual. This represents a slightly more restricted use of the term "image" than that adopted by Alexis and Wilson.

> Between a stimulus or cue, and the ultimate action that follows lies a filtering system, or "image" as Boulding has termed it. The image is a construct of relationships, experiences, values, and emotions. It is characterized by a capacity to grow from within as well as from the retention of external experiences. . . . The image . . . which has become integrated into that part of the central nervous system standing between stimulus and response, is a key element in cognitive behavior. . . . The decision-maker's behavior reflects his perceptions of people, roles, and organization, in addition to his own values and emotions. Even the most intelligent of us act on the basis of images that include more than the objective facts of the decision situation.[12]

Viewed in this context, decision making takes on an entirely different perspective than that provided by the "rationalists." Given the high degree of incomplete knowledge frequently confronting the decision maker, subjective choices characterize the entire process from data collection to the final decision stage. However, this is not to suggest that such preferences need represent arbitrary, capricious, and/or irrational behavioral patterns. Subjective preferences can be quite functional in a positive and meaningful sense. For the individual decision maker they can provide a certain degree of confidence as a hedge against the feelings of anxiety and tension that normally result when high-risk events are associated with correspondingly high degrees of uncertainty. The important qualification that must be placed on the use of subjective values by decision makers is that the preferences selected must be consonant with the preferences of the organization. As a result of the internal learning process, decision makers are expected to act in the best interests of their respective

[12] Alexis and Wilson, *op. cit.*, p. 158.

organizations. In this regard, organizational values become an integral part of the overall decision-making process. To the extent that the individual is aware of these value preferences and acts on them as his own, he is able to utilize, intelligently and rationally, a full range of operationally applicable subjective preferences. In the absence of objective data, subjective preferences are frequently the most reliable guides available for decision makers to follow. Indeed, one of the basic dilemmas which plague most successful corporation executives when they assume positions within the governmental bureaucracy is *not*, as is so frequently assumed, that they deal with the "human" problems of government in terms of the calculated, dispassionate orientation of the efficiency-minded business world. Few top-level corporation officials are either that objective or dispassionate. Instead, the real dilemma encountered by many of these people as they come to Washington is that the subjective preferences which they automatically employ in their new governmental decision-making environment are, for the most part, the products of an entirely different organizational system and environment. The subjective preferences which were learned in one setting become inappropriate guides to decision-making behavior when applied to an entirely different organizational surrounding.

### Nonrational Decision Making

Once it is recognized that subjective factors are present in the decision-making process, then a whole new area of investigation unfolds. The entire, complex, psychological structure of the individual then becomes a pertinent area of inquiry concerning how decisions are made. Gore's heuristic model of decision making is one example of this type of inquiry. For Gore, decision making is basically an emotional, nonrational, highly personalized and subjective process. Within this context, therefore, ". . . the factors validating a decision are internal to the personality of the individual instead of external to it." The key word in this statement seems to be "validating"; it is intended to convey a sense of personal, psychological approval or acceptance. The optimum situation is to select that decision alternative which creates the least anxiety or disruption to the individual's basic needs, wants, and desires. In effect, therefore, every "objective" decision should be modified or adjusted to meet the emotional needs of the various members of the organization who will be affected by the decision. The more extended passage from which the above statement was excerpted should be considered in order to provide a more complete insight into Gore's heuristic decision-making scheme.

> Whereas the rational system of action evolves through the identification of causes and effects and the discovery of ways of implementing them, the heuristic process is a groping toward agreements seldom arrived at through logic. The very essence of the heuristic process is that the factors validating a decision are internal to the personality of the individual instead of external to it. Whereas the rational system of action deals with the linkages between a collective and its objectives and between a collective and its environment, the heuristic process is oriented toward the relationship between that private core of values embedded in the center of the personality and its public counterpart, ideology. The dynamics of personality are not those of logic but rather those of emotion.[13]

In other words, although logic and reason may be the basic intellectual tools needed to analyze a given problem or to structure a series of solutions to a given situation, logic and reason may not prove to be completely effective in establishing intraorganizational agreement in connection with any given decision. Organizational decisions may (and usually do) have significant consequences insofar as the established internal behavioral

[13] Gore, *Administrative Decision-Making, op. cit.*, p. 12.

patterns of any bureaucratic structure are concerned. As noted previously, behavioral patterns of the individual are only partially based on formal rules and regulations. The socialization process at work within every organization is most effectively implemented through the informal, unofficial, and subjective levels. It is specifically designed to control the individual by exploiting his fears and satisfying his psychological needs. Thus, an organizational decision which may alter the variously established behavior patterns of the individual can only be effectively implemented if the individuals involved are satisfied that the proposed change will not jeopardize their own personal well-being. However, in this latter context, one is referring to emotional or psychological fears and anxieties which cannot be resolved or soothed on the basis of logic or reason alone. Hanson Baldwin relates a telling point in this regard in one of his articles on the Defense Department.

> A second factor causing delay and difficulties [in our overall defense policy] is the attempt by . . . the numerous assistants [to the Secretary of Defense] to eliminate what they call goldplating, or unnecessarily high performance figures or standards. The attempt is laudable, but it is sometimes carried to extremes, and it has been difficult as Adm. George W. Anderson, former Chief of Naval Operations, pointed out, for men in uniform to adjust to the idea that a 10-mile-an-hour speed differential between our own aircraft and enemy planes may not—in the eyes of the Department of Defense—be important. To a pilot, that 10 miles an hour, even though costly in terms of dollars, may be the difference between life and death.[14]

Thus, the main point that Gore seems to be making is that emotional needs or anxieties can only be satisfied with a corresponding emotional type response.

[14] "Slowdown in the Pentagon," *Foreign Affairs*, vol. 43 (January 1965), p. 262.

The use of emotionally, integrative, non-rational techniques creates a different tone or climate in an organization than their tougher, more formal rational equivalents. . . . a discussion in terms of non-rational devices often induces a climate of opinion "real" in terms of aspirations, goals, and symbols that have particular identities for members of an organization, rather than "real" in terms of the way others see them. Although this private inner organization is known only in the hearts of its members, it is "valid" as the context for the next steps which involve choices whose costs are paid in the coin of this inner realm.

So, decision-making is not a smooth flowing process dispensing choices when and where they are required. Rather, it is a twisted, unshapely, halting flow of interactions between people, interactions that shift constantly from a rational to a heuristic mode and back again. Sometimes tortuous, sometimes effortless, these interactions face in two directions at once.[15]

One interesting contradiction does seem to emerge from this proposition, however. As Gore observes,

A significant characteristic of decision-making is its intermittentness and discontinuousness, in contrast with the regularity of productive activities. Much rational behavior tends to be habituated and well-integrated. Heuristic behavior is marked by improvision, spontaneity, and accommodation. These surface differences seem to penetrate to basic functions; rational activities often reinforce the status quo and remain relatively stable and ideologically conservative; heuristic processes tend to press the status quo and imply change and ideological liberality.[16]

Despite the logical development of Gore's argument, it does seem reasonable to suggest that a completely contrary conclusion could be drawn from the nature of the heuristic decision-making process. Specifically, could it not be argued that the rational

15 Gore, *op. cit.*, pp. 78–79, 21.
16 Gore, *op. cit.*, p. 28.

behavioral patterns of "administrative man" give rise to innovative, imaginative programs while the subjective, emotional,
nonrational aspects of man tend to reinforce the status quo and
resist change.

The heuristic approach emphasizes the importance of the
conscious and the subconscious nature of man. If, as Gore
suggests, "factors validating a decision are internal to the
personality of the individual," then what we are talking about
are the myriad of values, attitudes, and beliefs which the individual carries with him as a result of a lifetime learning experience
—an experience that, incidentally, is noted for its extremely
effective reinforcing capacity. But, in addition to one's learned
responses we are also talking about the innate psychological
forces of man which are expressed in such gross forms as love,
hate, fear, and so forth. "Rational man" is expected to be able
to control the manifest expression of these forces, at least to the
extent, for instance, that love is modified to friendship, hate to
dislike, fear to anxiety. Within modern organizational settings
the individual's needs that must be satisfied are of a sophisticated
psychological nature such as security, status, prestige, influence.
The only difference between organization man and Stone Age
man is in their respective responses to stimuli which threaten
their psychological security.

In this respect, the heuristic model which emphasizes the
emotional element in the decision-making process provides an
essential insight into the true nature of that process. Deprived
of this perspective one can hardly be expected to understand
many of the actions that take place within any organization, and
particularly those within the political sphere. For example, the
often bitter and vehement opposition which normally accompanies most executive branch reorganization plans can be viewed
in terms of an emotional, nonrational reaction to a decision
which may be viewed by those directly affected as a severe threat
to their psychological security. In short, the heuristic method of

decision making is a "pattern of interactions between individuals through which the social mechanisms that sustain effective collective activity are developed and maintained."[17] The "social mechanisms" referred to in this statement would certainly seem to include the search for consensus, the willingness to accept compromise solutions, the responsibility to accept consensual decisions as binding, and, as Gore himself notes, the ability to be able to accommodate to the needs, wants, and desires of others.

As valuable as these "social mechanisms" may be within an organizational setting, it is difficult to conceive of them in terms of change, innovation, or ideological liberality. Although a certain degree of emotional content is an important ingredient in any rational framework, there is ample justification for us to conclude that the emotional aspects of man's personality may just as easily drive him in a conservative, even reactionary direction— or, even worse, in a direction of absolute intolerance. By the same token, adaptively rational behavior may indeed be used to fortify the status quo, but, again, sufficient knowledge is available to suggest that it can be used as the battering ram against the citadels of tradition and firmly established behavioral patterns.

This point will be developed more extensively in a later chapter; for the present it is sufficient to note that decision making is an integral part of any organization, and the heuristic, or nonrational, aspects of man are an integral part of decision making. The speculation that emerges is that the heuristic aspects of decision making enjoy a much more prominent position within the political organization than within the private sphere.

## Summary

This brief discussion of a few of the most basic theoretical aspects of the decision-making process should be sufficient to permit a more meaningful understanding of executive branch

[17] Gore, *op. cit.*, p. 130.

decision making specifically. Four of the main propositions developed in this chapter can easily be applied to the executive bureaucracy to determine their relevance. First, real limitations are imposed on the decision maker which seriously restrict the extent to which he is capable of objectively selecting that alternative which would yield the most desirable consequences in relation to his goal objective. Second, in the absence of objective knowledge, the decision maker is frequently forced to rely heavily on subjective judgments as his primary decision-making guide. Third, the nonrational fears and anxieties which may plague the individual within his organizational setting can have a very real effect on the manner in which he fulfills his decision-making responsibilities. And, finally, the decision maker is forced to operate in an environment of varying uncertainty which he may attempt to manipulate in either a satisfactory or optimal fashion. That is to say, one method of minimizing the degree of uncertainty is to seek satisfactory solutions to various problems—a tactic which may be most effectively utilized when low-level, low-risk, noncomplex situations prevail. However, it may be further hypothesized that under high-risk, complex conditions, in which the uncertainty and risk associated with the consequences of one's decisions are equally high, the attempt may be made to seek optimal or maximum solutions to problem situations. Used in this context "optimal" is taken to mean the best of all *known* and *available* alternatives. The manner in which decisions and the decision-making process within the federal bureaucracy are affected by each of these four factors will be explored in the following chapter.

# 5

## Executive Branch Decision Making

The President of the United States has often been described as a most lonely and forlorn figure simply because conflict situations, once they reach the President's desk, have nowhere else to go. As usual, Harry Truman described it best: "The buck stops here." So, the man who is situated at the apex of the federal bureaucracy is presumed to be the nation's foremost decision maker, at least in matters political. But the President does not operate in a vacuum, and lonely though he may be as he experiences the anguish and anxiety of making fateful decisions, he is no modern-day Philosopher King. To a very real extent, his decisions are not made—they evolve; and more often than not, the primary decision-making responsibility of top-level executive officials, including the President, is to decide which decision to accept. This, of course, is not always a responsibility easily borne. Even Harding, during his brief tenure as President, did not escape the horns of this dilemma: "I listen to one side and they seem right, and then I talk to the other side and they seem just as right, and there I am where I started—God, what a job!"

Nevertheless, it is a job that somehow must be done, and given the nature of our political system, plus the manner in which conflict normally must be resolved within the executive branch, it should come as no surprise that the executive decision-making process functions within an equally decentralized and bargaining-type atmosphere. With this in mind, each of the basic decision-making aspects examined in the previous chapter will be applied specifically to the executive bureaucracy. First, however, the fact alluded to above that decision making in the federal government is actually the end result of an involved, complex process of evolution will be examined in more detail. In truth, of course, decision making in any context is the result of a composite process; it is simply that within political organizations its composite aspects are more pronounced than in other situations.

## Composite Process

No organizational setting can demonstrate the full extent of the multifaceted decision-making process better than the federal executive bureaucracy and, within that setting, probably no better example can be found to illustrate the complexity of the process itself than that associated with the growth and development of American foreign policy in recent years. Since the end of the Second World War the United States has assumed many economic, military, and political responsibilities in the international sphere. As a result foreign policy considerations have come to command a significant segment of the resources, time, and attention of the executive bureaucracy. The increase in the foreign-policy role of the federal government can be seen in both the quantity and scope of our involvement. The tangible resources allocated to the formulation and implementation of our foreign policy have constantly increased—money, manpower, material—as has the number of nations, alliances, and organizations with which the United States has become involved in one way or another. The sheer complexity of our international affairs, both in terms of policy making and the administrative implementation of policy, is in itself a demanding task. But these demands are made all the more complex as a result of an increasing overlap between the foreign and domestic policy spheres. What this means, of course, is that very few meaningful foreign-policy decisions can be made by top-level executive officials which do not involve a varying range of domestic or internal considerations. By the same token numerous "domestic" policy decisions—income taxes, minimum wages, farm prices, transportation subsidies, labor-management problems—can have serious ramifications far beyond the continental limits of the United States. As a consequence, farmers, bankers, industrialists, labor union officials have become involved—either directly or through their representatives—to an unprecedented extent in the overall public policy decision-making process.

As a further illustration of the composite nature of the executive decision-making process, one need only consider the other major group which is "external" to the federal executive— Congress—which has also become increasingly involved in the integrated foreign domestic policy sphere. As Carroll pointed out some time ago, virtually every House Committee is involved to some degree with foreign policy questions.[1] What is true of the House is true also of the Senate. The extent to which the House and the Senate, acting collectively or through their designated committees and subcommittees, are capable of influencing the executive decision-making process is limited, for the most part, to negative and indirect means. Nevertheless, negative influence is influence, and the extensive preparation that goes into any one of the President's major programs in an effort to tailor it to the preferences of Congress wherever possible

[1] Holbert Carroll, *The House of Representatives and Foreign Affairs* (Pittsburgh: University of Pittsburgh Press, 1958).

is ample indication that anticipated reactions to public policy proposals frequently become an integral part of the executive decision-making process.

Finally, in terms of major foreign policy decisions, the executive branch itself has become a maze of interrelated administrative patterns. At the present time, the State Department must share its formerly semiexclusive function—and incidentally, influence—with the Departments of Defense and Treasury, and, to a lesser extent, with the Departments of Agriculture, Commerce, Labor, Justice, and Interior (which has jurisdiction over our nation's external possessions). Thus, as President Eisenhower announced his approach to the conduct of foreign affairs, composite decision making was virtually assured as a result of the organizational pattern which he devised.

> The overall foreign affairs reorganization which I desire to achieve is designed to emphasize the primary position of the Secretary of State. . . . It will be my practice to employ the Secretary of State as my channel of authority within the executive branch on foreign policy. Other officials of the executive branch will work with and through the Secretary of State on matters of foreign policy. . . .

Isolated from the remaining portion of the directive, the above statement certainly seems to centralize all authority and responsibility for the conduct of foreign affairs exclusively with the Secretary of State. However, as one continues to read the directive the clarity of the above statement disappears, and the impression of a centralized authority over foreign affairs in an all-inclusive sense becomes, in effect, only an illusion.

> . . . I shall look to the Secretary of Defense as the cabinet officer responsible, within the framework of foreign policy, for advising and assisting me in the formation and control of military policy. Similarly, the Secretary of the Treasury, within the

framework of foreign policy, shall continue to be the cabinet officer responsible for advising and assisting me in the formation and control of monetary and financial policy.

The Secretary of State, the Secretary of Defense, and the Secretary of the Treasury, as appropriate, shall review plans and policies relative to economic and military assistance programs, . . . and legislative proposals of the Foreign Operations Administration[2] . . ., to assure that in their conception and execution, such plans, policies, and proposals are consistent with and further the attainment of foreign policy, military policy, and financial and monetary policy objectives.[3]

Eisenhower's administrative approach was basically characterized by a strong emphasis on delegation of decision-making authority. Placing a heavy reliance on staff and executive subordinates, the President expected to be presented with a limited number of composite, well-reasoned alternatives and the consequences of each.

Composite decisions were also a pronounced characteristic of the Roosevelt years, although the difference between the two Presidents (Roosevelt and Eisenhower) in arriving at the final decision was striking. Roosevelt apparently was as unorthodox in his handling of the bureaucracy as Eisenhower was predictable and stable. The chain-of-command concept, valued so highly by Eisenhower, was merely a pesky encumbrance which

[2] The Foreign Operations Administration was the first foreign aid agency created by Congress during the Eisenhower Administration. It was established in 1953, replacing the Mutual Security Agency, which was the direct descendent of the original Economic Cooperation Administration. Eisenhower's first foreign aid director, who headed the FOA until it was replaced by the International Cooperation Administration in 1955, was Harold Stassen.

[3] *Mutual Security Legislation and Related Documents*, House Committee on Foreign Affairs, Committee Print, 83rd Congress, 1st session, 1953, pp. 196–99.

had to be circumvented by Roosevelt. Schlesinger writes of Roosevelt,

> His complex administrative sensibility, infinitely subtle and sensitive, was forever weighing questions of personal force, of political timing, of congressional concern, of partisan benefit, of public interest. Situations had to be permitted to develop, to crystallize, to clarify. The competing forces had to vindicate themselves in the actual pull and tug of conflict; public opinion had to face the question, consider it, pronounce upon it—only then, at the long frazzled end, would the President's intuitions consolidate and precipitate a result.[4]

The major difference between Roosevelt and Lyndon Johnson in their decision-making approaches appears to be one of means and ends. For Roosevelt, consensus building seemed to represent one feasible means that could be employed to achieve certain policy ends, although it seems clear that Roosevelt did not view consensus building as the only option open to him in the decision-making process. However, if a high sharing of values and wide agreement over methods of operation become ends in themselves—i.e., if consensus itself becomes a top priority goal to be achieved—as seems to be the distinguishing characteristic of the Johnson approach, then composite decision making is very likely to develop an even greater degree of complexity.

The search for consensus by President Johnson has been given elaborate attention. Perhaps he has given the term unusual prominence in his public statements, but the term itself and its central position in American politics is certainly not new. Indeed, as a characteristic of all organizational decision making —public as well as private—consensus building becomes an essential tactic. Manipulated persuasion, as discussed earlier, is

[4] Arthur Schlesinger, *The Coming of the New Deal* (Boston: Houghton-Mifflin, 1958), p. 528.

simply a means by which organizations seek to develop consensus. A basic difference does exist, however, between public and private organizations as to the function served by consensus. In private organizations, consensus is sought to maximize internal operating effectiveness, whereas executive branch officials, and particularly the President, must normally obtain consensus within various external groups simply to gain acceptance of a particular policy proposal. In the former instance, consensus serves as an important means to a desirable end—e.g., internal harmony and willing subordination to top-level policy decisions. However, if this goal cannot be achieved through the manipulation of consensus, then it can be achieved directly; that is, it can be unilaterally imposed. In the government setting, however, consensus building can quite easily become an all-important end in itself simply because agreement not obtained through persuasion or bargaining is not likely to be obtained at all. Under these circumstances, consensus becomes the critical amalgam of the public policy process, and executive branch decision makers can ill-afford to minimize its importance. As a result, the composite nature of executive branch decision making becomes extremely complex.

## Limitations on Executive Branch Decision Making

The limitations imposed on rational and objective decision making as discussed in the previous chapter are equally applicable to the executive branch. Goals are frequently vague and nonoperational, and this places any pretense of rational decision making on rather hopeless grounds to begin with. Data may be collected, stored, consolidated, and analyzed for obscure purposes, as well as for conflicting purposes. Available alternatives may be unknown or, worse, ignored. And, finally, time works its pressure on executive officials without discrimination. Under these circumstances—and given the vast expanse of the executive bureaucracy—top-level executive officials become almost totally dependent upon subordinate administrative officials in an effort to minimize the degree of uncertainty associated with complex problem situations. At the same time, however, the dependency placed on subordinates by top-level executive officials contributes to the maintenance of the limitations that are imposed on the decision-making process. This situation is just as inevitable as the composite nature of the decision-making process. Indeed, if one is prepared to accept two basic assumptions concerning this situation, the reversed dependency relationship need mean nothing more than a very simple delegation of data-collecting responsibilities to various subordinate officials within any organization. The two assumptions referred to are: (1) the individual responsible for collecting and supplying the necessary information will act in a totally objective and unbiased manner with a strong commitment only to thorough, complete, and accurate reporting; and, (2) the top-level executive officials who receive the information will be able to discern if the imperatives of the first assumption are not being satisfied. The first assumption involves the transmission of information; the second involves the ability to be able to determine the creditability of the information transmitted. In both instances some very real obstacles must be surmounted if either assumption is to be realized within the governmental structure.

For instance, in the upflow of information it is not unusual for subordinates to suppress, totally or partially, that data which may place them in an unfavorable position. To hide one's mistakes is an understandable temptation, particularly if the individual has high aspirations for advancement within the organization, or if his lateral mobility to other organizations is severely limited. Thus, Guetzkow reports the findings of a particular study investigating this problem in industrial organizations in which the researcher demonstrates a strong *negative* correlation

(−.41) between the mobility aspiration of subordinate executive officials and the accuracy of their upward communications.[5]

Aside from the motivation of advancement within the organization, subordinates may withhold information simply because of a tendency to discount the reliability of unfavorable information of any kind. As far as can be determined, no study has been conducted in the federal bureaucracy to test the validity of this proposition, although in a totally different context, Pool, Bauer, and Dexter present strong evidence of support in connection with constituency mail received by congressmen.[6] The findings of this study suggest that congressmen select those constituent messages which reaffirm their own attitudes, while at the same time they tend to ignore or discount messages which carry conflicting viewpoints. Similarly, Dearborne and Simon conclude from a study conducted by Bruner that the individual, when confronted with complex problem situations, perceives what he is "ready" to perceive, and that as the degree of complexity increases the perception that emerges is determined more by "what is already 'in' the individual and less by what is in the stimulus."[7]

In many instances, of course, the subordinate cannot invoke the option of suppressing "bad news." The amount of discretion enjoyed by subordinates to report or to withhold information is in most instances, severely restricted. This is especially true within the domestic area of public policy where far too many different and independent communications systems are at work

[5] Harold Guetzkow, "Communications in Organizations," *Handbook of Organizations, op. cit.,* p. 555.

[6] Raymond Bauer, Ithiel de Sola Pool, and Lewis Anthony Dexter, *American Business and Public Policy* (New York: Atherton Press, 1963), pp. 414–24.

[7] Dewitt Dearborne and H. A. Simon, "Selective Perception: A Note on the Departmental Identifications of Executives," *Sociometry,* vol. 21 (June, 1958), pp. 140–44.

reporting the same event to allow an executive subordinate to suppress important information. Consider the amount of publicity the poverty program has received since its inception and one can begin to appreciate the dilemma in which a subordinate would surely find himself if he attempted to withhold unfavorable information from his superior. With the assistance of the nation's news media, countless numbers of interested organizations across the nation have disclosed the effectiveness or ineffectiveness of the program as it has been implemented at the local level. What is true of the poverty program is true also of virtually every other major domestic governmental program. In the event of a malfunction or inequity at the operating level, congressmen, interest groups, and the news media will inform each other of the situation. Under these circumstances it is difficult—but by no means impossible—for a subordinate to attempt to suppress information from his superior.

A broader degree of discretion is available to executive subordinates who must report information relating to the administrative implementation of American foreign policy. The factor of proximity, the absence of interest groups, the limited effectiveness of the news media, and a distant Congress all permit a more flexible attitude insofar as the subordinate executive official is concerned when it comes to suppressing unfavorable information. But even in this type of situation the risk of discovery is ever-present. In most of the foreign countries, U. S. Ambassadors head teams of missions representing the regular diplomatic corps, the military advisory groups, the foreign aid officials, the Peace Corps representatives, and the U. S. Information Agency, all of whom are expected to report back to their respective superiors in Washington. Under this type of organizational arrangement, there is a high probability that unfavorable information, even if suppressed by the responsible mission team, will find its way into the Washington reports of one or more of the other "team" members.

Information can be withheld, however, without any deliberate intention whatsoever to suppress. This is probably one of the most serious administrative problems which face top-level decision makers. On the one hand the problem of "self-apparentness" is ever-present; on the other hand, the problem of "filtering" is inevitable. The late Robert F. Kennedy's controversy with FBI Director J. Edgar Hoover over the wiretapping activities of the Bureau while Kennedy was Attorney General, represents a good example of a top-level executive official who evidently was innocently "victimized" by a key subordinate as a result of the "self-apparentness syndrome." The following news story illustrates this point.

> Former Attorney General Robert F. Kennedy's top rackets buster said Tuesday: "Sure I knew for years that the FBI was making widespread use of electronic 'bugs' in organized crime investigations. But the top brass of the bureau would flat-out lie to me, denying it, whenever I officially asked about it."
>
> William G. Hundley, head of [the Justice Department's] Organized Crime Section from the GOP days of 1958 until this September, insisted that he never discussed his knowledge of the bugging with Kennedy while Kennedy was Attorney General, "and for a very good reason:
>
> "I began to suspect as early as 1959, from talking to various FBI agents who were good friends, that they were using 'bugs' in rackets cases.
>
> "And by '61 and '62, when I'd been running the Organized Crime Section for three or four years, I had learned about the 'bugs' with certainty.
>
> "But when the bureau officials kept lying to me about their use, denying it, I figured that this was obviously so delicate that it must be something that was just between the AG (Attorney General Kennedy) and the Director (FBI Director J. Edgar Hoover), as it is with 'national security' wiretaps. So I never talked about it."
>
> Hundley said the subject of bugging didn't come up in a

direct conversation between him and Kennedy until early this year, during one of his occasional visits to Senator Kennedy's Capitol Hill office.

"Bob said to me, 'Say, did you know that the FBI had been using bugs?' and I said, 'Sure, I knew,' and he said: 'Well, why the devil didn't you tell me?' and I explained to him that I assumed he knew all along."[8]

The problem of "filtering" is just as serious as is the situation in which the subordinate "assumes" his superior is aware of certain information. To repeat the oft-used analogy, a wide range of data enters into the base of the organization's inverted communications funnel, although not every "unit" of information which is introduced into the system will necessarily make its way to the apex. Indeed, as a result of deliberate and rational planning, one of the primary functions of a hierarchal structure is to eliminate and/or consolidate information as it progresses upward through the various organizational echelons. Thus, a built-in filtering process should be effectively at work in every complex organization. Assuming maximum operating efficiency in this regard, and if top-level executive officials depend exclusively on their intraorganizational communications network for data, then a very real risk is present that vital and important information will be filtered out in its upward transmission by subordinate officials who are unaware of, or unimpressed by, the relevance of certain information. To a very real extent, this is an inevitable consequence if one depends exclusively on line subordinates for information. Within the government bureaucracy particularly, it is not a simple task to guard against this contingency. The whole "ethos" of complex organizations places heavy stress on the proper delegation of authority. Furthermore, a basic administrative maxim stresses that top-level policy makers must be freed from the details of daily

[8] Philadelphia *Inquirer*, December 14, 1966, p. 1.

operations. Thus, there is a solid rationale for both the President and his Cabinet Secretaries to expect their subordinates to relieve them of the routine aspects of administration. But one of the inevitable "routines" normally assigned to subordinates is the screening of information and, because of the wide variety of variables at work within any organization, one can hardly assume that in screening out certain information the executive subordinate is always applying the same standards and criteria that would be applied by the Departmental Secretary or even the President. As Neustadt observes, "Presidents are always being told that they should leave details to others. It is dubious advice. Exposure to details of operation and of policy provides the frame of reference for details of information. To be effective as his own director of intelligence, a President need be his own executive assistant."[9]

In other words, for top-level government officials, and especially the President, to maximize the effectiveness of the decision-making process, access to the widest range of accurate, pertinent, and reliable information is needed. But in order to realize this goal, the President and his executive subordinates may frequently have to behave, within the organization setting, in a decidedly "dysfunctional" manner.

Franklin Roosevelt obviously was a master administrative craftsman in this regard. As recorded by Schlesinger, "he deliberately organized—or disorganized—his system of communications to insure that important decisions [and information] were passed on to the top."[10] In one sense, Roosevelt could easily be classified as the worst Chief Executive in our nation's history. But if one can understand how the entire executive bureaucracy is structured to filter out a great deal of information as it progresses upward, then one can begin to perceive that many of the unorthodox actions taken by Roosevelt were

[9] Richard Neustadt, *Presidential Power* (New York: Wiley, 1960), p. 154.
[10] Schlesinger, *op. cit.*, pp. 527–28.

designed specifically to overcome this very formidable information hurdle. But, "Only a man of limitless energy and resource could hold such a system together. Even Roosevelt at times was hard put to keep it from flying apart."[11] Presidential dependence on subordinates is, as noted, inevitable, for one even as dynamic as Roosevelt. However, the scope and extent to which one is to rely (trust involves too many ambiguous connotations) on one's subordinates is an entirely different manner. Eisenhower's heavy reliance on a rather limited and exclusive group of advisers during his first term was the cause of many unfortunate administrative bungles. The one major characteristic of his second term was the extent to which his scope of reliance on others for information was greatly expanded. As John F. Kennedy began his short Presidential career, the Cuban Bay of Pigs situation became an administrative fiasco, not so much because he was forced to depend on subordinates for the information required to make the necessary decisions, but, rather, because he was forced to rely heavily on the judgments of the same individuals who supplied the information. Where dependence on information and reliance on judgment are vested in the same subordinate official, any top-level executive policy maker is placed in the unfortunate position of sacrificing a vital degree of executive flexibility and discretion. Dependence on subordinate officials for information is as inevitable as the composite nature of the decision-making process itself; reliance on the judgments of these same subordinates is not.

## Subjective Rationality

As stated previously, decision makers in every large bureaucratic setting must, on occasion, make certain decisions on the basis of subjective preferences. This means that they frequently must utilize the values, attitudes, and beliefs of the organization

---

[11] Schlesinger, *op. cit.* p. 532.

to decrease whatever degree of uncertainty may be associated with a pending decision. The main problem in the use of subjective preferences as decision-making cues involves the factor of consistency. If the individual will be forced to make decisions on the basis of subjective factors, what assurance is there that he will select the "right" preferences—i.e., those values, attitudes, and beliefs that are endowed and approved by the organization? In view of the importance of this aspect of the decision-making process, it is not surprising that most large, complex bureaucracies exert extensive efforts to insure that the individual will become an integral part of the organization.

Within private bureaucracies these efforts toward total integration can be noted clearly. As the administrative official advances through the hierarchy, he becomes increasingly indoctrinated by the subjective preferences of the organization as perpetuated by his superiors. If this integrative process works correctly, the individual can expect to develop an emotional commitment to the organization which—figuratively speaking —tends to make the individual and the organization almost indistinguishable. In private bureaucratic settings this process is relatively successful as promotions are made on the basis of—as much as anything else—the degree of confidence placed in the rising administrator by his superiors that his subjective decision-making orientation is an accurate reflection of the organization's dominant values, attitudes, and beliefs. In public or governmental bureaucratic settings, however, this generalization is much less valid.

For instance, the element of competition inherent in the free enterprise system and its function as a legitimate and necessary characteristic of the organization's goal objectives is essentially lacking in the federal executive structure. This is not to suggest that competition is lacking *within* the executive branch. As previously noted, the competition between government officials over resources, power, and prestige can be intense.

However, the executive branch *per se* is not engaged in competitive struggle with rivals over a share of the market. Hence it cannot utilize the competitive factor as an internal cohesive device in the same fashion as Macy's and Gimbel's, for instance. An obvious exception would be crisis situations of major proportions where the existence of the government is threatened by a hostile external force (military, social, economic, or political). In the absence of crisis, however, a cohesive set of organizational subjective preferences cannot depend upon a corresponding set of tangible, operational goal-objectives for its rationale, as is generally the case in private organizations. What, then, can provide the basis for a high sharing of values, attitudes, and beliefs throughout the governmental executive structure? The answer to this question is, unfortunately, nothing in any meaningful sense.

One might assume that the President of the United States could easily staff his Cabinet with individuals who were totally committed to his overall program, and who completely shared his own subjective orientations as to the direction and content of public policy decisions. Unfortunately, unless one is talking at a high level of generalization, this assumption is not valid. A close reading of Fenno's study of the executive branch Cabinet officers clearly suggests that at the present time the President may view the Departments of State, Defense, and Treasury as the most vital executive Cabinet posts which should be staffed with individuals who are in complete accord with the President's goals and subjective preferences. In connection with the various other Departments, however, the President may very well have to name individuals to his Cabinet who, in fact, may have surprisingly little in common with the President.[12]

The subjective preferences of top-level government executives are *brought into* the organization rather than *shaped by* the

[12] Richard Fenno, *The President's Cabinet* (Cambridge: Harvard University Press, 1959), Ch. 2.

organization over an extended period of time. As a result, conflicts over subjective preferences are not an unusual occurrence within the Cabinet group. The American Cabinet neither falls together nor stands together, Fenno notes. To a great extent this is true simply because there is no solidifying force—except in times of severe crisis—aside from the personal (i.e., charismatic) attractiveness of the President, that is capable of blending together the wide diversity of subjective preferences brought into the top executive structure of the government by these individuals.[13] But even if this wide plurality of preferences could be fashioned into a single, cohesive force, there is good evidence to suggest that even the most dominant Presidential figure would be inviting serious political trouble if such an attempt was made. Roosevelt, for instance,

> . . . had to keep a variety of interests satisfied, or at least hopeful. . . . Everywhere there was the need to balance the right and the left—let Corcoran and Cohen write the act establishing the Securities and Exchange Commission, but let Joe Kennedy administer it, but flank him with Jim Landis and Ferdinand Pecora.[14]

What is true of Departmental Secretaries is also generally valid insofar as Under, and Assistant Secretaries are concerned. Each of these individuals is, for the most part, pressed into government service from a variety of different backgrounds. As a result, a sense of organizational commitment, cohesion, and

[13] The influence of party allegiance has been cited as a force capable of adding a degree of homogeneity to the President's top-level executive group. Party allegiance may be exploited by the President in connection with certain members of his official group, but to suggest that the entire group of Cabinet and sub-Cabinet officials can be bound together on the basis of party loyalty seems quite unrealistic given the information that is available concerning the President's Cabinet and the nature of our party system.

[14] Schlesinger, *op. cit.*, p. 536.

continuity fails to emerge in any meaningful sense. One direct consequence of this situation relates to the decision-making process in that a void is created because of the absence of any organizationally approved standards of acceptable subjective preferences. If the decision maker is not trained to utilize the preferences deemed most appropriate and desirable by the organization, he will be forced to resort to his own or some other sources's preferences. Unfortunately, because of the inability of the federal executive structure to impose its "will" on that of the organization member, the individual bureaucrat is left to his own devices to meet the subjective demands of the decision-making process.

What this suggests in practical terms is that the middle- or lower-level executive decision maker thrives in a setting that permits him to determine which, or whose, subjective preferences he shall apply in decision situations. There are exceptions, of course, but most of these occur at the bureau level where cohesive, centralized internal control is evidenced. The internal structure of the FBI, for example, is effectively consolidated around a relatively precise set of subjective preferences as established and maintained by top-level Bureau officials. These preferences serve as constant guides for the Bureau's agents as they meet their respective decision demands. Kaufman's study of the U. S. Forest Service indicates that this bureau within the Department of Agriculture has also achieved significant success in integrating organizational and individual subjective preferences.[15] On the other hand, one need only consider the roles of the Customs Collectors before these positions were abolished, or the roles of the various members of the many foreign aid mission teams to realize that uncoordinated and even unregulated subjective preferences may abound within the executive structure. Although this rich diversity of opinion has been

[15] Herbert Kaufman, *The Forest Ranger* (Baltimore: The Johns Hopkins Press, 1960).

applauded by some, the cost of this diversity, has been—as viewed by others—disproportionately high.

## Nonrational Decision Making

As noted in the previous chapter, every individual possesses certain personal fears and anxieties which are affected by changes that take place within his internal organizational environment. This we refer to as the nonrational aspect of the decision-making process because these personal fears and anxieties may have a decided effect on the manner in which the decison maker fulfills his responsibilities. It certainly affects the subjective preferences —or, more precisely, whose subjective preferences—the individuals choose to employ.

Congressional committees and subcommittees have, for years, recognized the validity of this proposition. The fear of a congressional investigation has caused more than one executive bureaucrat to become more responsive to the preferences of the particular congressional subgroups to whom he is accountable, even in those instances when such preferences may have run directly counter to the preferences of his executive superiors, including the President. Likewise, the relationship which exists between many private interest groups and executive bureaucrats is one which is frequently forged out of a necessity for support and security on the part of the executive official. As Gore noted in this connection, the decision-making process is as much a matter of resolving internal emotional conflict as it is resolving a complex problem situation in a logical and rational manner; and the most enduring emotion is fear or personal anxiety concerning the security of one's role and position within his organizational setting.

Private bureaucracies are in a much better position to exploit this factor to their advantage than are government organizations. However, this is not to suggest that such feelings of anxiety are absent in government officials. Indeed, these emotions become important factors in the analysis of executive bureaucratic behavior simply because any discussion of the emotional forces within the individual must be examined in terms of the relevance that the outward manifestation of such forces may have for the organization. One of the most positive expressions of such emotions is in the form of personal loyalty directed to the organization. The late Eugene Burdick patterned one of his early novels around the political formula, fear plus hate equals power. What is being suggested here is that fear plus security equals loyalty. That is, the source from which the executive bureaucrat can gain the degree of personal security needed to eliminate or minimize the fears and anxieties that may develop in connection with his position, will receive, in return, the loyalty of the individual. In our political system, loyalty, like information, can serve as legal tender. Its significance, therefore, is not incidental, and, for this reason, additional discussion on this point will be deferred to the subsequent chapter.

## Optimizing-Satisfying

The proposition presented in the previous chapter suggested that decision-making actions designed to achieve satisfactory, or "good enough" solutions to problem situations would most likely occur under low-risk, noncomplex conditions. On the other hand, decisions designed to achieve maximum or optimal solutions would more likely result from high-risk, complex problem situations. Within the executive structure, both patterns are evidenced. At the middle and lower executive echelons, "satisficing" represents an effective decision-making device, especially in connection with the multitude of daily, routine problem situations. At this level, goals—through reinterpretation and re-definition—can be made relatively clear and precise, and conflict intensity associated with a given problem situation frequently is low, its scope narrow. As a result, a satisfactory choice is, more often than not, the most "rational" as well as the most economical decision that can be made. This proposition seems even more appropriate in instances when the uncertainty associated with the consequences of one's choice is low and/or the perceived risks in making a poor choice are also low. Most (but by no means all) Presidential appointments come under this category. In most of these instances, a satisfactory choice frequently represents the best alternative to avoid high intensity conflict. Furthermore, the uncertainty and risk associated with the nomination of John Doe as Assistant Secretary of Commerce for Domestic and International Affairs may be quite minimal in that even if the nominee is a complete stranger to the President, his responsibilities will be structured in such a way as to minimize the danger or damage to the administrative machinery which may result from the appointee's own ineptitude.

However, with an entirely different set of conditions prevailing, optimizing may be the most "rational" decision-making strategy to follow within the executive branch. When unique events occur, or special responses are needed, and/or when conflict intensity associated with the problem situation is high, then satisfactory solutions frequently appear not to be "good enough," and optimal or maximum alternatives become the object of intensive search. Given the nature of the political decision-making process, complex decisions frequently have to be made under rather adverse circumstances. In addition to the uncertainties and risks that may be associated with each possible alternative, top-level executive officials, and especially the President, must recognize the additional pressure caused by the fact that most top-level policy determinations require virtually irrevocable decisions. That is to say, once certain basic decisions are made concerning a particular policy program, the machinery of the executive branch is put into motion, and the momentum which it develops is extremely difficult to halt, much less reverse. Thus, Eisenhower, as the first Republican President in twenty years, left office in 1960 with most of the New Deal programs still in operation. In much the same way, the dominant imprint left by the Eisenhower Administration in the area of international affairs and foreign policy has been modified, but not obliterated or erased, by the subsequent Kennedy and Johnson Administrations. So the element of irrevocability is present in virtually every major executive policy decision. Given the millions of people who will be directly affected by such decisions, this decision-making responsibility can hardly be viewed in terms of "good enough" or satisfactory solutions. As Sorenson notes:

> As each President nears a final answer, he realizes that his choice is only a beginning. For each new decision sets a precedent, begetting new decisions, foreclosing others, and causing reactions which require counteraction. Roosevelt, according to Madame Perkins, "rarely got himself sewed tight to a program from which there was no turning back."
>
> But too often a President finds that events or the decisions of others have limited his freedom of maneuver—that is, as he makes a choice, the doors close behind him. And he knows that once the door is closed it may never open again—and he may find himself in a one-way tunnel, or in a baffling maze, or descending a slippery slope. He cannot count on turning back—yet he cannot see his way ahead.[16]

Under these circumstances risks are high, uncertainties abound, conflict intensities are strong, and goals are frequently unclear or conflicting. Add to this the near-irrevocable nature of most major policy decisions, and the net result certainly suggests a long, agonizing decision-making process in which the "best" of all known and available alternatives to problem situations of national and international significance is sought.

[16] Theodore C. Sorenson, *Decision-Making in the White House* (New York: Columbia University Press, 1963), pp. 20–21.

## Summary

As suggested in the previous chapter, decision making is a perfect complement to, and a logical extension of, organizational control patterns. In both areas composite processes result, a "reversed-dependency" relationship develops, and extensive reliance is placed on the subjective exploitation of emotional needs in an effort to maximize operating effectiveness. However, the difference between decision making in public and private bureaucratic settings is significant.

In the first place, given the differences in the selection and training of executive officials in the public and private sectors, political executives are forced to rely on the judgments of their subordinates to a much greater extent than their counterparts in private enterprise. Stemming from this point, a second basic difference emerges in that political executives are, for the most part, products of some other organizational environment; as a consequence, the experience, knowledge, responses, values, attitudes, and beliefs that they reflect have all been shaped and determined in an entirely different organizational setting. In numerous instances, these pre-formed behavioral patterns, which permit the individual to utilize with confidence a set of subjective judgments in the absence of objective data, are of limited usefulness within the governmental bureaucratic setting. Thus, a process of relearning must take place if the executive official is to develop a new set of subjective judgments which can be applied with confidence in evaluating the recommendations of subordinates. For many, of course, this relearning process never occurs; under these circumstances, total reliance obviously must be placed on the judgments of one's subordinates if perpetual conflict is to be avoided.

Simply by way of illustration, the Presidencies of Truman and Eisenhower provide support for the above proposition, although its applicability encompasses all middle- and top-level executive officials in the governmental system. Harry Truman was a relatively inconspicuous individual whose limited tenure as U. S. Senator offered scant preparation for the momentous task he was to assume. Filling out the unexpired term of Franklin Roosevelt, Truman appeared as a troubled and harried Chief Executive who was forced to rely almost exclusively on the judgments of his subordinates. As he moved into his own four-year term, however, he gained increasing self-confidence, primarily because he gradually developed his own set of subjective judgments which he could apply with confidence and accuracy in evaluating the recommendations of his subordinates.

President Eisenhower followed a similar pattern. It is no accident that contemporary political historians picture him as "The Chief" during the second, but not the first term of his Administration. In short, few people are what could be even generously called "prepared" to assume virtually any executive position within the political bureaucracy; whereas, by contrast, within private organizations a comparable situation would be a rare event, indeed.

As noted above, superiors are dependent upon subordinates in both public and private settings—but to a significantly and qualitatively greater degree in the public sector. Much the same can be said of the emphasis which is placed on, and the use which is made of, the subjective aspects of bureaucratic behavior. This represents the third major difference between the two spheres. Because of the highly decentralized and fragmented control pattern present in the executive branch; because of the frequent and extensive turnovers of top- and middle-level executive officials; and because of the absence of a cohesive and enduring set of overall organizational goals—the behavioral patterns that do develop within the executive branch are for the most part highly personalized in content. Excluding, of course, the big bulk of thoroughly routine procedures which go on day-in, day-out in an almost semiconscious fashion, the manner in which most new, unique, nonprogrammed situations are confronted and resolved within the executive bureaucracy can be explained in terms of a more highly personalized and subjectively oriented set of relationships than are evidenced within private bureaucratic structures.

The Bureau of the Budget has made significant strides in institutionalizing various administrative procedures designed to increase the formal management control of the President,[17] and similarly, the official power, prestige, and status of the Presidency has even become increasingly institutionalized.[18] However, power can never be completely institutionalized, particularly within a political setting; the ingredient necessary to activate power relationships between superiors and subordinates is a highly personalized one. Neustadt notes that Departmental Secretaries, despite their assumed loyalty to the President, frequently behave as though they were in business for themselves. To a very real extent they are, in fact, private entrepreneurs, and they have to behave as such in spite of the fact that they are also supposedly members of an executive team. Because of these political "facts of life," power, of necessity, becomes the power to persuade, and nothing more. Personal persuasion becomes the basic characteristic of superior-subordinate relationships throughout the entire executive branch. From the senior career levels of the civil service to the Cabinet level, every official when acting in his capacity as a subordinate is to a varying degree an independent operator. As a subordinate he enjoys a certain degree of independence from his superior, and as a superior he is aware that the same fact exists insofar as his subordinates are concerned. Thus, everyone becomes a bargaining agent to some extent, which in turn simply accentuates the highly personalized,

[17] Richard Neustadt, "Presidency and Legislation: The Growth of Central Clearance," *The American Political Science Review*, vol. 48 (September 1954); and, by the same author, "Presidency and Legislation: Planning the President's Program," *Ibid.*, vol. 49 (December 1955).

[18] Neustadt, *Presidential Power, op. cit.*, Ch. 1.

subjective, and frequently emotionally oriented relationships which develop within the executive bureaucratic structure. Thus, the fourth basic difference between the political and non-political decision-making processes is noted in the degree to which interpersonal relationships vary in their impersonal and semiobjective content.

Within the executive branch two problems continue to plague the overall effectiveness of the decision-making process. The first one can be referred to as a mechanical problem involving the actual transmission of objective and subjective information throughout the organization. The extent and nature of this problem has been examined in this chapter. The second problem is much more basic. As already suggested, this involves the question of one's personal sense of commitment to his organization, its goals and its leaders; it involves the personal fears and anxieties of the individual who is forced to operate in an extremely complex organizational setting; it involves the basic question of organizational loyalty.

The relationship between these two problems is relatively clear. Loyalty to one's organization permits many purely mechanical transmission defects and obstacles to be surmounted. In the absence of a strong sense of organizational loyalty, however, the best structural and procedural arrangement for the transmission of intraorganizational communications may be only marginally effective. As suggested earlier in this chapter, personal fears, soothed by a sense of security, can be modified and channeled into an emotional outlet called loyalty. The function that this type of emotion can serve in any organization cannot be disregarded, just as the dysfunction that may result from the absence of any sense of loyalty must be considered equally significant. For this reason, the following chapter examines the question of organizational loyalty as it applies to organizations generally, and especially the executive bureaucracy.

# 6

## Organizational Loyalty

The presence or absence of a feeling of loyalty on the part of the individual members of any bureaucratic structure can significantly affect their values and attitudes toward other members, their subgroup, the organization itself, and even other extra-organizational objects and/or concepts. Control patterns within any organization are made effective as a result of a willingness on the part of all members to accept the view that individual interests and goals can be satisfied only if organizational goals and interests are realized. Similarly, the organizational decision-making process will be effective only insofar as each member is prepared to accept the organization's values, attitudes, and beliefs as his own. Loyalty is, in effect, an essential, intangible quality which must be present if an organization is to represent something more than a mere assemblage of persons. For a wide variety of reasons, some of which have already been discussed in detail, the absence of a sense of loyalty within any organization can seriously impair operating effectiveness.

For instance, if one examines the administrative evolution of the United States foreign aid program since its inception in 1948, the evidence of organizational loyalty on the part of the individuals involved in that program ranges from high to low. At the outset, those who joined the initial phase of the European Recovery Program, as it was administered by Paul Hoffman through the official aid agency, the Economic Cooperation Administration (ECA), were motivated by a wide range of considerations, and the behavioral pattern which emerged within the agency during this initial period can be viewed in terms of strong organizational loyalties.[1]

The accomplishments of the ECA exceeded even the most optimistic expectations. In retrospect, the spectacular successes enjoyed by the agency in the initial years can be understood in terms of several factors. However, the most relevant point for our present purposes involves the extremely successful administrative operation that was performed under Hoffman's direction. In this regard, certain generalizations are suggested. For instance, one could note that Hoffman was very successful in bringing together a group of individuals who were intensely committed to him personally, as a result of a strong sense of personal admiration and/or basic loyalty; or who were equally committed to the program's goals, as a result of any number of possible motivations (altruism, personal adventure, self-interest, and so on); or, both. Whatever the motives, a relatively strong sense of loyalty prevailed in the agency, and a fairly cohesive organization emerged in a relatively short period of time.

Loyalty, of course, is not to be equated with efficiency. However, it is legitimate to view it as a factor which may significantly affect the goal-attainment function of any organization. It is in this latter respect that a sense of loyalty can be seen as an

[1] See Herbert Simon, "Birth of an Organization: The Economic Cooperation Administration," *Public Administration Review*, vol. 13 (Autumn 1953), p. 227.

important aspect of the early administrative operations of the aid program. The absence of a strong relationship between organizational loyalty and goal attainment can also be seen as one of the fundamental weaknesses which plagued the aid program in later years. By the middle of the 1950's, for instance, the aid agencies which had jurisdiction over the administrative implementation of the program were virtually devoid of any degree of organizational loyalty. Internal cohesiveness, the proud characteristic of the earlier years had, by the mid-1950's, virtually disappeared.

The initial impetus associated with any new program—particularly one which reflects bold, imaginative thinking and goals—is bound to diminish, or dissipate, as the unique gradually becomes routine. Planners, innovators, and visionaries are replaced in key administrative positions by technicians, stabilizers, and operators. While this type of transition is considered normal and is to be expected, it does not necessarily follow that the shift from the novel to the routine must also result in the elimination of a sense of organizational loyalty. The types of loyalty engendered by the two different periods may in themselves be quite different—one fervent, the other quite subdued—but some sense of loyalty or commitment to the organization and its goals is needed if any degree of internal cohesiveness is to be realized.

Organizational loyalty, then, must be viewed as a key administrative factor which has many ramifications when utilized within a bureaucratic context. Any factor which can affect operations, morale, control, and decision making can hardly be considered insignificant. For this reason, some special attention must be given to (1) how the term is to be used and defined, (2) how it is developed within an organization, and (3) the type of conflicts associated with it. After examining each of these points, the problem of organizational loyalty as specifically related to the executive branch bureaucracy will be discussed in detail.

## Organizational Loyalty Defined

The term loyalty as it is being used here in connection with organizations is intended to incorporate and connote the concepts of transcendence and subordination. For example, the individual is frequently faced with the responsibility of having to make a choice, i.e., make a decision, between two competing sets of demands. Under these circumstances the individual may proceed in a number of ways; first, he may attempt to satisfy both sets of demands at the same time; second, he may choose to ignore both; and, finally, he may select one and reject the other.

In connection with the first possibility, it is probably accurate to suggest that this is the immediate reaction that most of us have when confronted with a conflict situation—is it possible to satisfy both demands, contrary though they may be? Frequently it is possible to achieve this end. Such a delightful state of affairs is not always possible (or desirable), however. Normally the individual must make a choice, *or* he may completely withdraw from the conflict, ignoring its presence, and simply refuse to make a choice. Instances of this type are not infrequent among both public and private executive officials who are forced to face difficult decisions involving conflicting demands. This type of behavior could popularly be referred to as the "indecision-making process," and it is generally not considered to be a commendable characteristic of executive officials, except, possibly under very specialized conditions involving a series of strategic moves by a calculating decision maker, in which case to decide not to decide may, for tactical purposes, prove to be the most effective decision that could be made under the circumstances.

Although the individual may attempt to satisfy both conflicting demands, or simply withdraw and make no attempt to satisfy either, the fact remains that neither the first nor the second alternative represents a feasible option in the majority of instances when conflicting demands are present. In other words, within complex bureaucratic organizations, executive officials are, for the most part, expected to make decisions concerning conflicting demands that may be imposed on them. It is true that this does not have to be a zero-sum type decision, in which case one demand is totally accepted or satisfied while the other demand is totally rejected; on the other hand, as previously noted, it is not always possible or desirable to be completely equitable, either. Thus, a preferential choice has to be made—a choice which in effect recognizes the advantage or the superiority of one demand over the other. The question that is of interest to us here is the relevance of this observation to the problem of organizational loyalty.

To favor one demand over another conflicting demand is a matter of individual choice. A significant difference does or can emerge, however, in the manner in which the choice is made. The choice can be voluntary or it can be a Hobson's choice, in which case the decision becomes forced, i.e., involuntary. In the latter instance, the question of loyalty is not a major concern. An individual, without any feelings of loyalty whatsoever directed to his organization, may, nevertheless, place organizational demands over either personal or other nonorganizational demands if he is physically and/or psychically dependent upon certain tangible bureaucratic resources. If an individual's position within the hierarchal structure can be effectively intimidated by the organization, then he really has no choice but to give priority to the demands of his organization, vis-à-vis competing demands. But this does not involve the element of loyalty; subtle force in the form of coercion, intimidation, and threats achieve the desired end result, although the means employed are, as discussed in an earlier chapter, basically dysfunctional. Therefore, it is not surprising that complex organizations utilize substantial resources in an attempt to insure that subordinate executive officials will voluntarily give top priority to the demands of their organization when confronted with other, conflicting sets of external and even internal demands. What is required, of course, is a socialization process in which a maximum degree of identification is established between the individual and his organization. The organization's values become his own; the choices that have to be made are made voluntarily and with the understood approval of the organization. The intervening variable which distinguishes this situation from the former is the intangible quality of loyalty.

Used in this sense, then, loyalty (or the lack of it) is a term which can explain why an individual behaves as he does within an organizational setting. Furthermore, it can be used to locate the individual's primary frame of reference which commands his attention in the face of conflict. When the organization, *per se*, represents this primary frame of reference, then, a strong bond of loyalty has been established between the individual and his organization. Viewed in this context, *The Organization* represents the highest of all organizational values, and its demands transcend all others in the case of either intraorganizational or extraorganizational conflict.

As such, organizational loyalty is to be distinguished from such other, closely related terms as morale, cohesiveness, and job satisfaction. Loyalty is meant to imply a high personal commitment to, and identification with, the goals and objectives of one's organization. A certain degree of subjective allegiance is involved in the concept of loyalty, which suggests that it should be distinguished from morale (happiness), job satisfaction (personal satisfaction), and cohesiveness ("togetherness"). Each of these latter factors is an integral aspect of organizational loyalty to the extent that the evidence of low morale, minimum satisfaction, and/or low cohesion are not likely to result in high organizational loyalty. On the other hand, it is not legitimate to assume the converse—namely, that high morale, maximum satisfaction, and high cohesion automatically result in the expression of a strong sense of loyalty. For instance, an individual may be attracted to an organization for any number of possible reasons, none of which may be at all related to the goals or objectives of the organization. Substantial personal satisfaction may be gained from simply belonging to a particular organization, although any sense of loyalty directed to the organization may be absent. In other instances, group cohesiveness is frequently manifested as a self-defensive mechanism which permits organization members to tolerate other undesirable organizational characteristics. Morale, cohesion, and satisfaction may be present but loyalty does not necessarily follow. The organization itself—through its top-level executive officials—has to gain the loyalty of its members, and because of the high rewards usually associated with winning the loyalty of the individual, extensive organizational resources are usually allocated for this purpose.

## The Development of Organizational Loyalty

Although much has been written concerning the numerous factors that enter into any consideration of the nature of group or organizational behavior insofar as loyalty is concerned, personal stability, security, and an anxiety-reward balance are suggested here as three necessary prerequisites which must be firmly established before any enduring sense of organizational loyalty can be developed. To the extent that the organization is able to provide the individual an opportunity to work in a relatively stable, secure, and anxiety-reward balanced environment, efforts can then be directed by the organization toward securing the loyalty of the individual.

To achieve this desired state, the organization can exert—indeed, must exert—the initiative. A clearly stated set of goal objectives is required, along with a relatively unambiguous set of role expectations for every organization member. The reciprocal nature of role expectations has to be made clear as well. That is, the individual must know what the organization expects from him, but he, in turn, must know what to expect from the organization in the event that he does or does not fulfill the expectations that are imposed on him. Under these circumstances, stability tends to emerge as the actual and expected behavioral patterns of all parties tend to converge. Continuous high correlations between variables create reliability; thus, an essential aspect of stability is reliability.

But, of course, reliability can only be established over time; and for this reason the organization must behave in a consistent manner if reliability is ultimately to be achieved. Individual anxiety, security, and stability will be affected to the extent that organizational responses to given individual actions follow a consistent pattern; consequently, operating continuity must be maintained within the organization if individual stability and security are to be realized.

However, individual stability and security do not necessarily insure an anxiety-free organizational setting. An individual may feel completely stable and secure within his bureaucratic structure, and yet reveal a high degree of personal anxiety. A clerk earning $50 per week may have a job for life—a perfectly secure and stable situation—but may be anxiety-ridden simply because he is unable to support his family on his salary. The situation here is not that his job is insecure or that the organization is unstable, but simply that the rewards he receives from the organization are not sufficient to satisfy certain of his physiological and/or psychological needs. If his rewards could be increased—a raise in pay—his anxieties would be decreased. A balance has to be obtained between the individual's anxieties and organizational rewards. If such a balance can be achieved, which in this case means increasing his pay to the point where it might reasonably be expected that he could contain his anxieties within normal limits of toleration, then the organization is in an effective position to seek and obtain the loyalty of the individual.

The term anxiety-reward balance is used here in preference to the terms anxiety-free or anxiety-reducing factors as it must be recognized that for many individuals anxiety is viewed as a necessary burden that must be borne if other goals (personal or organizational) are to be achieved. Executive officials, for instance, at all echelons within any organization are expected to assume various degrees of responsibilities. With the responsibility goes authority to issue orders, directives, and to make certain ranges of decisions. Organizational demands on the individual create anxiety in terms of achieving quality performance while personal or family demands on the individual usually create anxieties in terms of improving or advancing one's position within the hierarchal structure. As one advances up the executive scale, greater responsibilities are assigned, expectations in terms of job performance are increased, and, certainly, anxieties do not disappear.

Within this context, therefore, organizational stability and continuity, as well as personal security, can be maintained only if a balance can be drawn between the degree of personal anxiety the individual is willing to endure for the organization and the rewards that the individual gains for the endurance of such anxiety. A wide range of resources may be at the disposal of the organization to compensate the individual for the anxiety associated with his organizational function. Salary increases, stock options, promotions, innumerable status symbols can all be used to manipulate and modify the anxieties of the individual. Insofar as nongovernmental executive officials are concerned, anxieties cannot be eliminated; however, the organization can manipulate its resources in such fashion as to create an attractive and appealing position in spite of the tensions with which it may be associated.

If an anxiety-reward balance can be achieved, the executive official is then placed in a receptive mood to receive organizational cues which reflect a high "ideological" content designed to win his loyalty or allegiance. This does not ignore that fact that, from the moment the individual becomes an official member of the formal organization, value-laden "messages" are received which are expressly designed to solidify his loyalty. However, the purpose of this discussion has been simply to suggest that the overall effectiveness of such "messages" cannot be maximized until the individual's own "stability-security-anxiety/reward balance" is aligned with that of the organization. After a basic alignment has occurred, the individual is then psychologically prepared to respond positively to organizational cues based on loyalty.

## Competing Loyalties

The popularized literature of Whyte, Packard, Mills, and others creates the very strong impression of the mammoth, monolithic organization suppressing and conditioning the lone, insignificant subordinate executive official. The picture is, at the very least, distorted. Loyalty is a precious commodity; like information which is scarce, he who can obtain it may very well be in a position to influence the outcome of events or to influence the actions of others. For this reason it is understandable why large organizations attempt to monopolize the loyalty of their members, and, by the same token, why they tend to place great rewards on tangible demonstrations of loyalty. Presthus' observation in this regard is significant; ". . . loyalty seems to have become the main basis for bureaucratic succession. Like seniority, loyalty enjoys the advantage of wide acceptance, for it is a quality almost everyone can aspire to."[2] A loyal associate is a trusted associate; one whose behavior can be counted on to be highly consistent with the goals, values, and attitudes of the object of his loyalty, i.e., his primary frame of reference. Because of the value normally associated with the commitment of loyalty, it is unrealistic to assume the organization automatically wins each person's loyalty, as though through default. As with any

[2] Presthus, *Organizational Society*, p. 49.

other valuable commodity, the demand exceeds the supply; as a consequence, the individual's loyalty is sought after from many sources. In the world of the private organization, the executive official is a member of a subgroup which performs a specific function within the overall organization. A claim for his loyalty is clearly imposed on him from this source. In addition, membership in professional organizations, select clientele groups, church, civic and political groups, and the family may result in the emergence of conflicting claims for his loyalty.

Logically, it would seem that the organization should have many more tangible resources at its disposal than any of its rivals to reward loyal subordinates. The reason why this factor alone is not sufficient in and of itself to eliminate all other competing groups or objects is due to the fact that many subordinate officials do not have to depend upon the attainment of these rewards. It is, of course, possible to have an individual who is in no way dependent upon the organization for his need or goal satisfaction, and still be totally loyal to the organization. It is also true, however, that loyalty based on such independence cannot be considered the most secure partnership.

In addition to the virtually unlimited resources the organization has at its disposal to win the loyalty of its members, one must also consider the ultimate sanction, which is indeed monopolized—or at least should be—by the organization: the power of dismissal. But even the power of dismissal, like the effectiveness of tangible rewards, is limited. There are those for whom the threat of dismissal represents no threat at all as a result of a high degree of vocational or professional mobility. In many other instances, such as when one's immediate work group represents his primary frame of reference insofar as his loyalty is concerned, this sanction becomes extremely difficult to impose.

Despite these limitations, private organizations do indeed have a big advantage in the competition for the individual's loyalty simply because the rewards that are offered for one's loyalty normally cannot be matched by any other source, and the punishments are usually severe enough to insure a fairly high degree of conformity. Exceptions do result; deviations do occur; outright "subversives" do appear now and then within the ranks of some private bureaucratic structures. For the most part, however, the private hierarchies are in a relatively strong position to maximize the virtues and advantages of loyalty. The extent to which the same conclusion can be validly made in connection with public bureaucracies is the question to which we can now direct our attention.

## Executive Branch Loyalty

As we have already noted in connection with the basic problem of organizational control, conflict resolution within any bureaucratic structure is most effectively accomplished when the techniques and mechanisms of control can be monopolized by top-level executive officials. Much the same can be said in connection with the problem of organizational loyalty; unless the organization can command, i.e., monopolize, the complete allegiance of its members, then the effectiveness of the organization's appeals to its members on the basis of an implied sense of obligation can be seriously weakened. As noted, an individual may feel obliged to act the way his organization wants him to act on the basis of intimidation; on the other hand, his "correct" response or action may be simply the result of a totally loyal commitment to act always in the best interests of the organization. Within the executive branch of the federal government it is extremely difficult to accomplish either alternative.

Theoretically, of course, the President is located at the apex of the federal executive hierarchy; he represents the Chief Executive officer of a vast bureaucratic structure, and it might be expected that he would personify all of the organizational characteristics considered essential in developing a shared sense of organizational loyalty among his subordinate executive officials. The truth of the matter is, of course, that the executive structure rests on a base of an involved and complex set of semiautonomous operating subunits. Periodically, a group of individuals is selected from widely diverse organizational environments to fill the top levels of this hierarchal structure. Leading this group is the President who, like most of the other members of his "official" top-level executive family, is not a product, so to speak, of the organization which he is expected to direct. Under these circumstances, it seems apparent that executive branch loyalty, if it is to emerge at all, has to be gained or "won" on the basis of a highly personalized approach by the President and his Departmental Secretaries. In other words, the situation in the executive branch virtually requires that personal characteristics rather than institutionalized factors be utilized to develop any sense of organizational commitment.

This is not to suggest that the President and top-level Cabinet officials can obtain the type of responses they seek from subordinates only on the basis of personal loyalty, although in numerous instances this does represent the dominant motivating force for many subordinates. Programmatic loyalties can be developed and utilized successfully if channeled in constructive directions. Thus, many individuals involved in the administration of the poverty program are motivated by humanitarian considerations as opposed to any sense of personal commitment to either the President or the Director of the Office of Economic Opportunity. In addition, one must assume that the majority of executive bureaucrats are guided to some extent by a generalized and vague sense of responsibility to the body politic. By appealing to a subordinate on the basis of his responsibility to the public interest, top-level executive officials quite frequently are able to solicit the desired behavior or action.[3]

Simply by discussing the various tactics that can be employed by top-level executive officials to achieve some degree of subordinate loyalty serves to illustrate the basic thesis set forth by Richard Neustadt that Presidential power is, in fact, nothing more than the power to persuade, and that the bulk of Presidential energies have to be directed toward getting subordinates ". . . to believe that what he wants of them is what their own appraisal of their own responsibilities requires them to do in their interest, not his."[4] What is true of Presidents is also applicable to Departmental Secretaries. Each of these individuals has various resources at his disposal which can be utilized under appropriate circumstances to gain support and cooperation from subordinate executive officials. But, as noted in previous chapters, these "resources" have to be utilized within the context of either pure persuasion or pure bargaining techniques. Moreover, there are various (one might even say inherent) aspects of the executive structure which are quite effective in diluting the power to persuade. The real test, therefore, confronting any President or Departmental Secretary is to establish an effective sense of organizational purpose and commitment in the minds of subordinate officials in spite of the severe limitations imposed on them by the system. This is the challenge of executive leadership within the governmental bureaucracy, and it should not be surprising that few executives can claim total success in this area.

### Factors Which Limit The Power To Persuade

THE CIVIL SERVICE COMMISSION. Probably the most controversial aspect of executive branch management focuses on the

---

[3] According to published reports, this was the tactic apparently used by President Johnson in getting Chief Justice Earl Warren to head the public commission to investigate the assassination of President Kennedy.

[4] *Presidential Power, op. cit.*, p. 46.

philosophy of the merit system and the role of the U. S. Civil Service Commission. The Civil Service Commission is an independent regulatory body, composed of three members who are appointed by the President to serve six-year, staggered terms. It was created in 1883 with the passage of the Pendleton Act, which is the basic civil service statute of the federal government. On the basis of the Pendleton Act, as subsequently amended, the jurisdiction of the Commission now covers a wide range of activities affecting government personnel problems. The commission is directed to provide competitive examinations for job openings, to fill personnel vacancies, to establish standards for admission to the federal service, to establish policy concerning the dismissal, transfer, reinstatement, and promotion of federal employees, to conduct security inquiries when required, and to administer various specific acts which relate to veterans status, job classifications, life and health benefits, award incentives, and retirement programs. The most controversial aspects of the Commission's jurisdiction involve, as one may expect, the selection, classification, promotion, and dismissal of federal employees.

Although the Civil Service Commission does not enjoy monopolistic control over all federal employees,[5] the Civil Service Classification Act of 1949 does include the biggest proportion of federal government employees. For this reason, the following discussion will focus on the personnel problems that have been associated with the Civil Service Commission.

The Classification Act of 1949 established what is referred

[5] Personnel employed by the following executive branch subunits are covered by personnel systems specifically designed for their respective subunits, and are completely divorced from any connection with the Civil Service Commission: State Department Foreign Service and Foreign Service Reserve Officers, all military personnel, employees of the Tennessee Valley Authority, Atomic Energy Commission, Central Intelligence Agency, and the Federal Bureau of Investigation. The Post Office Department has its own distinct pay schedule for its Postal Field Services.

to as the General Schedule of graded responsibility. Ranging from G.S.-1 to G.S.-15—not including the supergrade positions of G.S.-16, 17, and 18, as subsequently established—each grade carries its own minimum and maximum salary range. G.S.-1 through G.S.-4 generally include all low-level clerical employees. Grades 5 through 7 are usually filled with college graduates, and may be considered the lowest executive echelon. Positions which fall within the G.S.-8 to G.S.-12 categories may be viewed as middle management officials. Top-level career officials (excluding the supergrades) are generally found in the G.S.-13, 14, and 15 grades. These are the senior careerists who have significant supervisory or managerial responsibilities, and/or professional or staff roles. As for the supergrade positions, appointments to grades 16 and 17 require the approval of the Civil Service Commission, and Presidential approval is required for all G.S.-18 appointments.

The literature examining the details of federal career service in depth is extensive.[6] Depending on one's point of view, the overall system is generally described as either stable and secure, or rigid and stagnant. The defenders of the Civil Service Commission and of the entire rationale behind the concepts of the merit system—who, incidentally, are extremely well organized[7]

[6] For introductory purposes see: Wallace Sayre (ed.), *The Federal Government Service* (Englewood Cliffs: Prentice-Hall, 1965); W. Lloyd Warner *et al.*, *The American Federal Executive* (New Haven: Yale University Press, 1963); Marshall and Gladys Dimock, *Public Administration* (New York: Holt, Rinehart, and Winston, 1964), Third Edition, Ch. 14; John Pfiffner and Robert Presthus, *Public Administration* (New York: Ronald Press, 1960), Fourth Edition, Part IV; Felix A. Nigro, *Modern Public Administration* (New York: Harper Row, 1965), Part IV; and John D. Millett, *Government and Public Administration* (New York: McGraw-Hill, 1959), Ch. 11.

[7] In addition to the Civil Service Commission itself which has consistently resisted major innovations in the federal career process, the House and Senate Post Office and Civil Service Committees have, for the most part,

—seek to maximize individual security and protection against arbitrary personnel decisions. They agree that effective and efficient administrative actions can only be realized within a relatively stable organizational environment in which individual anxieties and tensions generated by feelings of occupational insecurity have been significantly eliminated. If one can remove the causes of such anxiety—threatened dismissals, reductions in rank, arbitrary reward allocations—then personnel security can be realized, administrative continuity develops, and operating efficiency increases.

As viewed by the critics of the system, an artificial and highly dysfunctional type of stability is achieved by statutory dictates at the expense of qualitative performance. As a result, while the system is designed to protect the individual against arbitrary treatment—a function which has been quite successfully accomplished—it cannot, at the same time, maximize a reward and incentive system designed to encourage imaginative planning and dynamic administration. As a consequence, the critics of the system see complacency stemming from stability, mediocrity resulting from security, and a generalized conservative bias permeating the entire system which is committed toward the maintenance of the status quo.

To a very real extent, of course, these two positions have been reconciled to the satisfaction of all concerned. Everyone agrees that the routine job should be protected and the policy-making position should not. As long as one examines only the extremes of the policy-administration continuum, no serious

sought to maximize the security and stability aspects of the system. These groups have, over the years, been effectively supported by—and occasionally prodded by—such groups as the National Civil Service League, the National Federation of Federal Employees, the Naval Civilian Administrators Association, the National Alliance of Postal Employees, the National Postal Transport Association, the American Federation of Government Employees, the National Association of Letter Carriers, and the United Federation of Postal Clerks.

difficulty is encountered; as one moves toward the center of the continuum, however, an ambiguous situation develops, which in many instances totally obliterates any meaningful dichotomy between the two functions. A fine line divides the Assistant Secretaries (political appointees) and the senior career officials Assistant Secretaries are a part of the executive policy-making apparatus, appointed by the President, usually to supervise the administrative functions of operating units. However, to serve this function effectively, the line Assistant Secretaries must, almost of necessity, rely heavily on their chief subordinates, the senior career officials. Insofar as these career bureaucrats are concerned, security, status, and influence are an inherent part of their positions, and, for the most part, they are independent of any obligation to higher political appointees as long as they engage in no criminal, subversive, perverted, or insubordinate acts. The top-level careerists are, in a very real sense, the private entrepreneurs of the executive structure, and although the legal and theoretical strength of their positions can be traced to the Civil Service Classification Act and its attendant Pendleton philosophy, their political strength, which provides both security and bargaining power, may be derived from a variety of sources other than the President or some other politically appointed superior.

For example, the Consular Treaty, signed between the United States and the Soviet Union in 1964, was not ratified by the U. S. Senate until 1967. Many political factors delayed the final ratification vote by the Senate, but probably the most formidable obstacle was the position assumed by the Director of the Federal Bureau of Investigation, J. Edgar Hoover. As the head of a bureau within the Justice Department, and theoretically accountable directly to the Attorney General and his Deputy assistant, Hoover informed a House Appropriations Subcommittee in 1965 that the ratification of the treaty would make the work of his bureau more difficult in view of the fact that the treaty, if ratified, would permit the Soviets to enhance their intelligence operations within the United States. As the first session of the 90th Congress began in January 1967, the treaty again was scheduled for hearings by the Senate Foreign Relations Committee. At that time, Secretary of State Dean Rusk made public an exchange of letters written in September 1966 between himself and the FBI chief in an effort to modify the forceful impact of Hoover's previous pronouncement. This prompted *The New York Times* to comment editorially:

> Even after publication of the curious correspondence between Secretary of State Rusk and J. Edgar Hoover, it is far from certain that the Administration will be able to override the veto Mr. Hoover has hitherto exercised against the long-stalled Soviet-American consular treaty.
>
> There can be few, if any, precedents for the spectacle that correspondence presents: the Secretary of State, in effect, asking a Federal police official of sub-Cabinet rank to stop blocking United States foreign policy, and then receiving a reply so cryptic and ungracious that it can only further encourage opponents of the Administration policy. It is a reminder of the magnitude of Mr. Hoover's power, with implications that go far beyond the immediate issue.[8]

Thus, the stark reality of personnel management that confronts every President is the "elite" cadre of senior civil servants whose basic loyalty to the United States may be unswerving, but whose sense of allegiance to the President and his particular programmatic aims may very well be less than enthusiastic.

COMPETING CLAIMS FOR EXECUTIVE LOYALTY. Implicit in this discussion is the suggestion that if an individual's loyalty is not directed to the President or his program, or some other factor associated with him, such as his administration or his party, then it may very well be directed to some other primary frame of

[8] January 23, 1967.

reference. As we have already noted, this "other" frame of reference may indeed be one's self and one's efforts to maximize one's own self-interests. On the other hand, it should be recognized that various other groups external to the executive organization are not unmindful of the value of winning the loyalty of a strategically placed career official. These would include the many pressure groups that seek to influence those aspects of public policy which directly affect them, and the congressional committees which are constantly in search of career executive officials who are prepared to view the problems of a particular congressional committee sympathetically and with understanding. The reward for the individual bureaucrat who chooses to direct his loyalty to one of these external groups is not insignificant. Any executive official who can depend on the support of one of the strong national interest groups in the event of a conflict between the individual and his political superior, is in a fairly secure position, depending on the specific circumstances, of course. Similarly, Frances Knight's ability to rally significant congressional support in her dispute with Assistant Secretary of State Abba Schwartz should give every politically appointed executive official pause to consider just how weak the executive branch chain of command really can be.

But why, in fact, do middle- and lower-level bureaucratic governmental officials frequently turn to these external sources for support in return for loyalty? Aside from philosophic differences which may develop between the individual career official and the President whose program the individual is called upon to defend, are there other reasons which might explain why any individual would shun a close identification with the top-level political officials of his organization? In this connection, a third limitation is suggested.

THE LACK OF RECIPROCAL LOYALTY. To a very real extent, loyalty like so many other organizational relationships and behavioral patterns is reciprocal. Loyalty is expected to extend upward from every member and to converge at that single point known as the organization. However, loyalty to an organization, like loyalty to any other object or person, cannot be maintained long without some kind of tangible or intangible reward, and in this regard the organization is in the excellent position to provide most organization members with two of the most basic needs—approval-acceptance and protection-security. In return for his loyalty the organization member should reasonably expect his superiors to protect him, for instance, from any external threat which may result from the use of his discretionary judgment. Thus, the defense of subordinates by superiors becomes an integral aspect of the larger problem of organizational loyalty. In this connection, one reason, at least, can be found to explain the relatively low and weak sense of organizational loyalty that one finds throughout the executive branch.

Unfortunately, given the nature of our political system, it is difficult—or, more precisely, strategically unwise—for top-level executive officials to become involved in too many conflicts that may develop at the middle and lower operating levels within the executive structure. The President, as well as his Departmental Secretaries, may enjoy significant prestige, but the power and authority made available to them through formal investiture is severely limited. Whatever power, or authority, or even influence these individuals may be able to put together results, for the most part, from combining their personal leadership qualities with the limited formal authority granted to them. In this type of artificially contrived leadership structure, many top-level executive officials, including unfortunately the President, are extremely reluctant—for a wide variety of reasons, one may assume —to be too anxious, or too frequent, or too intense in their defense of subordinates against external attack, particularly when such an attack originates either from Congress or from a powerful and influential private interest group. New Haven Mayor Richard Lee touched directly on this point when he stated:

A man in public life can't possibly take on every issue as a major personal issue. He has to pick his battles and choose his struggles and select his wars. You have to postpone a lot of your battles until your army is ready. And you'll find sometimes that when your army is ready, the battles don't need to be fought.[9]

It has been stated repeatedly by the sage scholars of politics that Presidential power or influence, like currency, cannot be hoarded indefinitely without fear of the loss of value; thus it must be utilized, i.e., circulated. However, power and influence, again like money, will surely be lost if expenditures exceed income. So the moral of the theory on power is always to keep a bit of it in circulation simply to maintain the vitality of the power held in reserve. Specifically applied to the President, this is usually interpreted to mean that he should be extremely reluctant to allow himself to become involved in every kind of conflict that may develop *within* the various elements of the executive structure and/or *between* these various elements and the major external groups. The theoretical rationale behind all of this, of course, is that top-level executive officials should save their power, prestige, and influence for the really big conflicts in which they will inevitably be involved, and not dissipate these valuable currencies by becoming involved in every trivial conflict involving middle- and lower-level subordinate officials. The validity of most of these assumptions is questionable. No systematic studies have clearly demonstrated that power and frequency of its use always correlate negatively. Nevertheless, it is true, that over the years many of our Presidents and Cabinet Secretaries have acted as though these propositions were in fact absolute truths.

Deprived of many of the tangible resources that private organizations can utilize to develop a sense of loyalty among its

[9] Bernard Asbell, "Dick Lee Discovers How Much is Not Enough," *The New York Times Magazine*, September 3, 1967, p. 42.

executive corps, top-level governmental executives (including the President) must depend almost exclusively on being able to persuade subordinate executive officials that desired administrative behavior is also the most desirable behavior. But as already noted, significant limitations inhibit the power to persuade in the federal executive structure. Therefore, to a very real extent a void is created and, given the Civil Service Classification Act, the competing loyalties, and the lack of reciprocal loyalty within the executive structure, it is not surprising that Congress emerges as one of the dominant influences seeking to fill this void. As in each of the other areas of administrative behavior examined thus far, the interrelationship between Congress and the executive branch assumes an important role. This is particularly true in connection with the issue of organizational loyalty.

### Congressional Influence on Executive Loyalty

In one respect, Congress can be viewed as a structured system, much like the executive hierarchy. The House and Senate, acting in their collective capacities, speak with full authority. For practical purposes this authority is delegated to the standing committees which in turn may assign their responsibilities to subcommittees. On the bottom rung of the legislative ladder—at least in terms of formal authority—stands the individual member of Congress. If all the units within the legislative system were weighted in accordance with their hierarchal position, then executive branch officials could validly conclude that directives emanating from subcommittees carry greater weight than those coming from individual members of Congress; full committee actions should outweigh subcommittee determinations; and the collective expressions of the total membership of either the House or the Senate should enjoy priority over full committee decisions, only to be subordinated to the collective decisions jointly arrived at by both full memberships of the House *and* the Senate.

In fact, however, the various congressional units which occupy any one level in this structured setting are not weighted in accordance to their hierarchal position. Consequently, some subcommittees (i.e., House Appropriations subcommittees) are more "powerful" than other subcommittees and even some full committees. By the same token, not all full committees stand on an equal basis; by any number of criteria—status, prestige, influence, cohesion—some committees rank higher than others. An understanding of the congressional system as it in fact exists is extremely important, therefore, if executive branch officials are to provide an adequate degree of support for their subordinates.

Within the executive structure the traditionally rational organizational maxim prevails in that authority is generally inversely related to the degree of specialization, while within the congressional system a direct relationship generally develops between these two variables. For this reason, one proposition which is suggested is that congressional committees and subcommittees are usually in an extremely advantageous position when dealing with lower-level bureaucrats; they are at least in a competitive position when dealing with middle-level executive administrators; and they only are placed in a disadvantaged position when they are forced to deal with top-level executive officials. Four examples should be sufficient to illustrate this point.

ONE. In the first instance, a House Government Operations Subcommittee (Foreign Operations and Monetary Affairs) undertook an investigation of the use of State Department funds to finance a series of public opinion polls conducted for the State Department by a private opinion research organization.[10] In addition, the subcommittee also sought an explanation for the transmittal of official government information and data by subordinate executives to selected private interest groups for the

10 Hearings on *State Department Public Opinion Polls*, 85th Congress, 1st session, 1957.

express purpose of being used to alter negative congressional attitudes in connection with the United States foreign aid program.

In both cases, the subcommittee's evidence was conclusive, and the wisdom of the executive decisions which created each of these conflict situations was, at best, highly questionable. Nevertheless, in each instance, subordinate executive officials merely carried out the top-level policy decisions made by their superiors. The subordinate officials involved in this case were the middle- and lower-level administrators assigned to the foreign aid agency, the International Cooperation Administration (ICA). The most direct and immediate superior of these individuals was the Director of the ICA, John Hollister; others included numerous top-level State Department officials, including the Secretary of State, John Foster Dulles.

The policy directives established by these top-level executive officials, and expected to be implemented by the middle- and lower-level subordinates, included the cooperation with and supervision of the activities of the National Opinion Research Corporation (NORC) in the preparation, evaluation, and analysis of the public opinion polls taken by NORC on the attitudes of the American public toward various carefully selected topics dealing with American foreign policy. The executive subordinates within the ICA were, in addition, directed by higher authority to establish within the ICA an effective public information program as soon as possible. In both instances, subordinate zeal led to the expression of sharply critical attitudes from within some congressional groups. One such group was the House subcommittee mentioned above. Various members of this subcommittee created a clear impression that taxpayer's money was being promiscuously used to finance popularity polls for the Secretary of State, and to intimidate various congressmen, who were opposed to the continuation of the aid program. As a result, the chairman of the subcommittee,

Congressman Porter Hardy, Jr. (D.-Va.), scheduled a complete investigation of both activities.

Before the conflict officially developed, both Hollister and other top-level executive officials indicated their unwillingness to become involved in the controversy. As a consequence, the middle- and lower-level administrators who were left to face the subcommittee hearings alone were generally unable—given the burden of proof that fell on them—to maintain a balanced conflict. Indeed, when top-level State Department officials, in an effort to avert the subcommittee inquiry, ordered the NORC contract canceled and the key public information consultant to the ICA dismissed, any illusion of top-level support was shattered. From that point, subordinate executive officials within the ICA were reasonably confident that they would be solely responsible for their own defense. As a result, within the foreign aid structure, the concept of organizational loyalty was essentially lost.

TWO. An entirely different sequence of events occurred in a second instance involving the same congressional subcommittee and the Development Loan Fund (DLF). The DLF was created in 1958 as an autonomous agency with sole jurisdiction over foreign aid loans. One of the primary functions of the DLF was to review every loan request thoroughly, and to authorize loans for projects which were economically sound and technically feasible. It was assumed that extensive preliminary engineering studies and other supporting data would form the basis of the DLF decision.

The Hardy subcommittee became interested in the operations of the DLF when, on several occasions, the DLF "earmarked" loan funds to a particular country. "Earmarking" funds was a descriptive term applied to the DLF practice of committing certain amounts of money to a particular country in advance of receiving the detailed engineering and economic feasibility studies. The subcommittee viewed the practice as a subterfuge which enabled the DLF to award "grants" rather than loans. State Department and DLF officials defended the practice in terms of political considerations, the need for flexibility, and other practical factors. Nevertheless, the Hardy subcommittee felt an investigation was warranted, and formal hearings began.[11]

Specifically, the subcommittee's attention was directed to foreign aid funds which had been "earmarked," or committed in advance to Spain as part of a joint Development Loan Fund-Organization for European Economic Cooperation package aid arrangement for that country. The subcommittee attempted to direct the full force of its inquiry at the chief administrative officer of the DLF, its managing director. If left alone to his own devices, this individual was ill-equipped to defend the policies and practices of the DLF. De facto leadership and policy direction for the DLF came from a more elevated source—Under Secretary of State Douglas Dillon. It was Dillon, for instance, who informed Congressman Hardy, after subcommittee investigators were denied access to certain specified DLF documents, that although the executive branch was "most anxious to cooperate with congressional committees," it could do so only "in a manner consistent with its recognized constitutional duty and power with respect to the disclosures of documents and information."[12] As the subcommittee intensified its investigation of the DLF–OEEC loan to Spain, Managing Director Dempster McIntosh revealed his wariness of congressional reaction to the "earmarked" transaction when he advised Dillon in a memo, "that no fixed DLF amount be allocated as part of the U. S. contribution." Continuing in his memo, he reminded Dillon, that "such a line of credit is contrary to the basic approach of the DLF and may aggravate the difficulties we have had on the Hill

[11] Hearings on *Operations of the Development Loan Fund*, 86th Congress, 2nd session, 1960.

[12] *Ibid.*, pp. 37–38.

with similar cases in the past."[13] In his reply to McIntosh, Dillon acknowledged the need for discernment in such matters, but he added,

... arrangements of this sort looking to the stabilization of monetary and fiscal policies of friendly governments are often of overriding importance to the United States, and it is essential that we maintain the greatest flexibility as a government in carrying out our share of the responsibilities under them. Therefore, neither the Export-Import Bank nor the Development Loan Fund can adopt any hard-and-fast rule as to how they will proceed in a given case, but must look on each case on its merits at the time, taking into account the overall interests of the United States. This position should be maintained in any testimony before congressional committees.[14]

Dillon's statement contains two important directives to his subordinates : (a) a relatively unambiguous policy decision which states that in the allocation of DLF money, political flexibility is to be given priority over economic justifications and engineering specifications, and (b) a clear directive to all DLF officials to maintain this position in the face of any congressional inquiry. But, as was noted in the previous example, to issue a directive to subordinate executive officials completes only part of the equation; to achieve maximum operating effectiveness, and, indeed, maximum organizational loyalty, superiors issuing directives to their subordinates must be prepared to support and protect, if need be, their administrative assistants.

Thus, seeing that his managing director of the DLF was faced with a high-anxiety situation as the Hardy subcommittee attempted to fix total responsibility for the earmarking practice with the managing director, Dillon involved himself in the conflict by assuming full responsibility for all actions of the DLF.

[13] Hearings on *Operations of the Development Loan Fund*, p. 595.
[14] *Ibid.*, p. 596.

The subcommittee was then more-or-less forced to direct its inquiry to the one individual who could speak simultaneously as the third ranking official in the State Department, the overall coordinator for the entire U. S. foreign aid program, and the Chairman of the Board of Directors of the Development Loan Fund. Under these circumstances, the full thrust of the Hardy subcommittee inquiry was effectively offset by the willingness of a single top-level executive official to speak authoritatively and positively in defense of the administrative actions of his subordinates.

THREE. The third example to be cited involves a similar request for information, originating in this instance from the Senate Government Operations Subcommittee on Investigations. The use of foreign aid funds was again the focus of investigation, and the agency involved in this case was the Foreign Operations Administration which was headed by Harold Stassen in the early years of the Eisenhower Administration (1953–1955).

In an effort to achieve a high degree of cohesiveness, and loyalty, within his agency, Stassen, shortly after assuming his position as Director, issued an agency directive to all FOA employees instructing them that prior approval from the Director would have to be obtained before any information or data from within the agency could be released to any individual or group outside the agency. Furthermore, Stassen directed that no FOA employee was to appear before any congressional committee or subcommittee without being accompanied by the agency's legal officer.

This directive received its initial test when the Senate subcommittee sought all files, documents, and information relative to a specific aid project in Pakistan.[15] Before the question of access to information was directly encountered, however, the

[15] Hearings on *FOA Grain Storage Elevators in Pakistan*, 84th Congress 1st session, 1955.

second part of the directive was tested. The key witness, as seen by the subcommittee, was the FOA project manager who had made certain basic decisions in connection with the Pakistan project. Appearing before the subcommittee as requested, the project manager was accompanied by the FOA Deputy General Counsel, Leonard J. Saccio. The then-counsel for the subcommittee, Robert F. Kennedy, entered a vigorous protest against Saccio's presence, and he advised the subcommittee chairman,

> I would like to point out that we are looking into a matter that affects the heads of various departments, and possibly Mr. Stassen himself, and to have a representative of his office present is very apt to affect the answers that a witness could give to the staff. It certainly would make it more difficult, Mr. Chairman, and it has never been done in the past to my knowledge.[16]

The chairman, Senator John McClellan, concurred, but he advised the witness that he was welcome to appear before the subcommittee with his personal attorney (". . . if you feel that you need one . . ."). Saccio, in an attempt to defend his role in the hearings, stated,

> It is my feeling that the men of any government agency in the executive branch, have to carry out their duties, and be free of any feeling that they will be called upon to explain any recommendation that they may make, that the head of the agency and its executives are responsible for the operation of the agency, and these men should not have any feeling during the day-to-day operations of the agency that they will be questioned or criticized for what they have done in carrying out their duties.[17]

The subcommittee overruled Saccio's advisory opinion, and then proceeded to request all pertinent information relating

[16] Hearings on *FOA Grain Storage Elevators in Pakistan*, p. 11.
[17] *Ibid.*, p. 4.

to the Pakistan transaction. Again in compliance with the Stassen directive, agency officials refused to yield the requested information without first obtaining the approval of the Director and, as a consequence, Stassen himself was subpoenaed to appear before the subcommittee with all pertinent data requested. Honoring the subpoena, Stassen directed to the subcommittee a statement which touched the very core of the philosophical basis of organizational loyalty.

> . . . there is a very important principle involved. We are under the President's instructions on the confidential and privileged communications within the executive branch. . . . The point that is involved here is that in this matter . . . different individuals on the staff will make diverse recommendations and they must be free to recommend as they see fit. Then when the top executive . . . makes the decision, he has to be responsible for it. . . . I accepted [the responsibility] and it is in my judgment not only a bad practice but not correct to endeavor to then go back on the individual member of the staff and go into the question of each individual recommendation they made. This is the point that is involved here.[18]

As noted in the beginning of the Stassen statement, the implication is suggested that he, as FOA Director, assumed that his agency directive would enjoy the support of top-level executive officials, including the President. If there was an expectation of this type on the part of Stassen, it was never realized. Consequently, despite the efforts by Stassen to insulate his subordinates from the anxieties of ex post facto congressional investigations, he had none of the resources that were needed to "shore-up" his intentions. As a result, the subcommittee ultimately received all but two of the documents relating to the project, and Stassen's effectiveness as an executive administrator was somewhat weakened by the extremely sharp criticism leveled at him in the final report of the subcommittee.

[18] Ibid., pp. 46–47.

In the investigation of this case, the subcommittee was hampered by the delaying tactics of Mr. Stassen. . . . He was most uncooperative for a public official, as illustrated by his attempts to hinder and impede the legitimate functions of this subcommittee.[19]

FOUR. The fourth and final case that is cited to illustrate the importance of the concept of organizational loyalty as a critical factor in obtaining a state of equilibrium in executive-legislative conflicts involves various middle-level Defense Department officials and the full Senate Armed Services Committee. A clear contrast emerges between this and the previous example.

In the early years of the Kennedy Administration, various top-level executive officials—particularly those in the Defense and State Departments—became seriously concerned over the increasing number of written and oral public statements by military officers which were in varying degrees critical of U. S. foreign and defense policies. Finally, after several exceptionally critical statements were released by various officers, top-level Defense department officials decided on a policy which required that all military officers obtain prior clearance from appropriately designated Department of Defense officials for any public speech or statement to be released.[20]

In practical terms the policy directive meant that every military officer who planned to speak before any public group had to submit his proposed talk to the Defense Department for review by a small group of middle-level executive officials who rather ingloriously became known as the censors, or "muzzlers." These individuals were authorized to delete any passage which could

[19] FOA *Grain Storage Elevators in Pakistan,* Senate Government Operations Subcommittee on Investigations, Senate Report No. 1410, 84th Congress, 2nd session (1956), p. 12.

[20] *Congressional Quarterly Weekly Report,* vol. 19, No. 37 (Sept. 15, 1961), p. 1588.

possibly embarrass the Administration, or which might tend to contradict existing Defense or State Department policies.

Obviously, a certain degree of discretion was involved in this task, and of the many deleted phrases and passages that were brought to the attention of the Senate Armed Services Committee, few seemed objectionable when viewed in isolation from the rest of the speech. For an undertaking of this sort to be completely understood, a high sharing of values among all concerned was necessary. Unfortunately, the Armed Services Committee did not share the same values which were used to guide the Defense Department editors.

The committee sought to have the "muzzlers" appear at its hearings so that each subordinate official could explain the criteria he used to evaluate the speeches and, hence, provide an understanding as to why particular words, phrases, and passages were deleted. But, as indicated, the whole function of subordinate protection by superiors as related to organizational morale and loyalty would have been destroyed if this request by the committee was honored. As a result, Secretary of Defense Robert McNamara appeared before the committee and agreed to cooperate fully with the committee's investigation; like Stassen, McNamara assumed full responsibility for the actions of his subordinates; and, like Stassen, he refused to comply with the committee's specific request, i.e., supply the names of the individuals who were assigned the task of review. Later, McNamara modified his position somewhat by submitting the names of his "review staff" to the committee. Nevertheless, he refused to identify the individual staff members who deleted specific remarks from various speeches. "I believe today," he said, "that it is not sound management practice to pin the blame on subordinates for responsibilities which are mine."[21]

The lines were thus drawn between the Department of Defense and the Senate Armed Services Committee, or, to

[21] *Idem.*

personalize the conflict, between Secretary McNamara and the chairman of the committee, Senator Richard Russell. As viewed from within congressional circles a Departmental Secretary— or any appointed executive official for that matter—may, with propriety, respectfully decline a request for information from a congressional committee or subcommittee, but he cannot refuse a demand for information. McNamara was directed to supply the sought-after data by the committee in a manner which closely resembled an ultimatum. To maintain the strength of his own position, McNamara had to obtain additional support. For this reason, he sought, and received the support of President Kennedy. It was the President who finally stepped into the controversy—just as Dillon stepped into the controversy between the Hardy subcommittee and the Managing Director of the DLF—by invoking the doctrine of executive privilege which generally permits any President the privilege of withholding any information from Congress which he may consider contrary to the best interests of the nation.[22]

McNamara was able to obtain the support of the President, whereas Stassen was not; or, to put it somewhat differently, Stassen—no less committed to the principle of singular responsibility than McNamara—was, nevertheless, unable to protect his executive subordinates due to the fact that he himself was unable to obtain additional support when it was needed. The chain of command works in many different ways. Thus, organizational loyalty within the executive branch is something more than a simple exchange of identification and rewards for conformity and dedication. Superiors must be prepared to protect or defend

[22] For good accounts of the historical evolution of the executive privilege doctrine see Cornelius Cotter, "Legislative Oversight," in *Congress: The First Branch of Government*, Alfred DeGrazia (ed.) (Washington: American Enterprise Institute, 1966), pp. 54–58; and, Robert Kramer and Herbert Marcuse "Executive Privilege—A Study of the Period 1953–1960," The *George Washington Law Review*, vol. 29 (June 1961), p. 830.

subordinates who, by virtue of their tenuous positions within the porous hierarchal structure, are vulnerable to attacks on their own organizational loyalties by any group that is capable of penetrating the flimsy executive screen. Frequently, and unfortunately, it may be decided by top-level officials that the effort to defend subordinate administrators may not be worth the costs involved; under these circumstances organizational loyalty is severely impaired. Nevertheless, the trump card, in the person of the President, is in the hands of the executive branch, and the nature of the individual who occupies this office can, to a great extent, set the tone of the nature of organizational loyalty throughout the executive structure.

### Defensive Behavior

When subordinate administrative officials discover that support from the top of the executive hierarchy is either a token effort or totally absent, this, to use the terms of the psychologists, should result in an immediate signal to the individual that his previous behavioral patterns should be revised and corrected in accordance with the newly obtained information. The individual, in short, will be wise if he devises his own self-defensive mechanisms to guard against becoming an administrative "casualty" in any open hostility which may follow. Generally this means that the rational individual will seriously restrict the extent and scope of the degree of discretionary behavior which he may have engaged in previously, and second, it generally means that left alone to his own devices, the subordinate executive official who is rational as well as wise will seek support from other sources—and, unfortunately, all too often this means from *any other source*. Let us examine each of these points separately.

RESTRICTING DISCRETIONARY BEHAVIOR. As mentioned in a previous chapter, an effective decision-making process depends on the extent to which top-level policy makers are afforded access to a constant source of qualitatively and quantitatively valuable information. In this respect, executive policy makers are quite dependent on middle- and lower-level subordinates who have the original responsibility of selecting that information which they judge to be important, or of making certain evaluations of various situations and individuals, and passing this data on to their superiors. Subjective judgments frequently have to be made by the reporting officials and, in line with the discussion in the previous chapter on this point, let us assume that top-level governmental officials have complete confidence in the judgments of their subordinates reporting from the field. There is no substitute for candor in the reporting of events, no matter how harsh the truth may be. Thus it may be extremely important to know, insofar as the success of our foreign policy is concerned, if the President of the United States and the Secretary of State are viewed by the various peoples around the world as trustworthy men, the pillars of integrity, or as devious Machiavellians who are planning the conquest of the free world. It may also be extremely important to know if the head of state of a nation which is receiving substantial economic and military assistance from the United States is utilizing these funds with maximum effectiveness and success or if he is an incompetent charlatan who is actually siphoning off most of the American assistance into his own private coffers. The point is that if the individiduals in Washington are to be expected to make intelligent adjustments to existing policies and to initiate new policies to meet other pressing needs, they must have at their disposal accurate and reliable information about any given situation in any part of the world at any given time. If top-level executive officials are apprised of programmatic deficiencies, but make no adjustments in their foreign economic and military assistance programs, for example, then it is they who can legitimately be held accountable by Congress in the event of a subsequent inquiry. However, it is hardly fair to hold these same individuals accountable for failing to make whatever adjustments might have been necessary to correct these defects if, in fact, they were not informed by their reporting executive subordinates. Under these circumstances, the fault obviously rests at the source of the report.

However, consider the position of the subordinate executive official who, having been in Nation X for the past six months, has gradually developed the rather firm impression, based on fairly substantial evidence, that the goals of the assistance programs are not being realized. How does one proceed to incorporate this bit of information into a written report, particularly if the viewpoint to be expressed runs contrary to all existing attitudes of Nation X held in official government circles in Washington? It represents an extremely sensitive situation for the field investigator, and the way that he words his report will be determined by the extent to which he believes that his Washington superiors will protect his professional and personal integrity against any external conflict that may develop as a result of his communication being made public. If he is confident that he will be protected, as McNamara protected his "censors," then there should be no hesitancy in getting the vital information in its most accurate and candid form to Washington as soon as possible. However, if the individual is confident that he will have to defend himself before a congressional investigating committee for example, without any visible support being supplied by his superiors, and without being permitted, because of national security considerations, to cite the pertinent evidence that he has collected to support his evaluation, then one may begin to appreciate why he would choose to portray the economic and military assistance programs in Nation X in an entirely satisfactory manner. Under the circumstances, one can certainly understand the individual's desire to protect his own self-interest; it is equally apparent, however, that the cause of administrative efficiency and policy-making effectiveness in the executive hierarchy has been weakened in the process.

SUPPLEMENTARY SUPPORT. The second point that was made in connection with the development of certain self-defensive mechanisms on the part of the executive subordinate involved the search for support from other sources. This is not to imply that governmental bureaucrats are to be viewed as mercenaries who are prepared to "sell" their loyalties to the highest bidder. What we are talking about, however, are the "natural" alliances that are established among individuals of like interests who share similar goals. In this regard there are two directions the administrator can follow in an effort either to supplement the support he does get from the upper levels of the executive bureaucracy or to fill the void that may be created as a result of the complete absence of top-level support. First, the individual can turn to outside interest groups; second, he can seek aid and comfort from Congress.

Interest groups, as we have mentioned before, represent logical, natural, and, usually, quite willing allies for executive administrators. Whether they may be especially influential or valuable as a source of support is another question entirely, but the point to be considered first is that nearly every executive agency, bureau, or office does have contacts with a particular group or set of groups which are, in turn, directly affected in some way by the actions and/or decisions of the executive unit. The nature of this relationship may vary considerably in every dimension, but the very basis of the group process theory suggests that every group is anxious to obtain any advantage it can in the public policy process. Indeed, the fact that interest groups concentrate their efforts for this precise purpose represents nothing more than a political truism. So obvious is this expected pattern of group behavior that frequently one loses sight of the reversed process of an administrator seeking group support, i.e., protection.

The second direction in which the individual bureaucrat can

turn is toward the congressional committees which have jurisdiction over the activities of the administrator's agency or
bureau. In this regard, committees of Congress are very much
like interest groups in that they too have valuable resources at
their disposal that can be effectively utilized to supplement the
support received by the executive official. A bureau chief or
even an Assistant Secretary will, in all probability, not be able to
alter a budget decision made within the executive branch by the
Bureau of the Budget in connection with the individual's own
administrative operations. Either one of these individuals, on the
other hand, may be quite capable of having the deleted funds
restored by simply appealing—indirectly of course—to "his"
congressional subgroup. Wildavsky's modest effort on the budgetary process is filled with examples illustrating this point.[23]

In other words, the opportunities are available for executive
officials to develop a base of support independent of the executive office of the President; indeed, lower- and middle-level
bureaucrats—if they are at all aware of the limitations of Presidential power—begin to build this auxiliary type of support very
early in their careers. The persuasive powers of the President are
somewhat like a radio signal being transmitted: the signal grows
weaker as the distance from the transmitter increases unless the
power is increased. But insofar as the President is concerned,
very real limitations are imposed on his transmitting cacpacity.
Those at the lower and middle echelons of the bureaucratic
structure may receive only a weak "signal" from even an extremely dominant President. Consequently, supplemental support may be sought simply to strengthen one's own capacity to
transmit as well as to receive various signals. And this support is
normally readily available from the two major sources that have
been discussed.

[23] Aaron Wildavsky, *The Politics of the Budgetary Process* (Boston: Little,
Brown & Company, 1964).

## Summary

The differences between organizational loyalty within private and public bureaucracies is striking. Loyalty is an organizational by-product of continuity, stability, clear-cut goals, the fear of sanctions, the need for security, status, and protection. In short, it is a composite response to a wide range of tangible and psychological factors which cause the individual to conclude that his own best interests will be served by working to maximize the best interests of his organization. Although this description may represent something of an ideal model, it does seem reasonable to conclude that private bureaucracies are in a much more tenable position to approximate this ideal type than are public or governmental bureaucratic structures. Indeed, given the many competing claims on the loyalty of the executive branch administrator, the lack of a clear set of goal objectives, the relatively frequent turnover of top-level executive officials, and the highly decentralized, personalized, and substantially weaker sanctions at the disposal of the President, it is—or at least it should be for the thoughtful citizen—a source of surprise and satisfaction that the vast and sprawling executive branch complex is able to function as well as it does.

To a great extent this can only be explained in terms of the executive-branch bureaucratic system itself. It is essentially a conservative system in that its primary goal is to preserve itself. In this sense a basic loyalty does exist among professional administrators. Resistance to change, of course, is a normal response even within private bureaucratic settings. However, as noted in Chapter 2, although the private administrator who is to be adversely affected by a proposed change is expected "to put up the good fight" in opposition, the truth of the matter is that the resources at his disposal are severely limited, as are the prescribed boundaries of acceptable behavior within the private organizational setting. By comparison, as this chapter has attempted to demonstrate, the governmental bureaucrat has, relatively speaking, a much wider range of resources at his disposal, as well as many more alternative directions to follow than his executive counterpart in the private bureaucratic systems. Is it valid, therefore, to characterize the public bureaucrat as being much more susceptible to organizational "sclerosis" than management officials in the private world of corporate finance and industry?

In order to answer this query, one is forced to examine bureaucratic behavior within the context of the forces of change. When viewed from this perspective, classical examples of conflict emerge. In fact, some of the most revealing and significant data on organizations can be obtained by examining the internal responses that develop toward the forces of change. For this reason, the chapter that follows is designed to present a theoretical model of organizational change that, hopefully, can then be applied to examine change within the executive branch specifically.

# 7

# Organizational Change— A Conceptual Model

The manner in which every organization reacts to the forces of change should be considered an essential area of inquiry from which certain basic premises of administrative theory can be established. Control mechanisms, decision-making procedures, and organizational loyalty are, indeed, fundamental components of the complex structure we refer to as bureaucracy. However, the way in which any organization responds to changing internal and external demands may provide us with certain insights into the nature of bureaucratic behavior that are not generally visible if one's attention is focused solely on one single aspect of organizations. This assumes, of course, that organizations may react to the demands for change in different ways, and that these differences can be identified. The purpose of this chapter is to develop a conceptual model that can serve as a theory of change, applicable to all organizations in general. The two subsequent chapters represent an attempt to apply this model to the executive branch specifically.

## Two Forces of Change

An essential first step toward a theory of organizational change can be achieved by utilizing one aspect of the theoretical underpinnings of Parsons. To borrow Parsons' conceptual scheme of functional requirements,[1] and to alter it slightly to fit our present needs, we can state that every organization must meet four basic functional requirements:

1. The ability to maintain, preserve, and reproduce the organization's basic patterns of behavior (*pattern maintenance*).
2. The ability to adapt to environmental change (*adaptation*).
3. The ability to achieve organizational goals (*goal attainment*).
4. The ability to minimize intraorganizational disruption and conflict, and to maximize intraorganizational stability and cooperation (*integration*).

*Adaptation*

Every organization, no matter how hard it may try to maximize internal stability, is forced to respond to certain forces of change simply to survive as an organization. One reason for this is the rather obvious fact that no organization is able to exert complete control over its external environment and, second, the external environments of all organizations are themselves in a perpetual state of change. Thus, the changes that occur within the external environment create pressures on the organization to respond in the form of organizational change.

In terms of private enterprise, the changing nature of consumer-buying habits relates directly to organizational

[1] Talcott Parsons, "An Outline of the Social System," contained in *Theories of Society*, vol. 1, Parsons *et al.* (eds), (New York: The Free Press, 1961), pp. 30–79.

changes involving product diversification, packaging, distribution, and price. Insofar as price is concerned, the basic law of supply and demand represents the centuries-old recognition of this simple causal relationship between environmental and organizational (external-internal) change. This does not mean to suggest that this causal relationship is always a simple one; on the contrary, as a result of overlapping clienteles or customers, numerous organizations, public as well as private, may be forced to respond to change in a single group or in a single environment. The small, neighborhood grocer's external environment is composed primarily of his neighborhood customers. If the socio-economic characteristics of his external environment are altered unfavorably (i.e., become depressed) this should cause the grocer to decrease his prices and/or services by decreasing his costs. This is a relatively simple and direct relationship. However, if the external environment is expanded to include all residents of a large city, and the socio-economic indices drop, a wide range of different changes may result in the numerous organizations which view segments of the population as part of their respective external environments. For instance, the school drop-out rate may tend to increase, and this should place corresponding demands on the local school system to respond to this changing situation. An entirely different set of demands will be placed on the local police department under these same circumstances, especially if an increase in the incidence of juvenile delinquency is associated with the increased school drop-out rate. Real estate valuation may decrease causing a decrease in revenue for the city government. Local government officials must respond to this change by either decreasing the extent of city services and/or shifting the tax burden to other sources. If the tax burden is shifted to local industry and manufacturers, these organizations may be forced to respond by either increasing their prices or relocating in other communities. This little chain reaction is re-enacted daily in local communities across the nation, and it is just one illustration of the central proposition that every organization, no matter how hard it may try to stabilize its internal structure and operations, is forced to respond to certain forces of change originating in its external environment if it is to survive as an organization. The extent to which an organization is able to respond successfully to changes in its external environment shall be referred to as its *adaptation ability*.

## Integration

Similarly, it may be stated that no organization can prevent changes from occurring within its own internal hierarchal structure. And, as a consequence, the same central proposition stated above in terms of the external forces of change applies when one is considering internal aspects of change; namely, every organization, no matter how hard it may try to stabilize its internal structure and operations, is forced to respond to certain forces of change originating within its internal environment if it is to survive as an organization.

Stated in its simplest form, organizational change will inevitably result from a normal attrition process. New members replace charter members, young men replace older men, new ideas replace old rules, prohibited behavior becomes permitted, impersonal relationships replace personalized friendships. In short, just through the simple processes of maturation and subsequent aging, the organization must be prepared to respond to the inevitable forces of change from within if it is to survive. In a prior, less complicated era, a high school education might have been sufficient to put a young man on the bottom rung of the management ladder in many organizations. Few companies today continue this practice. On the other hand, as a result of advanced technological gains in industry and business, many operating procedures have become so thoroughly routinized that high school graduates are capable of performing tasks that previously were assigned to college graduates. Internal change can be precipitated by a wide range of internal forces. Internal change, however, can also be precipitated by the types of external forces cited above.

For instance, the neighborhood grocer may discontinue delivery service, thus dispensing with the need for a delivery boy. The school board may interpret their problem of increasing drop-outs in terms of a need for younger principals who would be more sympathetic to the problems of the school children. Thus a reshuffling of principal assignments may be indicated. For the police department, a juvenile delinquency squad may be created and staffed by patrolmen who formerly walked beats or directed traffic. In each instance, overt external forces caused deliberate and conscious changes to be effected within the given organizations. By the same token, however, changing social or cultural norms and attitudes may be indirectly and covertly revealed within the organization in the form of internal demands precipitating external change.

For example, there are numerous small cities throughout the nation that, because of their geographic location, access to natural resources or modes of transportation, or an available labor market, are extremely attractive as potential locations for business and manufacturing firms. Although each city may have one or more four-year, fully accredited colleges in its immediate vicinity, few could probably be expected to be within the immediate vicinity of accredited universities. This may represent an obstacle for a company that is considering a particular location, especially if a significant number of lower- and middle-level executives, engineers, or other specialists are to be assigned to the new location. Company promotion policies and, in many instances, social recognition are frequently dependent upon an individual's ability to obtain an advanced degree. But if a particular location does not have the facilities to meet this need, a prospective company might conclude that it would incur a severe competitive disadvantage in hiring and retaining bright and promising young executives and engineers. Consequently, in many localities of this description, a wide range of forces have been focused on the local college or colleges to establish graduate programs that would be especially appealing to the young executive-type. It is possible, in other words, for the forces of change to stem from, as well as focus on, the organization.

But for the most part, we shall be primarily concerned with the organization's response to change that is precipitated by either external or internal actions, and in this regard it seems reasonable to suggest that some degree of internal conflict is associated with all efforts by the organization to respond to change regardless of its source. Internal organizational conflict in the face of impending change is virtually inevitable simply because even the most insignificant change will heighten the degree of personal anxiety and tension for at least those individuals who will be affected by the change. Viewed in this context, it can be stated that the extent to which the organization can effectively avoid the development of an internal conflict situation while adapting to the forces striving for change shall be referred to as its *integrative ability*.

The successful organization, therefore, must be able to keep these two interrelated variables balanced at some equilibrium point. It must, in order to survive, be responsive to change to the extent that it is able to adapt to changing internal and external environmental conditions. At the same time, however, just as demands for change may be inevitable, so, also, can the organization be reasonably sure that the manner in which it chooses to respond to change will generate conflict and resistance from within its own membership ranks. Thus, it must not only be able to adapt to change, but it must also be able to minimize effectively, if not eliminate, the degree of intraorganizational disruption and resistance that will be associated with change. To do this it must be able to integrate the new with the existing behavioral patterns.

In a sense, what we are saying at this point is that at least two of Parsons' functional requirements—adaptation and integration —*must* be achieved to some degree by *every* bureaucratic organization, and although the degree and extent of adaptation and integration may vary from circumstance to circumstance when viewed over time, the organization cannot rationally invoke the option not to adapt or not to integrate if it wishes to survive (a company which chooses to go out of business before consenting to union demands, for instance, is an example of rational choice of this option). The organization does have an option, however, in the manner in which it will respond to change. Viewed in the simplest terms, the organization can follow one of two directions; it can, on the one hand, rationally choose to follow a direction of *responsive change*, or, on the other hand, it can, in the same deliberate and rational manner, choose to follow a direction of *anticipatory change*. The differences between these two directions of change are significant in that, as noted at the outset of this chapter, they do provide us with certain insights into the nature of bureaucratic behavior that are not generally visible if one's attention is focused solely on a single aspect of organizations. For this reason, each will be developed in detail below.

## Two Directions of Change

One way to view the problem of organizational change is to visualize the organization acting in response to clearly perceived stimuli. A second way to view the same problem is simply to visualize organizational behavioral patterns and operating procedures being changed in anticipation of a definite and direct expression of the forces of change. Little need be said about the meaning of responsive change; it is intended to convey the same meaning that is normally associated with the basic psychological concept, stimulus-response pattern. A stimulus is received, and a response to that stimulus follows. As applied to organizational settings, responsive change means a stimulus for change is received from either an internal or external source, and the organization responds accordingly to that stimulus. A rising crime rate in the city creates pressures on the police department which trigger a response within the department designed to halt the rise in crime. Satisfied that the demand for mini skirts included more young ladies than those few on the "screwball fringe," ladies' clothing manufacturers across the country responded to that demand completely. A demand is expressed and an organization responds to that demand in some manner—this is the essence of responsive change.

The meaning that is intended to apply to the term anticipatory change may be a bit more difficult to transmit. Essentially what is being suggested is that forces of change, external or internal, may be anticipated by the organization which is then in a position "to respond" to the change even before—i.e., in anticipation of—the actual expression of a demand for change by either external or internal groups. This does not mean to imply some psychic power is required if anticipatory change is to be achieved. In actual fact, however, the laws of statistical probability, the techniques of economic forecasting, the increasing use being made of data processing equipment, the fairly stable behavioral patterns of man, all strongly suggest that, within limits, relatively accurate assessments of future needs can be anticipated. By the same token, organizations should be able—again, within limits—to anticipate the type and intensity of the forces of change, external as well as internal, that will be generated in the foreseeable future. The ability to act or respond *before* the force becomes an overt and formally organized expression is what is meant by the term anticipatory change.

Of course, the organization does not have to assume a completely passive role in the manner in which it chooses to react to the forces of change. Through the strategic use of resource allocations in the form of advertising, public relations, and capital expenditures, for example, the organization may be able to exert a significant degree of control over its internal and external environments. That is, hopefully it may be able to modify the magnitude of the forces of change as well as to increase its ability to predict the frequency of change. The effort to control one's environment, however, is characteristic of all organizations regardless of the manner in which they choose to react to the forces of change. Thus, anticipatory and responsive change will, at this point, still be viewed as alternative patterns that can be employed by an organization apart from the resources that can be allocated in an effort to control its environments.

Two examples are immediately suggested that should permit both of these terms to be viewed in their proper perspectives. The automobile industry provides an excellent example of *anticipatory change* in that the new models that come out every year reflect fundamental anticipatory decisions made 12–24 months previously. The entire policy planning structure of the individual companies is geared to anticipate future market needs and desires well in advance of their formally articulated expression. The same industry, however, also offers excellent examples of *responsive change*, as when the impact of the small foreign car on U. S. car sales was initially unanticipated, or as when, more recently, the issue of automobile safety became a general public policy question. In both of these latter instances, the automobile industry did not anticipate the demands as they ultimately developed, and in both instances the industry was forced to respond to the demands after they became cohesively formed.

Within the scope of the model being developed in this chapter, the differences between these two contrasting modes of organizational change are viewed as being significant. In this respect, the differences between organizational change in response to positive forces—internal or external—and change in anticipation of the manifest expression of such forces may be characterized by the different types of organizational processes associated with each.

### Consolidation

Stated most directly, responsive change is generally characterized by the type of organizational processes associated with consolidation.[2] Used in this context, consolidation means those attempts to satisfy the forces (internal or external) for change by (1) re-ordering or revising existing, well-established performance programs, or, if this is not possible—that is, if a totally new performance program must be devised—then (2) devising a new performance program which would fit within the framework of existing organizational values, norms, and attitudes to the maximum extent possible. In other words, when referring to consolidation, we mean the deliberate and conscious effort on the part of organizational officials to resolve demands for change regardless of source (and hence to resolve the conflict that inevitably is associated with the forces of change) solely within the context of existing organizational structures, if at all possible. Thus stated, the basic component of consolidation is a strong commitment toward moderation, compromise, negotiation, and accommodation. Consolidation, then, very simply suggests that the organization places a high value on behavioral stability and conflict avoidance. On the one hand, both of the goals—behavioral stability and conflict avoidance—may be justified in terms of organizational continuity and operating efficiency; stability maximizes continuity which, in turn, maximizes efficiency. On the other hand, both of these values may be justified solely in terms of resistance against change; internal stability and interpersonal harmony maximize social congruence

[2] The manner in which the terms consolidation and innovation are used here resembles, to some extent, the manner in which they were applied by Theodore Lowi in his article, "Toward Functionalism in Party Systems," *American Political Science Review*, vol. 57 (Sept. 1963), pp. 570–83.

which in turn tends to maximize the value of maintaining the status quo. Regardless of how the goals of stability and conflict avoidance are justified, however, it is being suggested that both of the values are integral characteristics of consolidative behavior. Furthermore, as viewed within this context, consolidative behavior, which is to be viewed as the dominant manner in which responsive change is expressed within an organization, represents a basic similarity to Parsons' third functional requirement —*pattern maintenance*. Therefore, consolidative behavior is the direction the organization may take when choosing to react in response to external or internal demands if the ability to maintain, preserve, and reproduce the organization's basic patterns of behavior (pattern maintenance) is viewed by top-level organization officials as an all-important goal to achieve.

### Innovation

As may be expected, innovation serves as the converse of consolidation; thus, anticipatory change is generally characterized by the type of organizational processes associated with innovation. As used here, innovation is defined as (1) the conscious awareness on the part of organizational planners of the need for a new program that cannot be satisfied by utilizing any combination of existing, well-established programs, and (2) the ability to satisfy that need in anticipation of a formal and organized demand for change, coming either from within the organization, itself, or from its external environment.

Innovation represents the deliberate effort on the part of executive officials to search for improved performance programs, to diagnose organizational weaknesses in advance, and to predict as accurately as possible the consequences of innovative change. The essential difference between consolidative and innovative behavior is that within the former setting, organization officials are almost exclusively preoccupied with finding solutions to manifest problems, whereas the latter pattern places a much greater emphasis on the active search and identification of the problems themselves, before they become overt expressions of internal or external demands. Thus, within the conceptual framework that is being presented here, innovation is closely related to the concept of anticipatory change, just as consolidation is basically related to the essential aspects of responsive change. However, in an effort to maintain a clear distinction between these two concepts, a conceptual proposition dealing with what is referred to as the *scope of awareness* is suggested.

Basically, it is being suggested that in defining and identifying innovative behavior, it is important to stress the restricted scope of awareness of the need for a new performance program. Innovative behavior, as conceived here, implies the activities of a limited number of individuals in search of future problems and demands, and the activity of organizations in gaining acceptance of the solutions advanced for these future problems and demands prior to the actual manifestation of the demands. When the need for a new performance program becomes a generally recognized and accepted fact within the organization—i.e., when the scope of awareness expands greatly—anticipatory change gives way to responsive change, and innovative efforts are replaced by consolidative patterns of organizational behavior.

As viewed within this context, therefore, innovation suggests something much different from a strong organizational commitment toward moderation, compromise, negotiation, and accommodation. To a very real extent, the basic characteristic of innovation is its essentially "radical" nature in its willingness to depart from existing behavioral patterns. Within an innovative setting, the key values to be emphasized are not behavioral stability and conflict avoidance but rather intellectual initiative and creative vigor in the constant search for new and improved performance programs. Thus, innovative behavior becomes directly related to anticipatory change, and both can be viewed as the organizational characteristics which would emphasize Parsons' fourth functional requirement—*goal attainment*. If establishing goal objectives to satisfy internal and external needs and demands in anticipation of their actual expression is viewed by top-level organization officials as an essential objective to be achieved, then innovative behavior represents the most logical direction to follow.

## Interrelationship between Forces and Directions of Change

To pose the two forces and two directions of change as we have is to invite a possible conclusion that four distinct and un-related patterns of organizational behavior are being discussed; on the contrary, the four functions are integrally related within virtually every large, complex organization. One way to examine this mutually inclusive relationship is to proceed deductively. Thus, it seems reasonable to state at the outset that since every complex bureaucratic structure is inevitably confronted with both external and internal demands for change, then it must, of necessity, allocate a certain share of its resources to the functions of adaptation and integration. These two functions, therefore, can be viewed as "givens" in any organization. The problem then becomes one of determining the predominant reaction pattern(responsive-anticipatory) which the organization chooses to utilize in conjunction with the forces of change. In other words, will the functions of adaptation and integration be used to supplement responsive change and, hence, serve as a base support for consolidative behavior? Or, will the same functions, when combined with a generalized pattern of anticipatory change, be combined to supplement the organization's commit-ment toward innovative behavior?

Obviously, the effort to suggest an either/or choice in this situation is unreal and certainly meaningless. Organizations do not consciously and deliberately select one behavioral pattern of change and exclude the other. Every organization, no matter how strong its commitment to innovation may be, cannot anticipate every single internal and external demand for change; indeed, every organization will, on various occasions, behave in a manner that is primarily designed to avoid conflict and maximize internal stability. By the same token, no major, complex bureaucratic structure, regardless of its commitment to consolidative behavior, has ever functioned without having some opportunities to anticipate problems and demands, and to meet

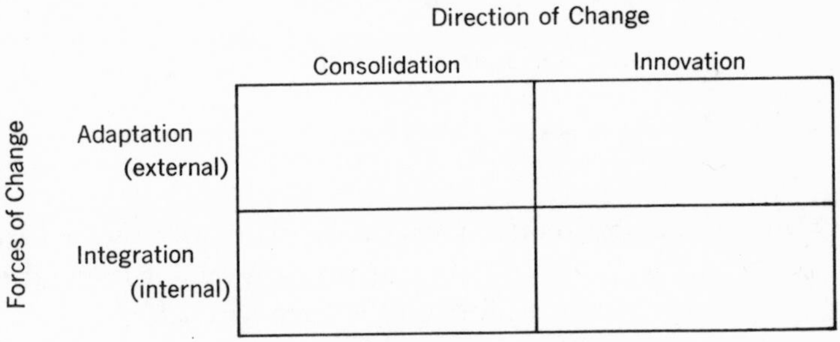

Direction of Change

|  | Consolidation | Innovation |
|---|---|---|
| Adaptation (external) | | |
| Integration (internal) | | |

Forces of Change

Figure 7-1

them through innovative means. Thus, what is being suggested here is that all organizations, although limited by a 2 × 2 (four cell) set, as noted in Figure 7-1, enjoy maximum discretion in the range of responses that can be assigned to this set. If one can view these responses not in terms of absolutes but rather in terms of relative degrees of emphasis, ranging along a continuum from high to low (emphasis), then a multiresponse situation prevails.

Within this four-cell matrix, it is possible to chart sixteen combinations if one limits the classifications to the extremes of each continuum—namely, using only high or low as classifying designations, with no consideration being given to gradations falling between these extremes. The sixteen logical combinations would be as follows:

**Table 7–1**

| | | |
|---|---|---|
| 1, 2 | H L | L H |
| | H L, | L H |
| | | |
| 3, 4 | H L | L H |
| | L H, | H L |
| | | |
| 5, 6 | H H | L L |
| | L L, | H H |
| | | |
| 7, 8 | H H | L L |
| | H H, | L L |
| | | |
| 9, 10, 11, 12 | H H | H H … etc. |
| | H L, | L H, |
| | | |
| 13, 14, 15, 16 | L L | L L … etc. |
| | L H, | H L, |

Of the sixteen possibilities, most can be discounted on the basis of internal contradictions. An organization cannot respond to the external (or internal) forces of change with a high (or low) consolidative *and* innovative emphasis at the same time. Although there may be mixtures of both elements in every reaction to change, an organization can give predominate emphasis in only one direction. Likewise, although an organization may innovate in one instance and consolidate in another, the suggestion being advanced here is that the choice in the direction of change is not random. Thus every organization can be classified as either innovative or consolidative on the basis of its predominate pattern viewed over time. Within the context of the proposed scheme, therefore, cases number 5–16 may be eliminated.

Of the remaining four cases, case number 1 represents a model of consolidation

$$\begin{pmatrix} H & L \\ H & L \end{pmatrix}$$

and case number 2, an innovation model

$$\begin{pmatrix} L & H \\ L & H \end{pmatrix}.$$

This, of course assumes that the organization will respond in the same direction to both the external and internal forces of change. However, two other patterns that must be considered are represented by cases number 3 and 4. In the former

$$\begin{pmatrix} H & L \\ L & H \end{pmatrix}$$

the organization would reveal a high consolidative emphasis being directed toward external change and a high innovative emphasis in the direction of internal change. Case number 4

$$\begin{pmatrix} L & H \\ H & L \end{pmatrix}$$

would simply reverse this pattern. The relative frequency with which one might expect to find these four patterns in actual operation could be:

$$1st \begin{pmatrix} H & L \\ H & L \end{pmatrix} \quad 2nd \begin{pmatrix} L & H \\ H & L \end{pmatrix} \quad 3rd \begin{pmatrix} L & H \\ L & H \end{pmatrix} \quad 4th \begin{pmatrix} H & L \\ L & H \end{pmatrix}.$$

Although the first two cases could be reversed in terms of frequency, it would appear that most organizations would fit into one of these two patterns. Intuitively one suspects that fewer instances of totally innovative organizations would be found

$$\begin{pmatrix} L & H \\ L & H \end{pmatrix},$$

and fewer still of the last ranked pattern

$$\begin{pmatrix} H & L \\ L & H \end{pmatrix}.$$

Empirical testing could, of course, cause a shift in these rankings.

## Summary

As stated at the outset, the purpose of this chapter has been to develop an analytical model of organizational change. Every organization—and, specifically for our purposes, every large complex bureaucracy—must constantly face two ever-changing environments. As these environments change, the nature and extent of the demands imposed on the organization from each will also change. Except in the very short run, the organization cannot ignore the changing demands imposed on it either from the groups which constitute its external environment, or from those individuals and subunits which are included within its internal system. The manner in which the organization chooses to respond to these demands may vary according to the nature and extent of the demand, as well as numerous other factors. However, a basic assumption of this model is that over an extended period of time, one response will emerge as preferred and will enjoy a generalized, but not absolute, primacy over the other alternative. Because the choice between the two alternatives of consolidation and innovation is essentially a value choice— behavioral stability and conflict avoidance *versus* intellectual initiative and creativity—the choice may not actually be a free one, but rather one imposed on the organization as a result of the nature of its value structure. In any event, the pattern that does emerge as the dominant, or primary frame of reference for the organization is significant in view of the fact that the direction of all future organizational development and change will, to a great extent, be controlled by this primary frame of reference. The purpose of the following two chapters will be to examine the bureaucratic structure of the federal government within the scope of this model.

# 8

# Executive Branch Consolidation

One essential conclusion, which is suggested in the previous chapter, is that organizations, like individuals, are frequently beset with conflicting and even contradictory demands. Certainly a basic set of contradictory forces at work in virtually every complex bureaucratic surrounding are the forces of consolidation and innovation. For the executive branch especially, this represents an extremely difficult, and seemingly perennial, dilemma. As Neustadt notes:

> ... this institution [the Presidency] vividly suggests a basic conflict, probably irreconcilable, between bureaucratic claims upon the White House and a President's own claims upon officialdom. Agencies need decisions, delegations, and support, along with bargaining arenas and a court of last resort, so organized so as to assure that their advice is always heard and often taken. A President needs timely information, early warning,

close surveillance, organized to yield him the controlling judgment, with his options open, his intent enforced. In practice these two sets of needs have proved quite incompatible; presidential organizations rarely serve one well without disservice to the other.[1]

In essence, the dilemma that emerges within the executive structure revolves around the twin goals of creative planning and administrative efficiency. Stated most directly, the concept of inherent conflict built into the executive structure is premised on the assumption that innovative behavior must be subordinated if operating efficiency is the primary goal to be maximized; and, conversely, administrative efficiency must frequently be qualified if imaginative and creative innovation is to be encouraged and rewarded. Lawrence Chamberlain's analogy between executive-legislative relationships and a seesaw is applicable here. Is it true that as one end of the seesaw goes up, the other end must go down? Or, to restate the premise in direct causal terms, does a linear, negative correlation exist between bureaucratic efficiency and innovative planning? Obviously, such a statement, as it applies to the executive branch of the federal government, is an extreme oversimplification—and as a consequence, a distortion —of a complex set of organization relationships. Allowing for the complexity of the situation, however, the question still remains, can an organization be imaginative and stable at the same time; is the executive bureaucracy structured in such a way as to allow the simultaneous pursuit of policy innovation and administrative consolidation without sacrificing certain values in either direction? It is the purpose of this chapter to examine executive branch consolidation within the context of the model developed in the previous chapter.

[1] Richard E. Neustadt, "Politicians and Bureaucrats," in *The Congress and America's Future*, David B. Truman (ed.), (Englewood Cliffs: Prentice-Hall, 1965), p. 113.

Seemingly, there is a natural tendency in man to favor "consolidative" behavior. Admittedly, necessity breeds innovation; basic physiological and psychological needs have to be satisfied, and in the absence of such satisfactions, individual behavior may become extremely innovative even to the point of becoming markedly irrational. However, for most of us, once these basic needs (as well as more advanced and sophisticated needs) are satisfied, we tend to become increasingly concerned with the strategies of maintaining our gains. Consequently, our future behavior is, to a great extent, determined by our accumulated and consolidated knowledge gained from past experiences. Furthermore, as noted in the chapter on decision making, the consequences associated with the various alternatives in a particular decision represent varying degrees of risk. In this respect, as well, there is a natural tendency for each of us to protect against personal losses by seeking to minimize the degree of uncertainty, which is simply another way of suggesting that we seek that alternative that carries with it the most favorable and predictable consequences. When confronted with completely new demands for action, a natural response is that we simply try to fit the new demand into already known response categories. Thus, if this type of behavior is characteristic of individuals and the manner in which they conduct their personal lives, it should not be surprising to discover that organizations, being composed of individuals, reveal a basic tendency also to favor the known over the unknown, the predictable over the uncertain, the favorable over the unfavorable.

C. Northcote Parkinson, formerly Raffles Professor of History at the University of Malaya and author of the now-famous Parkinson's Laws, examines this tendency in his whimsical collection of essays on public administration.[2] According to Parkinson, there are immutable forces that direct all decision-making groups to spend the greatest amount of time on the least

[2] *Parkinson's Law* (New York: Houghton Mifflin, 1957).

important items. More individuals understand these relatively simple items, thus, the consideration of these points consumes the greatest amounts of time and discussion.

A nonsatirical treatment of essentially the same problem is presented by March and Simon as they propose their "Gresham's Law" of planning. As they view the problem of organizational innovation, two factors are suggested that affect the manner in which organization members choose to engage in an activity. "First, the greater the explicit time pressure attached to an activity, the greater the propensity to engage in it. . . . Second, the greater the clarity of goals associated with an activity, the greater the propensity to engage in it." On the basis of these two factors, they conclude:

> These propositions lead to a prediction that might be described as the "Gresham's Law" of planning: Daily routine drives out planning. Stated less cryptically, we predict that when an individual is faced both with highly programmed and highly unprogrammed tasks, the former tend to take precedence over the latter even in the absence of strong over-all time pressure.[3]

Parkinson, March, and Simon, each in his own way, are simply restating the thesis that individuals seek security in order to protect themselves against the unpredictable forces of their environment. When that environment happens to be their organizational setting, the search for security becomes no less important. Thus, any one of a wide range of individual actions may result in order to maximize security and minimize anxiety. Security may be found by multiplying organizational activity within one's administrative jurisdiction, thus creating the impression of indispensability and importance. Or, security may be found by selecting known tasks over completely new, unpredictable demands. Both examples lend support to the impression

[3] March and Simon, *op. cit.*, p. 185.

that within organizations there is a natural predisposition to favor consolidative, as opposed to innovative, behavioral responses.

Although March and Simon stress the consolidative tendencies inherent in organizations, they do not rule out the possibility that innovation can be achieved under certain circumstances. Banfield, however, is not even this optimistic insofar as rational planning, i.e., innovation, is concerned. As he defines his terms,

> A plan . . . is a decision with regard to a course of action. A course of action is a sequence of acts which are mutually related as means and are therefore viewed as a unit; it is the unit which is the plan. Planning . . . is to be distinguished from . . . "opportunistic decision-making" which is choosing (rationally or not) actions that are not mutually related as a single means.

A plan is rational if the basic elements of rational choice are present at each stage of the plan's development. The various steps involved would include the awareness of a need to be satisfied, the formulation of a goal objective, the gathering of pertinent information, the structuring of the various alternatives that could be utilized to achieve the goal, the consequences of each possible alternative, and the final selection of the alternative that would achieve the desired goal under the most favorable set of circumstances.

> If we now take this definition as a yardstick and apply it to organizational behavior in the real world we are struck by two facts: there is very little planning, and there is even less rationality.
>
> In general, organizations engage in opportunistic decision-making rather than planning: rather than lay out courses of action which will lead all the way to the attainment of their ends, they extemporize, meeting each crisis as it arises. . . . Moreover,

such plans as are made are not the outcome of a careful consideration of alternative courses of action and their probable consequences. As a rule the most important decisions—those constituting the development course of action—are the result of accident rather than design; they are unintended outcomes of a social process rather than the conscious products of deliberation and calculation. If there is an element of rationality, it is "functional" rather than "substantive."[4]

The theme is the same: consolidative behavior is simply more evident in organizational settings than its counterpart—innovation. And, as one may very well expect, the executive bureaucracy abounds with specific examples that can be used to support this premise. The major difference that sets Banfield apart from Parkinson, March, and Simon is that whereas the latter three directed their remarks concerning consolidative behavior toward the individual specifically, Banfield levels his evaluation directly at organizations. Thus, if a group of individuals join together to form a subunit within a particular organization, it is possible that the consolidative tendencies of each individual may be expressed in such a manner as to blend in to a dominant value preference for the entire subunit. In a like manner one may refer to overall organizations as revealing a definite preference for consolidative behavior. Within the executive branch specifically, numerous examples could be cited of consolidative patterns evidenced at each of these three levels— the individual, the intradepartmental subunits, and the departments and independent agencies. A few examples that best illustrate this point are presented below.

[4] Edward C. Banfield, "Ends and Means in Planning," in *Concepts and Issues in Administrative Behavior*, Sidney Mailick and Edward H. Van Ness (eds.) (Englewood Cliffs: Prentice-Hall, 1962), pp. 71, 73–74. Originally published in *The International Social Science Journal of UNESCO*, vol. II, No. 5 (no date).

## The Individual

Since the individual forms the basis of any organization, the system that recruits, trains, promotes, and rewards organizational personnel can have a decided influence on the development of the individual's organizational attitudes and values. Personnel management systems within any bureaucratic setting create a "framework" that is designed to complement the basic goal objectives of the organization. Within the federal bureaucracy, the individual enters into a management system that, as previous chapters have indicated, is, at best, highly decentralized. This is not to suggest that the relationship between personnel management and goal attainment is not an important consideration in the world of the federal bureaucracy. Indeed, for the many and varied groups that have a vested interest in the executive personnel system, this relationship becomes an essential element to the achievement of their own goals and values. Within this composite cluster of groups interested in executive personnel policies—congressional committees, interest groups, civil service reform groups, federal employees unions, the Civil Service Commission, and, of course, executive bureaucrats themselves—the President, as head of the overall executive structure, has a role in the personnel process, although the role he does enjoy is neither dominant nor exclusive. Thus, as a result of the diverse interests which converge on the executive personnel system, organizational behavior within the executive branch reflects a consolidative pattern because of the efforts of these groups to consolidate their own specialized objectives.

For instance, the Civil Service League and other like-minded reform groups are totally dedicated in their efforts to protect the federal career system against any form of possible political contamination. One way to achieve this objective (so it has been assumed) is to emphasize positions rather than individuals; find an individual for a job opening rather than a job for an individual. The difference between the two approaches is significant. In emphasizing jobs, position classifications become the currency of exchange between the Civil Service Commission, executive agencies, departments, bureaus, congressional committees, and other external groups. The primary task, under these circumstances, then becomes fitting an individual into an insulated administrative position in which monetary and other rewards are assigned to the position rather than to the individual. The de-emphasis of the importance of the individual creates an atmosphere at the outset that is not likely to spark imaginative and creative behavior, particularly at the lower and middle levels of the executive structure.

Until 1959, the Civil Service Commission, as the official governmental independent regulatory body charged with the responsibility of insuring a pure career system, traditionally shared the goal objectives of the external reform groups. But, in addition, it had its own vested interest to protect; namely, the continuation, if not expansion, of its own assigned jurisdiction. Consequently, the dominant apolitical system which the Commission attempted to maintain resulted in such personnel devices as elaborate job descriptions, pay scales, and appeal processes. All of these intricately devised personnel procedures became so completely institutionalized that the career official was virtually encrusted in a protectionist network which, as a result of its overall rigidity, inevitably reduced the individual to secondary importance in the overall scheme of executive management.

John Macy, Jr., who was appointed Chairman of the Commission by President Eisenhower in 1959 and reappointed by President Johnson in 1965, has directed many efforts at altering the uninspiring, negatively oriented personnel structure of the federal government. His success, thus far, has been significant. In 1966, for example, Congress codified all federal personnel laws for the first time, federal recruitment and examining procedures were thoroughly revised and modernized, and executive manpower management programs were formally adopted. In this latter regard, the Executive Assignment System represents a significant advancement, in that it centralizes the tasks of locating, developing, and utilizing executive manpower. As Macy stated

> For too long, we have trusted to luck and to limited searches in filling these most responsible of positions in the civil service. Too often the quest for qualified candidates has been confined to the agency in which a key job is located or to persons in other agencies whose abilities were known to the selecting officials.
>
> In limiting consideration to the career people close at hand —to the few he knows or has heard about—the selecting official sells himself short, his agency short, and certainly he sells short the eminently qualified executives who may work no farther away than across the street.
>
> The record shows clearly that executive selection in the past has been markedly agency oriented. Of 1,072 classification actions covering positions in the top three grades in a recent year, 964 (90%) were promotions or reassignments of agency personnel. Only 19 (2%) were transfers from other agencies: And only 39 (4%) were new hires.[5]

The Executive Assignment System is designed, first, to widen the scope in which the search for needed executive officials may take place. Second, it is designed to shift top-level career officials to positions within the executive branch where their skills are needed, thus negating the previous assumption that an individual is immutably bound to a particular department or agency. Third, it is designed to increase the recruitment rate of middle- and top-level management officials into government service.

The essential ingredient in any successful personnel system, however, is still the individual's perception of his "life" in the

5 John Macy, "Assurance of Leadership," *Civil Service Journal* (October-December 1966), p. 3.

organization. Existence may indeed have to precede essence in organizations as in individuals. Institutional structures can certainly affect attitudes and perceptions. But the attitudes and values fostered by the "old" civil service image are not automatically displaced by the recent efforts of the commission. Thus, it is not surprising that the individual may view his specific position with greater importance than his organizational affiliation. Loyalty was geared to the position, not to some vague and abstract concept as the organization or government service. To a great degree, rewards are realized to the extent that one satisfies the requirements of his particular job description. Given this type of personnel orientation two distinct consequences are suggested.

First, since individual performance is gauged primarily in terms of position specification, performance exceeding position expectations can only be meaningfully rewarded by advancing the individual to a higher *position*. If all higher positions are filled, however, advancement is blocked. The only other alternative is the creation of a new position—an alternative that can easily result in the development of a "patch-work" organizational structure. Thus, real limits are imposed on the extent of rewards that can be given for superior performance, and a primary incentive for quality performance is denied.

The second consequence which is suggested results from the nature of the system itself and its many variables which tend to insure behavioral conformity and consolidation. As noted previously, innovative executive performance at the lower and middle levels of the executive hierarchy will, to a great extent, depend on the degree of "top-level loyalty" that is directed downward to protect executive subordinates. In the absence of this downward loyalty, administrative innovation is not likely to flourish. Moreover, the multiforce demands coming from the interest groups and congressional committees frequently create a complex set of pressures on the executive bureaucrat which encourages cautious and deliberate actions. As Martin notes, the federal executive, "In most cases . . . accepts this environmental pressure as a 'given'; at times he attempts to change or modify it when he finds it too constricting; but usually the feedback from his actions becomes threatening, and he gives up such notions and turns to acceptance."[6] For the most part, however, federal bureaucrats, according to Martin, view their external environment favorably; it provides guidance, direction, support, and security. It is, in short, a beneficent composition of masters if one is inclined to cooperate with the elements.[7] Reimer concludes that "the major challenge to federal personnel administration today is the creation of conditions which will foster creative work in the federal service."[8] However, Warner and his associates suggest that such conditions would be difficult to realize. As they attempted to demonstrate, the federal executive, as a result of the many conflicting forces that center on him, and, furthermore, as a result of the various contradictory roles he is forced to assume, exhibits strong deferential attitudes.

> One tends to approach problems with care not to upset the state of affairs, not to call too much attention to one's self, not to push issues to the crisis stage. To do so may cause a retraction of the supportive and nurturing aspects of the system and a frightening pushing forward of its domineering side. In the coping mechanisms of most of the men, there is a strong element of system-deference.[9]

On the basis of the "job classification" philosophy that permeates the entire federal career structure, and the

[6] Norman Martin in Lloyd Warner, *et al.*, *The American Federal Executive* (New Haven: Yale University Press, 1963), p. 193.

[7] *Idem.*

[8] Everett Reimer, "Modern Personnel Management and The Federal Government Service," in *The Federal Government Service*, Wallace Sayre (ed.) (Englewood Cliffs: Prentice-Hall, 1962), second edition, p. 241.

[9] Warner, *op. cit.*, p. 247.

consequences that result from this situation, it is not difficult to conclude that federal executives tend to avoid making decisions whenever possible. Such a conclusion is neither sufficient nor accurate in describing the executive decision-making process. Decisions are a daily function in every bureaucrat's life. The difference emerges in the type of decisions that are made, be they consolidative or innovative. The point that has been developed thus far in this section is that the multifaceted federal system is most effectively supportive of consolidative decisions. Innovative decisions always involve a varying degree of risk and uncertainty. To expect innovative decision making to flourish, one would normally expect to find an organizational system wherein this type of behavior was not only expected but rewarded. The truth of the matter is that innovative behavior within the executive branch is, for the most part, neither expected nor rewarded except under special circumstances that will be discussed in the next chapter.

Within private business organizations, the emphasis placed on management techniques, skills, selection, training, and development is of an entirely different nature than that evidenced within most governmental organizations. Within the federal structure there are notable exceptions to this generalization, of course (the military and the foreign service career programs are immediately suggested). For the most part, however, the high value placed on management development in private business organizations simply has not, until quite recently, received comparable attention within the governmental system.[10] Basically, the executive bureaucracy is such that, "the sort of person who finds innovation in itself rewarding and stimulating cannot well fit the role."[11]

[10] *Improving Executive Management in the Federal Government*, Committee For Economic Development, Washington (July 1964), pp. 35–38.

[11] Warner, *op. cit.*, p. 248.

## Intradepartmental Subunits

Probably one of the most celebrated subunits within the entire federal bureaucracy is the Corps of Engineers of the United States Army. The assigned responsibilities of the Corps include, in addition to its obvious military functions, such water resource development purposes as flood control, navigation, water supply, river flow regulation, recreation, hydroelectric power, shore protection, information concerning flood hazards, and regulatory functions, including approval of plans for bridges and other works of improvement in navigable waters.[12] Insofar as these civil functions are concerned, the Corps' authority to approve plans for bridge construction and all other projects involving the nation's navigable waterways is substantial. The definitive analysis of the Corps is provided by Arthur Maass.[13] For our purposes, it is sufficient to note that all such plans approved by the Corps are included in its annual appropriations request presentation to Congress in the form of the Rivers and Harbors Bill, more easily identified by its colorful nickname, the "pork barrel bill."

Although the Corps is organizationally located within the Department of the Army which, in turn, is within the Department of Defense, it views itself primarily as a congressional agency— "the engineer consultants to, and contractors for, the Congress of the United States." By the same token, Congress sees the Corps as a specialized subunit of the legislative branch. As Maass points out, the continuous direct relations between the two Public Works Committees and the Corps have developed into a

[12] *United States Government Organization Manual*, June 1966 (Revised) (Washington: U. S. Government Printing Office), pp. 152, 160.

[13] "Congress and Water Resources," *American Political Science Review*, vol. 44 (September, 1950), pp. 576–593. This article became the basis for a later and more extensive study. See his *Muddy Waters* (Cambridge: Harvard University Press, 1951).

close identity of interests between the two.[14] As a result, the Corps stands as an interloper in the executive structure, completely protected by powerful external groups, including the congressional committees already noted as well as the dominant private interest group—The National Rivers and Harbors Congress. The extent of this support permits the Corps virtually to ignore any adverse ruling it may receive from the Bureau of the Budget that a particular project does not conform to the President's program. When adverse rulings are directed at any other executive branch subunit, Congress has rather faithfully followed the advice of the Budget Bureau; in connection with Rivers and Harbors projects, however, the Public Works Committees take their cues from the Corps, and not from the Bureau of the Budget.

Moreover, Congress has consistently isolated the Corps from any reorganization efforts by the President. Prior to 1949, the Corps (along with various other executive subunits) was explicitly exempted from all reorganization authorizations given to the President by Congress. The Reorganization Act of 1949 passed Congress with no agencies exempted. However, one other change in the 1949 Act virtually assured perpetual isolation of the Corps from any Presidential reorganization efforts. Prior to 1949 a reorganization plan of the President could be defeated *only* by a negative vote of *both* Houses of Congress. The 1949 Act altered this provision by making a negative vote of *either* House sufficient to defeat any reorganization plan. Congressional supporters of the Corps were satisfied that the amended Act simply made the Corps all the more secure from top-level executive interference.

Certainly as far as the Corps is concerned, consolidative behavioral patterns guide its actions in response to the local needs of Congress, as opposed to any innovative efforts by the President in an attempt to put together a coordinated and

[14] Maass, "Congress and Water Resources," *op. cit.*, pp. 579–80.

integrated national water resources program. Constituent needs, as expressed by legislative representatives, influence the behavioral pattern of the corps. As a consequence, the pattern of change that does emerge is almost exclusively responsive and, hence, consolidative.

Probably an even more extreme example of consolidative behavior was evidenced by the obscure locomotive inspection section of the Interstate Commerce Commission's Bureau of Railroad Safety and Service. Although placed within the ICC for functional, administrative, and fiscal purposes, the locomotive inspection section was virtually an autonomous operation headed by a director and two assistant directors, each of whom were *nominated by the President and subject to Senatorial confirmation.* Technically, therefore, these three individuals were on the same hierarchal level as the ICC commissioners, although they were only responsible for the operations of a section within a bureau of the ICC.

Created in 1911 as a result of the passage of the Locomotive Inspection Act, this section was able to maintain its own existence for 54 years despite rather spectacular data concerning its overall operations. For example, consider the following information:

### Table 8–1

|  | Number of Locomotives Subject to ICC Inspection | Number Inspected | Number Defective | Percentage Defective |
|---|---|---|---|---|
| 1946 | 48,467 | 112,777 | 11,836 | 10.5 |
| 1964 | 34,350 | 79,682 | 8,852 | 11.1 |

On the basis of these data, declining indices of output are indicated in all areas except the percentages of locomotives found defective. On the other hand, the annual appropriations assigned to the section followed an ascending pattern over the entire period. Appropriations for selected years were as follows:

**Table 8–2**

| | |
|---|---|
| 1946 | $543,605 |
| 1952 | 747,100 |
| 1953 | 709,500 |
| 1959 | 1,045,000 |
| 1961 | 1,160,428 |
| 1962 | 1,129,000 |
| 1963 | 1,170,800 |
| 1964 | 1,225,284 |

One could conclude that an important function of the locomotive inspection section in its later years was simply to maintain itself as an autonomous operation. In this respect it was undoubtedly successful. Its behavioral pattern was completely geared to respond to the needs of the railroads themselves. Its relationship with its parent organization, the ICC, was theoretical and its relationship with the President, who appointed the section's three top men, was fictional. Not until 1965, when President Johnson's Reorganization Plan No. 3 was passed by Congress, was this administrative anachronism eliminated.[15]

Equally significant in terms of consolidative behavioral patterns was the continuous debate for years within the State Department involving the unification of the Department's foreign service officer personnel system and the personnel system established for the individuals assigned to administer the foreign aid program. Top-level State Department personnel officers were strongly opposed to any suggestion that foreign aid personnel be incorporated within the scope of the Department's FSO system. Their opposition was based on the premises that foreign service officers were diplomatic generalists, not technical specialists, and they were career officials, not political appointees. Neither premise was entirely accurate, although there were sufficient elements of truth in both claims to insure the perpetuation of the stereotyped images for years.

[15] See *Reorganization Plan No. 3*, Hearings, Subcommittee of the House Government Operations Committee, 89th Congress, 1st session, 1965.

For example, in 1959 the Deputy Director of the International Cooperation Administration, Leonard J. Saccio, appeared before the House Foreign Affairs Committee to make his agency's annual presentation in the absence of the ICA Director, James Riddleberger, who was recovering from an illness. Saccio had joined the agency in 1955 as Deputy General Counsel. Although he managed to develop rather good rapport with the various House and Senate committees that had jurisdiction over the aid program, he was never completely able to alter his image as a political appointee involved in an area generally reserved for career diplomatic officials. Note, for instance, the not completely facetious interchange which took place between Saccio and Congressman Wayne Hays of the House Foreign Affairs Committee. Saccio was asked how long he had been with the ICA.

SACCIO: Four years.

HAYS: How did you get your job?

SACCIO: I came down and looked for it. I left a company in New Haven after eleven years of service as general counsel and officer of the corporation . . .

HAYS: Did you have to get anyone's recommendation to get your job?

SACCIO: I sought it.

HAYS: And did you get it?

SACCIO: I did.

HAYS: From Mr. [Leonard] Hall [Republican National Chairman] or some of his subordinates?

SACCIO: No, from the people I knew in Connecticut.

HAYS: That would be Mr. [Meade] Alcorn [Hall's successor]?

SACCIO: Yes, I think he was in charge at the time.

HAYS: And the organization you were with before was Berger Brothers?

SACCIO: That is right.

HAYS: That is a corset manufacturer?

SACCIO: That is right.

HAYS: Well perhaps there is some connection between that business and defense support.

SACCIO: They were known as Spencer Supports, sir.[16]

Because of this type of attitude which prevailed for years, both within Congress and the State Department, no progress was made at combining the two separate personnel systems, despite the fact that the foreign aid program was widely recognized as an integral part of U. S. foreign policy. As seen by State Department personnel officials, integration meant the dilution of a quality reputation associated with the foreign service system. It meant, also, a sharing of authority and influence with an "alien" group. Interestingly, ICA officials also opposed any change in the direction of combined personnel systems. Their stated reason was that their requirements for specialists simply could not be met by foreign service officers. On a more subtle level, however, they feared a loss of agency identity if the two systems were integrated. Moreover, various congressional groups also opposed the merger plan because an integrated personnel system would result in increased functional integration, and, for a number of reasons, these congressional groups preferred to keep the State Department and aid agency functions separate.[17] Thus, the resistance to change came from many different directions both within and without the executive structure. Until September 1961, the separate and distinct personnel

[16] *Mutual Security Act of 1959*, Hearings, House Committee on Foreign Affairs, 86th Congress, 1st session, 1959, p. 252.

[17] *Mutual Security Act of 1959*, Hearings, Senate Committee on Foreign Relations, 86th Congress, 1st session, 1959, pp. 803–804. For an excellent comparative description of the two personnel systems see Robert E. Elder, *The Policy Machine* (Syracuse: Syracuse University Press, 1960), Ch. 9.

systems were maintained despite the significant degree of administrative duplication, overlap, and confusion that resulted. The change that finally did come about was basically responsive and consolidative in that it attempted to meet the demands for a new program within the framework of existing behavioral patterns.

## Departments and Independent Agencies

Although subunits within the various executive departments and agencies may resist changes from established behavioral patterns in a purely consolidative manner, top-level executive officials themselves may be extremely resistant to changes that may be aimed at their respective departments or agencies. Indeed, even the creation of a new department or agency may be viewed as an exercise in consolidation, although this tactic must also be considered as one of the basic innovative devices at the disposal of the President—a point to be discussed in more detail later.

For example, the recent establishment of the Department of Transportation and the Department of Housing and Urban Development[18] represents responsive change carried out within a consolidative behavioral pattern. In both instances, the need for some type of functional consolidation had long been evidenced. Transportation, housing, and urban affairs programs had been scattered haphazardly throughout the entire executive structure. Therefore, neither plan proposed by the Johnson Administration could be considered an example of innovative or anticipatory change. Actually both plans sought to achieve their desired objectives with a minimum degree of internal displacement and disruption.

The HUD proposal, for instance, merely elevated an already existing executive agency—the Housing and Home Finance

[18] Public Laws 89–670 (1965) and 89–174 (1965), respectively.

Administration (HHFA)—to Cabinet status. In the process, the various component units of the HHFA—Federal Housing Administration, Public Housing Administration, Urban Renewal Administration, Federal National Mortgage Association, and Community Facilities Administration—were also transferred to the new Department. However, all of the other diverse urban programs spread throughout the executive branch were left undisturbed. In the short run, therefore, the only change involved an agency becoming a department overnight. One critic of the proposal viewed the change in terms that certainly suggest a strong consolidative orientation on the part of the Administration in connection with the HUD proposal.

> . . . the Congress has decided that you cannot create an executive department except by legislation. So the purpose [of this proposal] is to present as harmless a bill as possible that would have a minimum of opposition, and then use the reorganization plan method later to expand it to create a Department of Urban Affairs.[19]

The Deputy Director of the Bureau of the Budget, in responding to the implications of this statement, did not disclaim the validity of the suggestion as a possible future decision. Be this as it may, the point is that the creation of HUD was a clear example of high organizational adaptation on the part of the Administration. Every step in the process was calculated to adjust the proposed design to the external demands—a situation which was neatly illuminated by the manner in which the new department's official name was agreed upon.

In 1962, President Kennedy submitted to Congress a reorganization plan designed to establish a Department of *Urban*

[19] Statement by John C. Williamson, National Association of Real Estate Boards, *Department of Housing and Urban Development*, Hearings, House Government Operations Subcommittee, 89th Congress, 1st session, 1965, p. 143.

*Affairs* and *Housing*. This plan was rejected by the House on February 21 by a 264–150 roll call vote. President Johnson's bill (not a reorganization plan) sought to establish a Department of *Housing* and *Urban Development*. His bill was passed. John Williamson of the National Association of Real Estate Boards provided one man's interpretation of the change:

> Instead of a Department of Urban Affairs and Housing we now have a Department of Housing and Urban Development. The rearrangement of words in the title was dictated, we surmise, to satisfy an industry which conditioned its espousal of such a Cabinet rank department upon the assignment of some sort of priority . . . to housing.[20]

During House hearings on the bill, Deputy Budget Director Staats was asked if he drew any significance from the changed title and the changed attitude from opposition to support by the various housing associations. Staats replied,

> I would not know first hand whether this is related to the title, or whether or not they are now satisfied that the bill . . . meets the concern that they have previously expressed on the other proposals.[21]

The President of the National Association of Home Builders, who had previously opposed the Kennedy plan but who appeared before the Senate Subcommittee hearings in support of the Johnson bill, was not nearly as circumspect.

> SEN. SIMPSON: I noted that the bill is substantially the same except the word "housing" has been moved to the

[20] *Establishing a Department of Housing and Urban Development*, Hearings, Senate Government Operations Subcommittee, 89th Congress, 1st session, 1965, p. 159.
[21] House Hearings, *op. cit.*, p. 24.

front of the title. Did that have any influence upon
you?

MR. WILLITS: Well, let us say that that helped.[22]

The situation involving the Department of Transportation
was somewhat different in that the transfer of many diverse
executive subunits to the new department was achieved. As
finally passed by Congress, the Transportation Department
took on the appearance of a holding company. The new Secretary was restricted in his authority to develop a nationally
integrated transportation policy as a result of a shared desire on
the part of various congressional and interest groups to maintain
mutually advantageous relationships that had developed over
the years. Furthermore, as a result of House insistence, the
Maritime Administration was retained in the Commerce Department, thus depriving the Secretary of the new department of any
authority over this vital segment of the transportation field. In
short, although a certain degree of dislocation resulted from the
new design, this appeared minimal in that most transferred
functions were substantially insulated from whatever influences
one might reasonably expect to be generated from the apex of any
executive departmental structure. The move was basically
consolidative, the reaction, essentially responsive; consequently, established behavioral patterns were, for the most part,
preserved.

Even within existing departments such as the State Department, which, at least at upper echelons, has traditionally sought
to preserve its innovative imprint on the formulation of foreign
policy decisions, consolidative tendencies seem to have become
an increasing problem. "Gresham's Law of Planning" as Simon
uses the term is an apt description of the current State Department situation in that routine, programmed activity tends to

[22] Perry E. Willits appearing before the Senate Government Operations
Subcommittee, *op. cit.*, p. 157.

drive out available time that should be apportioned to non-programmed or planning activities. McCamy, for instance, devotes an entire chapter to this problem in his study of the administration of foreign policy.

> Recent change has brought more action than thought to the conduct of foreign affairs. The move from traditional diplomacy into operations abroad diminished the old central work of scheming. Without scheming, without the incessant analysis of what other nations were up to and how our nation should move, the conduct of foreign affairs became almost entirely routine.[23]

And elsewhere he notes,

> The practice of diplomacy itself had become almost entirely response, not foresight. Men who worked in political affairs divisions may have thought they were diplomats in the mold of de Callieres. They were, in fact, no more than reporters of events, assemblers of views, drafters of replies, attenders of meetings. Foreign policy was made in answering the mail.[24]

If "Gresham's Law of Planning" is applicable to the State Department, then one could reasonably expect that Gresham-type planners were manning the critical positions in the formulation of U. S. foreign policy. To this point, McCamy writes:

> The present men who control, below the top chiefs, are hired because they are good at foreign relations, not because they are interested in the large questions of foreign policy. They are chosen by examinations . . . that find aptitude for routine work that can be handled only by the most intelligent, most responsible, and most dedicated of men. . . . In truth, strange as it

[23] James L. McCamy, *Conduct of The New Diplomacy* (New York: Harper & Row, 1964), p. 249.
[24] *Ibid.*, p. 250.

seems, the United States in its years of anxiety, has no experts specially chosen, trained, and experienced in foreign policy.[25]

An innovative orientation is the only prescription that McCamy can muster as an essential element that must be introduced into the Department's policy planning process. Some individuals within the Department must be freed from the depressing and restricting routine of daily operations simply "to think candidly and fearlessly about basic policy, with originality and all the wisdom that our culture can muster." Such is the conclusion that McCamy offers, but, implicitly it seems, with not much real hope or expectation behind it. In a disheartened fashion he relates a conversation with a tired, old-styled diplomat, the essence of which aptly capsules the consolidative syndrome.

> Once I asked a Permanent Under Secretary of the British Foreign Office what he considered to be the biggest difference in diplomatic work between now and when he began 30 years before. . . . His answer to my question was immediate. It required no contemplation, for the man had suffered. "It is," he said, "the enormous amount of unnecessary work we do now."[26]

A similar conclusion concerning the State Department is reached by Robinson.

> It is this long-range thinking and projection for which, we are often told, the executive has difficulty in finding time. Interviews with policy makers in the Departments of State and Defense recurringly turn up the lament that they are so very busy with particular reactions to particular events that there is little opportunity to survey the future. Although there may be ways of insulating planning staffs from operating duties,

[25] James L. McCamy, *op. cit.*, p. 256.
[26] *Ibid.*, pp. 274–75.

attempts so far seem to have usually resulted in eventually drawing planners into making decisions.[27]

The willingness to give priority to programmed or routine matters is a malady probably common to all organizations, indeed if not to all organisms. Within the governmental structure, this preference inevitably results in a consolidative-type of responsive change which, under the circumstances of pressing details, limited time, and decision-making demands, is probably the best that can be expected. But on the basis of the various examples that have been discussed to this point, excessive routine demands may not be the only reason why organizations react to change in a consolidative manner. Also of significance is the fact that individuals, subunits, and even executive departments can—often with justification—feel threatened by impending innovations. The best means to offset such threats lie in the direction of entrenching a consolidative foundation solidly within the executive structure. For the most part, this tactic has been ably carried out. A third reason which helps to explain the consolidative orientation so dominantly reflected throughout the executive structure is the mutually compatible and advantageous relationships that have developed among executive subunits, congressional committees and subcommittees, and interest or clientele groups. One of the basic problems facing executive branch personnel officials in all departments and agencies is that only limited rewards are available to career bureaucrats who demonstrate a capacity and a willingness for innovative behavior. On the other hand, substantial rewards are generally available to the executive administrator who chooses to respond faithfully to the expressed needs of his clientele and congressional groups. In many respects it is the more rational alternative; but in any event, it solidifies a consolidative attitude and orientation within the mind of the administrator.

[27] James Robinson, *Congress and Foreign Policy-Making* (Homewood: Dorsey Press, 1962), p. 205.

# 9

# Executive Branch
# Innovation

Innovation was defined in Chapter 7 as the ability of an organization to anticipate, not just respond to, the external and internal needs for change. Innovation implies the conscious and deliberate effort to search for new problems, and to devise new responses to meet these problems. As the model in Chapter 7 sought to demonstrate, consolidation/innovation is not a zero-sum situation. Thus, just as every organization must, on occasion, respond to the forces of change in a consolidative manner, so also does every organization have opportunities to anticipate the need for change and to meet these needs through innovation. However, as has already been suggested, for innovation to occur on a consistent basis, some means must be available to reward those who would be expected to provide innovative designs. And in this regard the executive branch is severely disadvantaged. Because of the vast domain of the executive structure, legitimate concern is directed to such problems as organizational stability and operating effectiveness. These frequently become the sought-after goals that are worthy of reward simply because they carry with them the prospects of continuity, predictability, personal security, and environmental control. Within this context, therefore, innovation represents more of a threat than a blessing in that higher risks and uncertainties are inevitably associated with innovative behavioral patterns. Under these circumstances, how, then, can innovation hope to be achieved within the executive branch? Some of the methods that have been employed will be examined.

## Achieving Innovation

### Formal Planning Units

Nearly every major operating department and independent executive agency has a policy planning subunit buried somewhere within its internal structure. The extent to which such groups are utilized in a purely policy-planning capacity varies considerably, but a quick perusal of the *United States Government Organization Manual* indicates that virtually every top-level executive official has, on paper at least, relatively easy access to some type of innovation-directed planning group. For instance, the policy planning staff of the State Department is supposed to function in a quasi-intellectual vacuum, completely free from any operating responsibilities or decision-making functions. Its primary mission is to establish the long-range foreign policy goals of the United States, as well as the long-range means (i.e., programs) designed to accomplish these objectives. A critical assessment of the State Department policy planning staff results in a mixed response. Robinson, cited previously, assumes the position that even the best possible efforts on the part of the planning staff are wasted simply because the rest of the State Department organization has become geared almost exclusively to daily operating procedures. This suggests an obvious hypothesis concerning the effectiveness of such planning units—the success of any formal planning unit within any organization will depend on the extent to which its innovative designs are accepted by top-level operating officials. Planning units can be created, superbly staffed, and directed to anticipate changing needs long before they materialize. However, the effectiveness of such units is lost if their recommendations either cannot or will not be implemented. Because of the consolidative orientation that has developed to an increasing extent during the post World War II period within the State Department, many foreign policy observers no longer look to the Department's policy planning staff as a continuous source of rich, new ideas that may be infused into the foreign policy process. On occasion, of course, the planning staff has in recent years advanced innovative policies designed to anticipate future needs; the Marshall Plan, and the Truman Doctrine before it, the long-range policy objectives sought through the NATO proposal, and the work done by Chester Bowles for President Kennedy in reassessing the rationale behind the manner in which foreign aid funds were distributed in various nations, are a few policies of this type. On the whole, however, the role of the policy planning staff in the State Department has not been especially spectacular, and one suspects that most knowledgeable observers would be more inclined to agree than disagree with Senator Abraham Ribicoff: "Many people who have been in the policy planning work are very, very able men and women, yet I always have the feeling that this was almost an exercise in futility. The Secretary of State was always so busy and he has so much to do that he very seldom paid much attention to them in their work."[1]

The obvious conclusion concerning the efficacy of such formal planning units as a source of innovative policy is that their influence and impact on the behavioral orientation of any

[1] *Conduct of National Security Policy*, Hearings, Senate Government Operations Subcommittee on National Security, 89th Congress, 1st session, 1965, p. 145.

organization is directly dependent upon the manner in which their analytical efforts are received by the top-level operating executives whom they serve.

### Creation of New Operating Units

Because organizational "sclerosis" is commonly associated with bureaucratic development, change imposed within existing structures frequently incurs excessively high costs. Change is as much a state of mind as an actual event. The now-famed Hawthorne studies long ago established the validity of this premise. Therefore, since the negative consequences that may be associated with an impending change may very well exceed the positive gains anticipated from the change itself, other alternatives may be sought that would achieve the same objective but at significantly less cost. One alternative, not always open, however, is simply the creation of a completely new operating organization or subunit. In this fashion, the internal disruption and dislocation that may have resulted by implementing a new program within an existing bureaucratic unit may be avoided.

Or, to view the same problem from a completely different perspective, top-level executive innovation frequently requires expeditious and unobstructed implementation. Particularly within the scope of national defense or national welfare policies, the President and his policy advisers may desire immediate administrative action. If the responsibilities are assigned to existing operating units that, it seems clear, are overwhelmed with the routine necessities of daily operations, the prospects of prompt administrative action are considerably diminished. For this reason, necessity or urgency frequently dictates the establishment of a new administrative subunit.

Finally, a third consideration frequently leading to the creation of a new operating unit is suggested by the fact that the

President may decide to embark on a completely new program for which only broad guidelines can be initially established. In the absence of prior experience, the consequences of future behavior are nothing more than quasi-guesses. Under these circumstances, maximum administrative flexibility and discretion become absolute necessities. Such values can hardly be achieved by operating within existing units that function within their own well-defined and fully developed set of norms and "standard operating procedures."

Thus, anticipated resistance, urgent action, and maximum flexibility are three general reasons why it is frequently easier, wiser, and/or more reliable to create a new agency to perform a particular innovative task than to utilize already existing organizational units. Obviously these three considerations are not mutually exclusive; indeed, in most instances where existing executive structures have been bypassed in favor of a new unit, all three factors contributed in varying degrees to the decision. The most obvious example which immediately suggests itself involved the proliferation of the "alphabet" agencies during the Depression and World War II. During both of these crisis periods, new programs were constantly being devised to achieve a wide variety of innovative (as well as consolidative) goal objectives, and, in the process, new agencies were almost instantly created to assume responsibility for the implementation of these new programs. The Atomic Energy Commission was created to take advantage of the obvious need for flexibility and discretion, in addition to a need for technical expertise which could hardly be provided by any other existing unit. Likewise, in deciding on the manner in which the Marshall Plan would be put into operation, top-level executive officials created an autonomous agency, the Economic Cooperation Administration, instead of assigning the task to the State Department.

Nevertheless, although the desire to achieve an innovative goal objective frequently dictates the creation of a new agency, the creation of a new agency does not always signify the presence of innovative behavior. As noted, the ECA was created in 1948 to carry out the Marshall Plan. When the initial impetus behind this grand experiment began to wane, the Mutual Security Agency was created to supersede the ECA in 1951. The new Republican Administration felt the need to rid the aid program of all past Democratic remembrances, and in 1953 the Foreign Operations Administration was established to replace the MSA. Adverse congressional opinion began to develop over the operations of the FOA, and in an effort to restore some of the initial luster and confidence of the aid program, the International Cooperation Administration was created in 1955. In 1961, President Kennedy sought to give the aid program a new spark of vitality and still another agency was created, the Agency for International Development. Unfortunately, none of these changes represented innovative efforts on the part of the top-level executive officials concerned. Instead, each new agency was primarily a consolidative effort to meet changing needs essentially within the same established program patterns that existed previously.

On the basis of the foreign aid experience, at least one conclusion is suggested. Given the inevitable resistance, inflexibility, and sluggishness that one can reasonably expect to find in existing executive organizations, the creation of a new, fresh, imaginative agency to implement an innovative policy decision is certainly a reasonable and rational alternative. However, once the initial or exploratory phase of the innovative program has passed—once the nonprogrammed activity becomes thoroughly routine or programmed—then little advantage is gained by attempting to maintain the fiction of innovation simply by creating new agency names. Once an operation becomes essentially consolidative in its behavioral patterns, any pretense at innovation becomes a self-defeating exercise.

## Presidential Commissions and Advisory Groups

Resistance to change can stem from all levels within the executive branch and from the various external groups. Since the President and his top-level advisers must assume the responsibility for initiating innovative designs, they must also, naturally, assume the responsibility for having these policies and programs accepted. Unfortunately, the factor of acceptance is frequently jeopardized as a result of the suspicion that the Administration in power will gain some partisan political advantage from the innovative change. For this reason, the President, in order to have innovative measures effectively implemented, frequently has to assume unusually high risks in getting his plans stamped with the imprimatur of unquestionable sincerity, integrity, and nonpartisanship. To attain this heightened level of purity, one of the most effective, and yet, most unpredictable, means available to the President is the blue ribbon, star-studded Presidential Commission or Advisory Board.

Presidential commissions serve several important functions. In the first place, they may provide a consensus-building function in being able either to mitigate rising opposition from within legislative and/or interest group circles, or to establish a countervailing force of support. Second, they can provide an objective analysis of existing programs and operations. Third, they can provide the President with a set of recommendations which carry with them the impeccable credentials of a group of respected and knowledgeable citizens. Thus, in connection with a wide variety of executive problems, which inevitably arouse suspicions of partisan political maneuvering on the part of the President (e.g., foreign aid, labor-management relations, civil rights, and executive management procedures), the President's use of advisory groups permits him to accomplish from the outside, figuratively speaking, what would be extremely difficult if tried from within. More recently, President Johnson has made

extensive use of the commission device to accomplish
various Administration goals. The President's Crime Commission submitted a 340-page study following its 18-month
investigation. This study then served as the basis of the
President's message to Congress concerning crime in the United
States.

Superficially, it may seem quite reasonable to expect a high
correlation between the findings and recommendations of
Presidential Commissions and the ultimate goals of the President. Such is not always the case, however, and herein lies the
risk that must be assumed by the President who chooses to
utilize this device as an aid in his innovative design. For example,
in connection with the U. S. foreign aid program, both the
Eisenhower and Kennedy Administrations received serious set-
backs as a result of commission-type analyses made of the
program.

Kennedy's experience occurred following a very un-
spectacular record of achievement in the foreign aid area during
his first two years in office. In an effort to alter the essentially
negative image created by this AID operation, he created in
December 1962 an outside commission to undertake an immediate review of the entire aid program. The Commission to
Strengthen the Security of the Free World, as it was called, was
headed by General Lucius D. Clay, U.S.A. (ret.). The final report
of the "Clay Commission" (submitted to the President in March
1963) contained, for the most part, a series of generalizations
that essentially suggested that aid efforts could be reduced in
certain countries without impairing the overall quality of the
program. In addition, the Clay Commission delivered what it
probably felt was a modest suggestion: "AID informs us that
if our criteria were now in effect, present programs would be
reduced by approximately $500 million . . ." From the point of
view of the President, who had already requested $4.9 billion
for foreign aid in his annual budget message to Congress, this

statement could hardly be viewed sanguinely. Having established the Commission, however, the President felt an obligation to recognize its conclusions. Thus, in his foreign aid message to Congress, the President requested $4.5 billion, a reduction of approximately $420 million, which he hoped would impress Congress with his willingness and sincerity to follow the recommendations of the Clay Commission. Subsequently, a very long and complex debate developed between the executive and legislative branches over the foreign aid program. The ultimate result was that Congress finally appropriated $3 billion for the foreign aid program, a slash of $1.5 billion from the President's original request. And, as the intricacies of the legislative process were revealed in this instance, it was apparent that the Clay Commission report at the very least provided the fulcrum that maximized legislative leverage.

During the Eisenhower Administration, an outside appraisal of the foreign aid program also backfired, but the damage in this instance was borne almost solely by the President's first foreign aid director, Harold Stassen. Shortly after being named director of the aid program, Stassen sought to establish the same type of rapport that existed during the Hoffman years of the ECA between the foreign aid agency and American business interests. As a first step in this direction, Stassen contacted 55 leading business executives to serve as an advisory body for the overall aid program. This group divided into 12 evaluation teams, each assigned a specific country for intensive evaluation. For Stassen the strategy was clear, even though his timetable was tight: the individual teams would investigate their assigned countries, prepare their respective reports, reassemble in Washington to combine the team reports into an overall commission report, which Stassen could then use as the basis for his first congressional presentation in 1953. Unfortunately for Stassen, the plan had to be revised when he became aware that the final summary report would be extremely critical of the basic philosophical premises behind the aid concept. Having assembled a "blue ribbon," impeccable "jury," Stassen was more or less stuck with the verdict. In a hastily called meeting with his "committee of fifty-five," he was able to get a slight majority of the group to concede to a toned-down version of the final report, but for the most part the critical sting remained.

On balance, it is clear that under certain circumstances a commission-type approach can be an excellent vehicle to initiate innovative change sought by executive branch officials. However, it seems reasonable to suggest that a direct relationship exists between the potential value of the group and the potential risk associated with the use of the group. In other words, the type of panel that would be most effective would have to consist of individuals whose reputations for partisan noninvolvement and intellectual independence were unquestioned. With such a group, however, the possibility that it may reach an entirely different set of conclusions than those sought by the President or other top-level executive officials is by no means remote. At the other extreme, of course, this "risk" can be completely eliminated by assembling a group of "puppets" to voice the opinions of their executive patron. In this situation the value of any report or study is slight.

## Encouraging Innovation

Despite the emphasis on consolidative behavior and responsive change that one can find at virtually all levels throughout the executive structure, certain significant—albeit comparatively isolated—efforts have been made in recent years to encourage innovative behavior in the middle and upper echelons of the executive bureaucracy. The two major areas that have revealed the most significant developments in this connection are management development programs and the decision-making process.

### Management Development Programs

Many of the steps taken in this direction have been geared to correct the glaring deficiency of the lack of rewards for superior individual performance. The establishment of supergrade positions (G.S.-16, 17, 18) was an important first step in providing additional incentives for senior career officials. The designation "supergrade" carried with it the explicit definition that the position was essentially policy oriented or, in the case of scientists, research oriented. By 1966, approximately 5,000 supergrade positions had been authorized by Congress. Given substantial policy responsibilities, individuals nominated for these positions received salaries ranging from $19,000 to $25,000 annually. One difficulty persists, however; supergrade positions are established on the basis of slots, in accordance with general civil service policy. Thus, as was discussed before, even in these exalted positions, individuals are selected to fill specific jobs. In his 1967 State of the Union Address, President Johnson directed his attention to this point when he suggested that supergrade ratings be assigned to outstanding senior careerists who could then be moved within the executive branch in a manner designed to maximize their overall effectiveness.

In another area, marking a major break from a tradition that dated back to 1789, Congress, in 1965, approved President Johnson's Reorganization Plan No. 1, which frankly recognized that the responsibility for the operations of the Bureau of Customs fell almost exclusively on the shoulders of senior career officials. As a result, the historic pattern of appointing political loyalists to the positions of Collector of Customs was ended, the positions abolished, and the entire structure reorganized in such a way as to place top-level Bureau positions within the sphere of senior career officials. In this and in other similar instances, the goal has been (along with other practical economic considerations, of course) to increase individual incentive for increased quality performance.

In the area of providing management skills, the Civil Service Commission has taken several steps. In accordance with the Government Employees Training Act, the CSC established an Office of Career Development which, in turn, has created an Interagency Training Program. This effort is designed to promote and coordinate management training programs among the various agencies and departments throughout the executive structure. In this connection, agencies are encouraged to establish training courses and management development seminars in accordance with their own particular needs. Moreover, the Bureau of the Budget, General Services Administration, and the CSC give courses and seminars designed to accommodate the broad, general needs of the government. Institutes in middle-management problems, and executive leadership have been established. Special attention has been given to the career science executive in the federal government. And seminars in operations research, financial management, and data processing are offered routinely.

Furthermore, as a result of the 1966 Executive Order[2] issued by President Johnson, the executive assignment system discussed in the previous chapter will, hopefully, allow the Commission's newly created Bureau of Executive Manpower to effect a series of significant changes concerning top-level executive personnel. For example, long-range manpower needs of the federal government will be a primary concern of the new Bureau, in terms both of the scope of these needs and the means to satisfy them. In this connection the Bureau is expected to devise new executive search-and-selection procedures, which will focus on management resources outside of government in addition to the transfer of executive officials between agencies and departments. The executive assignment system is designed to maximize flexibility and increase the manpower resources available to the federal government. The attempt to shift the focus of search

[2] No. 11315, 89th Congress, 2nd session.

from job slots to individual qualifications is an important development, and, if carried out successfully, it could signify a major alteration in the executive branch personnel practices.[3]

In connection with the various steps that have been taken in an effort to develop a more professional management orientation within the executive bureaucracy, a few comments concerning the politically appointed executive officials are necessary. Certainly no indications of innovative changes have been evidenced thus far in connection with the traditional mode of selecting this group of executive bureaucrats. Presidential preferences continue to play an important role in determining, within broad limits, who shall serve in these positions. However, certain tenuous and admittedly speculative observations can be offered concerning some future changes that may be considered.

For instance, given the increasing recognition being directed to supergrade positions, and the increasing demands in many areas for high technical competence, the most vulnerable or, rather, the weakest link in the Presidential appointee structure appears to be the Assistant Secretary. Mann's study of this group[4] does suggest that given the background experience of the Assistant Secretaries, viewed collectively, their overall contribution to the bureaucratic process becomes marginal. In other words, if one considers the total management resources of the executive branch that have to be invested in the average Assistant Secretary to turn him into a truly productive executive official, and then balance this investment against his average tenure, the net gain from an administrative point of view is marginal, at best. Of course, to this formula must be added the political value gained by maintaining these politically appointed positions, but here again the impression is that the gain is

[3] See John W. Macy, "Assurance of Leadership," *Civil Service Journal*, *op. cit.*

[4] Dean E. Mann with Jameson Doig, *The Assistant Secretaries* (Washington: Brookings, 1965).

marginal as would be the political loss if the positions were filled by supergrade careerists. In any event, a thorough study of this proposition could conceivably lead to the formulation of executive management policies truly innovative in scope.

Another, somewhat more confident observation can be advanced. A general reassessment of the President's Cabinet structure is long overdue; not in terms, necessarily, of how individuals are selected, but rather which executive departments should be included in the President's highest council of policy makers. The discussion recently developed in connection with changing the status of the Post Office Department to that of a government corporation is a case in point. President Johnson's reference to a merger of the Commerce and Labor Departments is another example. Neither of these points represents particularly novel ideas, but they do emphasize the need for fresh, innovation insights concerning the Cabinet structure.

### Decision-Making Innovations

Any organization will be forced to follow a consolidative pattern of behavior if it does not have the facilities necessary to make innovative decisions. To anticipate the need for change before the need becomes a gross reality an organization must, at least, be able to make reasonably accurate long-range forecasts which will aid in discerning projected needs. For even the most efficiently organized bureaucratic structure this is not an easy task; for the executive bureaucracy, this type of long-range planning has, until recently, been generally considered an impossibility. With the continued advancement of automatic data processing equipment, however, the ability to gather, store, and order data has taken on an entirely new dimension. Theoretically, at any rate, the executive decision-making process may be able to project itself well into the future and to gain tremendous advantage from the multivariate analysis capable of being performed by advanced computer facilities.

In a more specific and directly related sense, the most significant device that has been introduced into the executive branch to anticipate changing needs has been the planning-programming-budgeting system—PPBS. Whether PPBS represents a dramatic innovation, i.e., "revolution," or simply a natural "next step" in the normal evolution of governmental budgetary practices need not really concern us at this point. It may be helpful to utilize a modest conclusion coming from a Committee for Economic Development report which certainly does not overstate the significance that must be given to this technique: "If carried through in all its implications. . . initiation of this . . . system may come to rank among the main events in federal budgetary history."[5]

The primary purpose of PPBS is to improve the rationality and to increase the degree of confidence that is reflected in the executive decision-making process. It is designed to insure that executive decision makers will be in a significantly improved position to select the most desirable, i.e., the optimum, program alternative related to a particular public policy decision. To the extent that PPBS represents a recognition of the integral relationship between policy decisions and budgetary decisions, it offers no departure from the administrative behavioral patterns developed during the New Deal period. As noted previously, the shift of the Budget Bureau from the Treasury Department to the executive office of the President symbolized, and institutionalized, the recognition of the budget as the central policy-making tool. This basic assumption remains unchanged; what has changed, however, is the manner in which budgetary data is collected and organized, and related to top-level policy decisions. Since the beginning of the New Deal, emphasis within the entire

[5] *Budgeting For National Objectives*, Committee for Economic Development, New York, 1966, p. 22.

executive branch was on administrative *performance*; PPBS, as the name implies, emphasizes *programs* and *program development*. The difference is fundamental.[6]

As Schich correctly notes, an administrative performance emphasis is purely management oriented. The performance budget that was developed and utilized during and following the New Deal Administrations was gauged to provide an accurate assessment of actual operating performance. It was a management tool in that it related budgetary decisions to other management-oriented categories; e.g., personnel, administrative expenses, operating expenses. Whereas this approach was effective in making particularistic, management-type decisions, it was not useful as an overall budgetary statement that could be meaningfully related to organizational policy goals. For example, the Bureau of the Budget receives annual budget requests from each executive department. Departmental budgets are composite budgets in the sense that each budget reflects the needs of each department's subunits. Performance budgets are thus consolidated as they make their way up through the departmental echelons. The Budget Bureau and the President then face the task of relating these various composite performance budgets to the overall program goals of the Administration. Or, as previously noted, it is at this point that the limitation of resources dictates the establishment of certain executive priorities. But, for the most part, the questions being asked at this stage of the process simply cannot be answered on the basis of the type of information that is available. Budget officials are unable to make intelligent, rational, and nonarbitrary priority decisions.

The main defect in the performance budget format is that it tends to emphasize essentially static conditions. Seldom are

---

[6] For a detailed evaluation of this point see Allen Schich, "The Road to PPB: The Stages of Budget Reform," *Public Administration Review*, vol. 26 (December, 1966), pp. 243-58.

alternative schemes submitted to budget officials; hence top-level executives are forced either to accept the budget in toto or to reduce the budget requests by imposing their own arbitrary judgments. For instance, as Capron notes,

> . . . there is not even available to the Budget Director and the President . . . the kind of information which allows one to judge the effect on a given program of either a decrease or an increase in the funding level finally recommended to Congress. The result of this is that the judgment of the Budget Bureau staff is often superimposed on the judgment of those presumably much more knowledgeable about the program.[7]

In order to avoid this basic dilemma, PPBS is aimed at increasing decision-making rationality by increasing the number of factors that can be used to provide top-level decision makers with a truly comparative analytical dimension. In a statement on August 25, 1965, President Johnson directed all executive departments and agencies to "retool" their budgetary habits in accordance with PPBS standards. As he informed all of his executive bureaucracy in that order, PPBS will enable us to:

1. Identify our national goals with precision and on a continuing basis;
2. Choose among those goals the ones that are the most urgent;
3. Search for alternative means of reaching those goals most effectively at the least cost;
4. Inform ourselves not merely of next year's cost, but the second, third, and subsequent years' costs, of our programs;

[7] William M. Capron, *The Impact of Analysis on Bargaining in Government*, Paper presented to the American Political Science Association Annual Meeting, New York, 1966, p. 5, mimeo.

5. Measure the performance of our programs to insure a dollar's worth of service for each dollar spent.[8]

Translated into the language of the PPBS advocates, the new system insures:

1. the evaluation of alternative program choices and the selection of that alternative which permits the realization of a given national goal at minimum costs;
2. the comparative analysis of the various governmental activities as they relate to broad national goals;
3. the formulation of national goals, alternative approaches to these goals, and supporting benefit cost data on a projected multiyear basis;
4. constant and immediate revision of all programs, goal objectives, and multiyear fiscal estimates in response to changing demands and needs, on the basis of cumulative experience.[9]

PPBS has its advocates, of course; but it has its critics, as well. In this respect, one of the most interesting aspects of the system that emerges from the literature of some of its proponents is the striking similarity of their visionary zeal to the apolitical, value-free, scientific precision of the "science of administration" vanguard of an earlier era. Dwight Waldo was the skeptic who

[8] Contained in *Planning-Programming-Budgeting: Official Documents*, prepared by U. S. Senate Government Operations Subcommittee on National Security and International Operations, 90th Congress, 1st session, 1967, committee print, pp. 1–2.

[9] Obviously, the intricacies of PPBS are much more complex than the oversimplified explanation presented here might suggest. More detailed and comprehensive treatments of this important subject are readily available. See, for instance, *Public Administration Review*, vol. 26 (December, 1966), entire issue; David Novick (ed.), *Program Budgeting* (Cambridge: Harvard University Press, 1965); Charles Hitch, *Decision-Making for Defense* (Berkeley: University of California Press, 1965).

effectively demolished the earlier scientific tabernacle; for the
present, at least, the most telling criticism of PPBS has been
directed by Aaron Wildavsky who, like Waldo before him,
probes to the heart of the PPBS viscera in an attempt to uncover
a normative bias.[10] An example of the purely objective, value-
free approach assumed by the PPBS advocates is provided by
Melvin Anshen. "The program budget is a neutral tool. It has no
politics."[11] Elsewhere Anshen cites the positive consequences
that may be expected from PPBS, followed by the usual dis-
claimer which certainly, and understandably, will draw cynical
responses from many political scientists. As seen by Anshen the
program budget is a tool that will "broaden," "sharpen,"
"illuminate," and "facilitate" the tasks and responsibilities of
decision makers, but that will *not* "answer problems," "make
decisions," "displace management judgment," "determine
objectives," or "judge performance."[12] Wildavsky, on the other
hand, sees politics and political choices still at the heart of the
budgetary process.

> It will be useful to distinguish between policy politics (which
> policy will be adopted?), partisan politics (which party will win
> office?) and system politics (how will the decision structure be
> set up?). . . . My contention is that the thrust of program
> budgeting makes it an integral part of system politics.[13]

"System politics" provides a convenient means to examine
many of the potential consequences that program budgeting

[10] "The Political Economy of Efficiency," *Public Administration Re-
view, op. cit.*, pp. 292–310. Waldo's critique is contained in his study, *The
Administrative State: A Study of the Political Theory of American Public
Administration* (New York: The Ronald Press, 1948).

[11] "The Program Budget in Operation," in Novick (ed.), *Program
Budgeting, op. cit.*, p. 370.

[12] "The Federal Budget as an Instrument for Management and
Analysis," in Novick (ed.), *Program Budgeting, op. cit.*, p. 23.

[13] "The Political Economy of Efficiency," *op. cit.*, pp. 304–305.

could have on the internal control and decision-making systems of the executive branch. The relationship between PPBS and administrative centralization immediately comes to mind. As presently conceived, program budgeting contains a centralizing bias, as seen by Wildavsky. And certainly judging by the manner in which PPBS has advanced thus far within the Department of Defense, this sentiment seems to be in no fear of being contradicted. Arthur Smithies, writing in the Novick volume, notes,

> Where programming and administration diverge, the way in which the organization as a whole works depends largely on the means employed to ensure that administrators in fact carry out programs. . . . The critical factor is the head of the organization. Without his authority and support, departments and bureaus are likely to go their own way. Moreover, programming can be a potent instrument for increasing the authority of the department head, as Defense Department experience has shown. In fact, some uneasy critics of Defense Department programming allege that this is its main purpose.[14]

This "centralization syndrome" associated with PPBS does indeed cause the greatest amount of unease among its critics. Even with the most generous interpretation being given to the implications of programming in the executive branch, it still would seem difficult to suggest that the President, the Bureau of the Budget, and other top-level executive officials would not stand to gain a significantly greater degree of centralized control over subordinate operating units. Nevertheless, William Capron tries.

> Potentially, at least, PPB will permit, if properly implemented, a rationalization of the centralized-decentralized relationships from the President . . . down to the sub-organizational units

[14] "Conceptual Framework for the Program Budget," in Novick, *Program Budgeting, op. cit.*, pp. 54-55.

which go to make up the federal hierarchy. As one moves up the hierarchy, if the inputs called for in the PPB system are adequately developed, it would be possible for the decision-maker at any level to make the choices among the elements for which he has responsibility, but to a large extent to devolve on the decision-makers below him responsible for each one of these elements the choices *within* each of these elements.[15]

As seen by Capron, a most extreme form of centralization is present in the existing decision-making process by virtue of the fact that top-level executive officials are frequently compelled to make choices—and hence, to veto subordinate decisions—in the absence of relevant and/or valid information.

> In short, the present system seems to me to lead to a pernicious and promiscuous kind of centralization all the way up the line, and it is this perverse centralization in the present system which hopefully, at least, PPB will go some way to correcting. PPBS when developed can be a powerful force for a rationalization of the federal decision structure and for decentralization.[16]

The threat of centralized control stemming from the program budgeting approach, whether real or imagined, certainly represents the major obstacle in its path within the executive branch. In this regard, a process of cumulative centralization seems to emerge—i.e., within any organizational structure executive officials at any hierarchal level will strengthen their control over all subordinate officials below them. As a consequence, even Departmental Secretaries would stand to lose much of their autonomy and discretionary maneuverability to the President and his budget control officers. An example of the type of response that might develop from department heads if

[15] *The Impact of Analysis on Bargaining in Government, op. cit.*, p. 7.
[16] *Ibid.*, pp. 7–8.

and when PPBS reaches the specific stage of compulsory adoption (at the present it is on a "as soon as possible" basis) can be detected in their individual responses to a legislative proposal originating in the Bureau of the Budget concerning the purchase and use of automatic data processing equipment by federal departments and agencies.[17] The proposal established the General Services Administration (GSA) as the central coordinator and manager of all executive branch data processing equipment. The first section of the proposal stated that the General Services Administrator was authorized and *directed* to coordinate and provide for the economical and efficient purchase, lease, and maintenance of all executive branch data processing equipment. The last section of the proposal created an ambiguous situation. On the one hand, it seemed to confirm the centralized power granted to the General Services Administrator in section one (his authority was subject to review only by the President and the Bureau of the Budget), yet on the other hand his power seemed to be advisory only in regard to intra-agency data processing decisions (he could not interfere with the determination of each agency's data processing needs, and he could not control in any way the use they made of their own data processing equipment). However, in the final sentence of the proposal, the centralization syndrome was reasserted ("In the absence of mutual agreement between the Administrator and the agency . . . such proposed determinations shall be subject to review and decision by the Bureau of the Budget unless the President otherwise directs.").[18] The responses of various top-level executive officials to this proposal are interesting in view of the innovative, anticipatory nature of the change being considered. Almost without exception every Departmental Secretary

[17] *Automatic Data Processing Equipment*, Report of the House Committee on Government Operations, 89th Congress, 1st session, 1965, House Report No. 802.

[18] *Ibid.*, p. 75.

and other invited respondents endorsed the goal of administrative coordination that the proposal sought to achieve. At the same time, however, each firmly reasserted the "sovereignty" of his own decision-making power. The excerpted statements below suggest the presence of a latent uneasiness even at this top level.

It is considered essential that determinations with respect to [data processing equipment] . . . involving national defense and national security be made by the Secretary of Defense. [Cyrus Vance, Deputy Secretary of Defense.]

. . . it is our belief that management decisions as to when and where data processing will be used are the prerogative of the agency concerned. [John Gronouski, Postmaster General.]

Agency heads are charged with the responsibility for the proper and efficient conduct of the programs. . . . It is not practicable to expect the Administrator of the General Services Administration to make or review decisions about agency data processing equipment needs . . . [Robert Giles, General Counsel, Department of Commerce.]

The agency responsible for the administration of operating programs must have the authority to select the equipment it needs in order to carry out its programs, and it should not be restricted in its utilization of equipment. [Wilbur Cohen, Assistant Secretary, Department of Health, Education, and Welfare.]

We have made a most determined effort to integrate the tools of data processing with the services we are responsible for providing. . . . As a result, decisions concerning the procurement of this . . . equipment, and the manner in which it is to be used are directly related to the success or failure of such programs. [W. J. Driver, Administrator, Veterans Administration.]

We believe that the functions to be performed by central agencies should involve . . . the issuance of policies, procedures, and guidelines for use by the various departments and agencies and that the responsibilities of . . . departments and agencies in managing their own data processing resources within such . . . guidelines should continue substantially unchanged. [John Vinceguerra, Atomic Energy Commission.]

It is essential that we retain effective control over the design, installation, maintenance, and utilization of these and other special systems used in our technical operations. . . . To transfer our control of these systems to the General Services Administration would seriously hamper our efforts to carry out our air safety responsibilities. [N. E. Halaby, Administrator, Federal Aviation Agency.][19]

The federal bureaucratic structure is, at the present, faced with an incipient innovative force that could be staggering in its ramifications if it ever reaches a fully developed stage. Emotions are mixed about PPBS and the use of data processing equipment as they relate to the traditional decision-making process. Moreover, the intensity with which many of the conflicting opinions are presented tends to obliterate much of the moderating dialogue that has taken place. There is much to be said for any management technique that would permit a greater degree of rational decision making than now is evidenced within top-level executive circles. Decision making is actually choice making, and the very least we should expect from our executive bureaucratic officials is that they make intelligent, rational choices. But this of course assumes that they will have at their disposal the proper facilities to make intelligent and rational choices; under the present circumstances, this assumption appears to rest on faith alone. PPBS at least contends that more refined analytical means can be introduced into the public policy

[19] *Automatic Data Processing Equipment, op. cit.*, pp. 46–66.

process. But neither does it seem unreasonable to assume that the consequences of its application could extend far beyond its programmatic intentions. The centralization of executive authority is not an unwarranted conclusion; executive reorganization could logically be considered; executive-legislative relationships could become recast; and Congress, itself, could certainly be forced to reassess its operating premises. In short, neither the scope nor the magnitude of its influence portend to be quite as modest as its most extreme defenders contend. If PPBS knows no politics, it can learn; the illusion of neutrality cannot last long. Political questions seek political answers. PPBS may permit policy makers to transpose political questions into an analytical framework from which analytical answers may be obtained. However, analytical answers generally do not serve well as responses to political questions; thus, some means must be devised either to sacrifice one to the other or to reconcile the two. At this stage in the development of systematic analysis within the executive hierarchy, the choice can be deferred; but eventually it must be faced if program budgeting continues to gain support. And in this respect to anticipate that need is in itself an invaluable innovative undertaking.

# 10

# Conclusion

The problem of "organizational change," as applied to the executive branch, has been the focal point of discussion in the previous two chapters. Certainly from within the behavioral sciences, the concept of change (i.e., the degree of variation in the substantive content of organizational behavior) commands serious attention as a key variable in the analysis of organized activity. The relationship between change and the three other factors examined in the earlier chapters should be apparent. The manner in which the executive structure is able to control internal behavior, make rational and intelligent decisions, and develop a sense of organizational loyalty will, to a great extent, be determined by the demands for change that are imposed on the organization. Likewise, the manner in which the executive structure does meet the forces of change shall, in part, be determined by the way in which these other three factors are organizationally developed within the executive structure. In other words, change must be viewed as both cause and effect, as a dependent and independent variable. As such, it may serve as a convenient summary vehicle to integrate the various analytical concepts that have been advanced in the previous chapters.

Specifically, four generalizations concerning bureaucratic behavior in the executive branch are suggested, with varying degrees of confidence.

## Relative Preference

First, it can be suggested that the organization's choice between an innovative or consolidative behavioral pattern is really no choice at all—at least to the extent that "choice" is taken to mean the deliberate, rational, and conscious selection of one alternative and the rejection of the other. Instead, it seems much more realistic to conclude that all large, complex bureaucracies reflect a composite mixture of both innovative and consolidative tendencies. "Pure" examples of both exist only as disparate models; otherwise, all functioning organizations fall somewhere between these two extremes. Within a single organization, different emphasis may be manifested at different times within different subunits operating on the same or different levels. With the introduction of PPBS into the executive branch, the Defense Department and the Bureau of the Budget assumed predominately innovative postures while many of the other executive departments responded in a more consolidative manner. Even within a particular department, innovative and consolidative patterns may be directed by functional responsibilities; ideally, research or planning groups are not expected to respond to the forces of change in a purely consolidative fashion any more than the offices of general counsel or comptroller are generally viewed as a primary source of innovative behavior. But of further significance is the direct relationship which should be evidenced between the hierarchal principle of graded authority and the innovation-consolidation scale.

In other words, as one proceeds upward in the organization to positions of increasing authority and responsibility, decision-making discretion, as previously noted, should also increase.

Increased decision-making discretion may also be interpreted as the organization's expectation that the individual will anticipate the need for change within his zone of responsibility rather than simply respond to the forces of change. Conversely, for low-level executive positions, it may be hypothesized that the organization's expectations run more in the direction of responsive or consolidative change because decision-making discretion is narrowly limited and innovative behavior at this level may actually become quite dysfunctional.

Organizations, of course, do not always conform to this generalized relationship. However, the main point to be stressed here is that regardless of the predominate orientation that may be revealed by the organization, the differences that exist between innovative and consolidative tendencies are relative rather than absolute. Executive officials are virtually precluded from an absolute rejection of either alternative, which is simply to suggest that except in unusual circumstances both innovation and consolidation must be viewed and utilized as mutually inclusive alternatives.

## Nonequal Alternatives

Because of the nature of the administrative responsibilities that are generally assigned to the middle- and lower-level executive echelons—e.g., the implementation of routine, programmed tasks—organizational rewards are generally allocated to the individuals at these levels for such behavioral traits as conformity to organizational norms, dependability, loyalty, and so forth. As noted previously, innovation, originality, and/or creativity are neither expected nor especially rewarded at these lower levels. Furthermore, at these operating levels, where program efficiency depends to a great extent on administrative proficiency, subunit continuity and stability become important administrative factors. However, where operating continuity and stability are realized, formal as well as informal behavioral norms are likely to be developed which substantially reinforce consolidative responses.

In other words, although it is reasonable to suggest that innovation and consolidation are both available as alternative directions that may be pursued to meet the forces of change, it may also be quite likely that they do not represent *equally* available alternatives. The executive hierarchal structure, with its dead-weighted lower tiers, has, so to speak, a very low center of gravity. The forces of consolidation, as a result, are much easier to follow than to reverse through innovation. As a consequence, significantly higher costs (time, effort, resources) may be expected if an innovative direction is followed. Given this hypothesis, the choice is by no means equal.

## Suggested Relationships

A third, and admittedly more tenuous generalization emerges when paired relationships are attempted between innovative-consolidative orientations and several other organizational characteristics that have been examined.

### Directions of Change and Decision Making

For instance, in relation to the decision-making alternatives of satisfying and optimizing, as discussed in Chapter 4, one hypothesis which is suggested is that a predominately consolidative behavioral pattern that emphasizes responsive change (and thus places primary importance on the maintenance of existing behavioral patterns) will encourage a preference for obtaining "satisfactory" decision-making solutions. And, conversely, a predominately innovative behavioral pattern that emphasizes anticipatory change (with primary importance being placed on goal attainment) will induce a preference for obtaining "optimal" decision-making solutions.

It may be recalled that the choice between these two decision-making alternatives was said to be a function of the degree of risk involved, as perceived by the decision maker. For top-level public policy executives, this element of risk may be viewed as the "support-opposition" ratio resulting from the various individuals and groups (internal as well as external) that may be affected by a particular policy proposal. For the most part, public policy decisions follow a consolidative pattern, selecting the alternative that is best designed to satisfy the stated needs of internal and/or external forces. Given the nature of our pluralistic political system, this has meant that a "satisfactory" alternative was one that satisfied at least the minimum needs or desires of the maximum number of groups directly involved. In this somewhat distorted Benthamite framework, the group theory of politics proceeds around the standard of at least a minimum good for the greatest number. Under the circumstances that have enjoyed—and still enjoy—wide legitimacy throughout the executive branch, innovative behavior is limited as an option open to executive policy makers because, as viewed by many, the primary function of the executive branch is solely *to respond* to the expressed needs of others.

As viewed by many other individuals, however, responsive change is self-defeating; to wait for a need to be expressed is simply to view the executive branch as a bobbing cork in the swirling eddies of our political, social, and economic currents. As one critic of this position, John Wilkinson, has noted,

Certain events that systematically affect all others *seem* to lie in the future but lie in fact in the past. The "future" is often a conventional, grammatical matter of tense, and already behind us as far as rational prevision and effective action are concerned, in much the same way that everything important has already occurred when an atomic reactor has heated up beyond the point at which it can be brought back under control by shoving in the lead shield. We must not, of course, remit our efforts to find solutions, for we can seldom be sure in a given case just whether a "due date" is or is not a past-due date, that is to say, whether or not we have yet passed the point of no return. But it is certain that *some* of the much debated cultural explosions of today are already irremediable historic events as surely as the death of Caesar. For example, "debate" about air pollution or the population explosion is probably hopelessly past-due, and all we have to do now is to pay the penalties, of which we do not even know the nature or magnitude.[1]

The post-World War II period of American politics has marked a slow but steady advance towards the nationalization of political issues, and hence, the nationalization of political conflict. The expression "national needs" now takes on more than simply oratorical significance as the demand to meet these needs currently falls almost exclusively on the executive branch. There is wide agreement today that the executive branch enjoys a virtual monopoly in the area of public policy initiation. Convincing arguments have also been advanced that the conflict resolution and even the representative functions traditionally considered the exclusive prerogatives of our legislative assemblies have passed by default to the executive domain.[2] Be this as it may, the point that does seem irrefutable is that the most pressing demands for change being made on our national government today simply cannot be met by responding solely from within a consolidative orientation that attempts to manipulate expressed needs within the context of existing behavioral patterns.

[1] "Futuribles: Innovation vs. Stability," *Center Diary: 17* (Santa Barbara: The Fund for the Republic, March–April, 1967), p. 18.

[2] Carl G. Friedrich, "Public Policy and the Nature of Administrative Responsibility," *Public Policy* (Cambridge: Harvard University Press, 1940); Norton Long, "Bureaucracy and Constitutionalism," *The American Political Science Review*, vol. 46 (September, 1952); Roger Davidson, "Congress and the Executive: The Race for Representation," in *Congress: The First Branch of Government*, Alfred DeGrazia (ed.) (Washington: American Enterprise Institute, 1966).

Although not totally obsolete, the basic inadequacy of an almost exclusive consolidative approach to the resolution of conflict is gradually becoming apparent. Charles Dechert correctly senses the new direction when he wrote,

> Legislation in the United States is becoming increasingly programmatic. Rather than legislation being proposed and passed on a piecemeal basis to handle specific and limited relationships, or to relieve concrete shortcomings and inequities within the society, individual items of legislation are represented as part of an overall pattern. Implicit in these programs are the faint beginnings of a "systems approach" to legislation.[3]

Indeed, the PPBS formula is designed to anticipate future needs in order to devise solutions to these needs well in advance of their positive expression. Under these new working assumptions of maximum administrative rationality, a much wider range of alternatives can be fully explored, and an "optimal" solution can be selected. Optimizing thus becomes an essential and integral part of the new decision-making scheme which promises to emphasize an innovative orientation that would anticipate future forces of change.

### Directions of Change and Conflict Resolution

Similarly, in relation to the two general categories of conflict resolution as developed in Chapter 3—manipulated agreement (with pure bargaining being included) and objective analysis—a relationship is suggested between the former and consolidative behavior. In this case, the proposition being advanced is that the control techniques of manipulation (and pure bargaining) are geared to cause the least amount of internal as well as external disruption and dislocation that may result

[3] "Availability of Information for Congressional Operations," in *Congress: The First Branch of Government, op. cit.*, p. 171.

from change. In this sense, then, it is suggested that the techniques of manipulated agreement and pure bargaining tend to reinforce the strength of existing behavioral patterns within the executive structure, and, thus, are much more conducive to the designs of consolidative change. On the other hand, an organization's commitment to an innovative orientation is significantly strengthened when the techniques of objective analysis become an integral part of the organization's control structure.

The primary feature of organizational control in which agreement is manipulated within existing behavioral frameworks is the preservation of continuity and the maintenance of a minimum level of outcome satisfaction for the involved participants. Even within private organizations where direct, unilateral control mechanisms are available, manipulated agreement frequently represents a more desirable solution. Within governmental bureaucracies, pure bargaining is evidenced in addition to manipulated agreement, and the basic framework in which both of these techniques are applied is consolidative in character.

Only at the problem-solving and pure persuasion levels— as these terms were defined in Chapter 2—can conflict be effectively resolved (and hence behavior controlled) through the techniques of objective analysis. Within this context, the role of value preferences is minimized by selecting a particular alternative on the basis of empirical facts and not subjective preferences. This approach was viewed as particularly well suited when applied by the lower executive echelons where specific operating decisions by small subunits could be controlled in a purely objective manner. As one advances up in the executive hierarchy, however, control becomes more difficult in that more variables of a nonquantifiable nature must be taken into account by subordinate executive officials. As a consequence, subjective preferences become an increasingly significant determinant in the executive decision-making process, just as manipulated agreement and pure bargaining become increasingly significant techniques in the control process. And the proposition being advanced here is simply that the use of subjective preferences within the executive branch decision-making process, and the reliance placed on the techniques of manipulation and bargaining as effective control mechanisms in the resolution of conflict, function in a symbiotic fashion with the consolidative orientation of the executive branch.

There is, of course, still wide acceptance of the assumption that the resolution of conflict and the decision-making process within the executive branch do not lend themselves to objective analysis beyond the most elementary type of problem that may be evidenced at the lowest operating levels. However, it seems reasonable to suggest that, at the very least, PPBS is capable of affecting a more orderly and a more conscious analysis of many extremely complex problems that confront top-level executive officials. PPBS proponents are quick to disassociate the PPB system from having any direct influence on the conflict resolution and the decision-making process. As seen by these individuals, PPBS may be viewed as an aid in the decision-making process; it may quantify data, order data, analyze data, and report results; but the actual decision must be made by the responsible executive officials. The point is that objective analysis can be made to work effectively at top-level executive levels as seen most dramatically in the Department of Defense. The effects of this approach on the traditional consolidative tendencies throughout the Department have also been widely proclaimed. With an essentially innovative orientation now being reflected by most top-level Defense Department officials, the anticipation of future needs—as defined by rather precisely stated goal objectives—has become predominately emphasized whereas the previous commitment to purely responsive change has been substantially reduced.

Insofar as the bargaining process itself is concerned—pure bargaining techniques characteristic of executive branch control

—one can only suggest that objective analysis of the type being discussed here is certain to have an impact on the efficacy of this traditional means of conflict resolution. Capron suggests that any time one or more "players" in the bargaining process employ systematic, explicit analyses of one variety or another, the rules of the bargaining game must inevitably be changed.

Even the most venal parochial party to governmental bargaining can be forced to take account of cogent systematic analyses —as long as some others at the bargaining table insist on making it part of the dialogue.[4]

In short, if objective analysis gains recognition as an effective means of resolving conflict and solving complex problems, then the organizationally conditioned subjective preferences may become less significant as decision-making determinants. Under these circumstances, it seems reasonable to assume that the consolidative behavioral patterns of the executive branch and their focus on manipulated agreement and pure bargaining will be assigned secondary significance to the innovative designs of the executive structure and its primary concern with attaining well-defined goals based on reliable estimates of future needs. Of course, the discussion of the application of objective analyses by top-level executive officials is still essentially a "futuristic" intellectual exercise. PPBS as an applied problem-solving, decision-making technique is still in its infancy as far as the executive branch is concerned, and despite the restrained optimism of many who are convinced that PPBS represents a genuine contribution to administrative development, it is not at all certain that its growth pattern will not be disfigured, stunted, and/or dissipated in the years ahead. More will be said in this connection later.

[4] William M. Capron, *The Impact of Analysis on Bargaining in Government.* Paper delivered at the 1966 Annual Meeting of the American Political Science Association, New York, pp. 3, 16.

## Differences Between Public and Private Bureaucracies

The fourth generalization that seems warranted is that, as an overall characteristic, the executive bureaucracy of our federal government reveals a much greater tendency to follow the consolidating-satisfying-bargaining patterns of organizational development than do the large, complex bureaucracies of private industrial and business corporations. To a great extent, the administrative hierarchies of this latter group reveal a stronger commitment to the innovative-optimizing-objective analysis pattern of organizational development. While this hypothesis is, in itself, a type of summary statement of the preceding propositions, it is offered as a separate generalization in order to discuss in detail some of the major causes of this basic difference; four will be mentioned.

### Lack of Control

Without doubt one of the striking differences between the two bureaucratic spheres is the basic inability of top-level federal executives to monopolize the usual resources that normally could be expected to be used to control the behavior of subordinates. Bennis argues forcefully over the ever-increasing democratization that is occurring and will continue to occur within private organizations.[5] However, in spite of the formal and informal liberalization that may be occurring within the most progressive corporations, the fact remains that the "man at the top" enjoys—at the very least—a residual type of direct control over his subordinate executive officials. A recent *Life* magazine feature examined the problems associated with getting a long-range master plan for production control introduced into IBM's Systems Manufacturing Division, composed of the

[5] Warren G. Bennis, *Changing Organizations* (New York: McGraw-Hill, 1966).

company's nine computer manufacturing plants. Representatives of the nine plants gathered together in a five-day meeting in an effort to work out their own solution, but the "keynote" talk by the Division's President left little doubt that unless a workable plan was devised within the Division, one would be "crammed down your throats by Headquarters."[6] Bennis himself reports an incident involving the president of a large retailing organization and his top executives who attended a T-group (laboratory training) session for management officials. The trainer of the group describes the event:

> In the afternoon, right after their second T-group of the day, when people were on their feet, the president rose and told everyone to remain in their seats and then delivered a twenty minute speech. He first said that supervisory training was an important thing and that the company had already spent a lot of money on it. He thought the participants were getting something from the company which they could not reasonably expect to get. Then he went on to say that these are critical times, that the competitive situation was worsening, and that success would require the greatest effort of everybody. This could be achieved, he said, by working hard and by following the given orders without questions—all the requisites, I thought, of a paternalistic management. He went on speaking then like a military leader. Then he referred to my short lecture on leadership, and said that there was one point he did not agree with at all. (One of the participants had asked whether a subordinate always has to follow orders to the word. I gave a qualified answer, trying to show that there are times when a superior could be questioned.) The president said that he most strongly wanted to emphasize that a subordinate had better follow orders—there was no question about that![7]

[6] "The Frustrating Warfare of Business," vol. 62, no. 18 (May 5, 1967), p. 46.

[7] Bennis, *op. cit.*, p. 159.

By contrast, of course, this type of direct control—whether made explicit or kept implicit as in the IBM situation—is just not available to top-level governmental executives, including the President. As Truman mused over the future of his successor, "He'll sit here, and he'll say, 'Do this! Do that!' *And nothing will happen.* Poor Ike—it won't be a bit like the Army. He'll find it very frustrating."[8]

> Eisenhower evidently found it so. . . . And this reaction was not limited to early months alone. . . . "The President still feels," an Eisenhower aide remarked to me in 1958, "that when he's decided something, that ought to be the end of it . . . and when it bounces back undone or done wrong, he tends to react with shocked surprise."[9]

But to suggest that lack of control is one explanation for the differences between public and private organizational patterns simply begs the question. Why do political executives have less control over their subordinates than do their counterparts in the private bureaucratic spheres? The basic reason, as developed in detail previously, is due to the additional "appeal" routes that are normally open to political subordinates who happen to oppose or seek to resist directives received from their superiors. In this connection the roles of Congress, congressional committees and subcommittees, and private interest groups are especially critical. Although the Board of Directors, the buying public, the labor unions, and the various other groups that may fall within the external environment of the private corporation have, under certain circumstances, made their preferences known to corporate executives in such a way as to modify or rescind certain company decisions, it is difficult to envision a disgruntled middle-level corporate executive lobbying any one of these groups directly in an effort to nullify his superior's directives.

[8] Neustadt, *Presidential Power, op. cit.,* p. 9.
[9] *Idem.*

Of course, it is important to stress the fact that control is a management device which, like fire, can be employed for good or evil. It can be activated only by an appropriate individual; to use Norton Long's expression, it becomes "a gun for hire" to be used according to the preferences of the man by whom it is held. Thus, control can obviously be used simply to reinforce an organizational preference for consolidation, satisfying, and manipulated agreement. But, by the same token, it can be used to direct a bureaucratic orientation towards innovation, optimizing, and objective analysis. It can, in other words, insure that current policies and programs be geared to the anticipation of future internal and external needs, and, as such, it becomes an essential factor for any organizational official who would value an innovative pattern of organizational change. Within the federal bureacracy—with its lack of real control power, its dispersion of authority, and its multiple appeal routes open to subordinate executive officials—the consolidative-satisfying-bargaining combination is virtually assured as being the dominant behavioral pattern.

### *Lack of Valid Measurements of Effectiveness*

For more than a century and a half American democracy has functioned without total interruption, although, on occasion, under severe stress. On the basis of this operating experience, the best we can usually say in its defense is that it works. But how well does it work? How effectively are the various public policies advanced by the President, evaluated and enacted by Congress, and implemented by the bureaucracy? The truth of the matter is that until quite recently intuition and election returns served as the only available measuring devices for operating effectiveness. Political effectiveness has, for the most part, monopolized the attention of the governmental bureaucrat while his nongovernmental counterpart has been forced to think primarily in terms of operating effectiveness. The distinction is significant in that the governmental bureaucrat is normally forced to consider that which appears politically desirable in addition to that which may be operationally feasible, and as Neustadt suggests, a disproportionate imbalance in favor of political desirability has resulted.

> ... it is fair, I think, to say ... that our public officers have been generally inclined to make the calculation without bothering their heads too much about their wherewithal in operating terms. Generally speaking they have tended to assume that if they could secure political assent, they could invent, or improvise, or somehow force the requisite responses from the men who actually would do the work, in government and out. The great machines of management would surely manage somehow if the necessary sectors of the public, or the press, or Congress, or the Cabinet ... were acquiescent.[10]

By juxtaposing political desirability and operating feasibility, a necessary second dimension is opened which has been generally ignored or subordinated within the executive decision-making process. It does suggest a third criterion which, when combined with the other two mentioned, could be used to analyze the differences in behavioral patterns between public and private bureaucracies. The third criterion could be called economic feasibility, and overall criteria could then be applied to both public and private organizations to determine to what extent proposed organizational policies are, first, desirable (politically or otherwise; is the proposal desired as well as desirable?); second, assuming it is desired and/or desirable, to what extent is the proposal economically feasible? (in relation to the costs involved, what will be gained?); and, third, assuming the

[10] Statement by Richard Neustadt before Senate Government Operations Subcommittee on National Security and International Operations, Hearings, *Conduct of National Security Policy*, 89th Congress, 1st Session, 1965, Part III, p. 121.

proposal is economically feasible, is it operationally feasible? (given the organizational resources which exist, can the proposal be carried out?).

Top-level executive officials in private corporations are in a relatively secure position to obtain reasonably accurate answers to the important second and third queries *before* a particular policy or action decision is made. Precise measuring devices and increasing proficiency and sophistication in the use of automated data processing equipment make such determinations fairly reliable. Assuming a proposal is approved, nongovernmental bureaucrats are then in an equally strong position to maintain a day-to-day account, if necessary, of changing environmental conditions. As a result, at any instant in the course of the program, adjustments can be made in the program on the basis of updated projected data and accumulated actual performance data in order to maintain a favorable benefits-cost ratio.

For top-level executive branch officials, however, the first query becomes the most important, and it is primarily answered on the basis of political considerations. As Neustadt suggests, if this all-important first question can be answered affirmatively, then it is generally assumed that the second and third questions will, somehow, be satisfactorily met. Political desirability, therefore, most frequently represents the primary decision-making determinant within the executive structure, while economic and operating feasibility can for the most part be determined only *after* the program has been put into operation, and even then, not accurately. This basic inability to be able to reach reasonably accurate estimates of economic and operating feasibility before a program is instituted seriously limits the extent to which innovative efforts can be programmed into the executive structure. Under the present circumstances, the best estimations of future effectiveness can be obtained by making incremental changes in existing programs. As a consequence, consolidative behavioral patterns are, again, reinforced.

*Lack of Clear Goals*

As discussed previously, the problem of ambiguous goal objectives can be examined in connection with private organizations as well as public bureaucracies. At least, the explicitly stated goals of nongovernmental structures often provide excellent examples of ambiguously stated principles. However, while many of these vague statements may prove to be functional in the sense of developing consumer loyalties, creating favorable perceptions, and so on, they are not designed to provide a clear and precise definition of organizational purpose that can be applied to gauge all organizational activity. For this purpose, large-scale business and industrial organizations are able to apply a wide range of accounting techniques that are capable of measuring all phases of organizational performance in terms of some profit-related standard, be it referred to as cost-effectiveness, cost-benefit, or cost-utility. Through the utilization of advanced computerized techniques and sophisticated management analysis, alternatives to pending policy decisions can be selected as a result of being able to relate the consequences of each alternative (costs) to the primary goal objective of the organization (maximum benefits). In this context, innovation does not become a totally unpredictable venture into a murky future; that is to say, given a particular standard or goal objective which all administrative officials recognize and comprehend and, given further, a high degree of confidence in the utility of the standard or goal objective, then decisions made by top-level officials on the basis of the standard become meaningful to other subordinate officials throughout the organization.

Within the governmental bureaucracy, however, precise standards or goal objectives that can be applied to the decision-making process are for the most part lacking. Moreover, the assumption—nearly viewed as absolute—has been that such standards are impossible to apply to governmental operations because of the nonquantitative nature of these operations. The first crack in this generally accepted theory has been delivered by PPBS which, on the basis of its limited application in the executive bureaucracy, suggests a different conclusion.

Ironically, however, the dramatic results of the Department of Defense experience with PPBS, have simply reaffirmed the convictions of many individuals that government is not in business to make a profit, and that operating efficiency should not be its most important concern. Viewed in this context, operating efficiency within the executive bureaucracy must often be subordinated to other—i.e., political, social, economic, ethical—considerations. An extended discussion of this value judgment can probably be handled more expeditiously and more effectively elsewhere. It does seem appropriate to note here that while this "humanistic" concept of governmental activity can, on occasion, give rise to innovative policy decisions (e.g., the Marshall Plan, Berlin Airlift, Lend-Lease, NATO), the weight of its persuasiveness is probably most effectively applied in maintaining existing behavioral patterns and, thus, a consolidative orientation.

### Necessity to Demonstrate Immediate Results

The fourth major difference between public bureaucracies and large, complex private organizations is that governmental executive units, much more so than private corporations, are under strong pressure to have operating performance coincide with promised expectations as soon as possible. To paraphrase Banfield slightly,[11] the extent to which federal executives may discount the present for future gains is extremely limited. This is not to suggest, that corporation executives have unlimited discretion in this regard; stockholders are not an immutably

---

[11] Edward Banfield, "Ends and Means in Planning," *Concepts and Issues in Administrative Behavior*, Sidney Mailick and Edward H. Van Ness (eds.) (Englewood Cliffs: Prentice-Hall, 1962), p. 77.

submissive lot. However, as a corporation's profit position improves, stockholders, satisfied that their initial investment is secure, are generally more receptive to the promise of future gains than immediate dividend increases. "Growth" is an important descriptive term for corporate officials, organizational executives, and stockholders. To grow, an organization must expand in some direction, and growth entails research, long-range planning, and *deferred benefits*. Innovative decisions are demanded, given the nature of the competitive system, but innovative decisions are, by definition, decisions designed to anticipate future needs. Hence, the rewards or benefits to be gained by these decisions must inevitably be deferred for the present.

Government executives, by contrast, enjoy little opportunity to defer immediate gains for future rewards. For several important reasons they are forced to respond to the exigencies of the present.

ONE. Executive administrators are rather effectively constrained to a twelve-month future by the congressional appropriations process. The annual budget hearings which involve nearly every middle- and top-level executive official restrict any serious consideration of future needs to an extremely limited cycle. From the congressional viewpoint, the annual sessions not only provide an opportunity to preview projected budget requests, but also (and probably more significantly) an opportunity to review the previous year's operating performance. In any event, the entire process is geared against abrupt departures from previous levels of appropriations, which in effect means that the entire process is characterized by a predominately consolidative orientation.[12]

[12] For more extensive treatment of this point see Aaron Wildavsky, *The Politics of the Budgetary Process* (Boston: Little, Brown & Co., 1964), and, by the same author, "Toward a Radical Incrementalism," in *Congress: The First Branch of Government, op. cit.*

TWO. Assuming for the moment that executive branch officials would favor the greater administrative freedom and flexibility that would be gained from an innovative orientation, Congress as the authorizing body is simply not geared—intellectually, temperamentally, or structurally—to adapt to an innovative design of the executive branch. Individual congressmen and congressional committees are almost exclusively conditioned to respond to current and immediate needs. On occasion, as with the moon project and the current supersonic jet transport program, both representing policy decisions based on estimated future needs, Congress will concur; but for the most part, congressional skepticism and disinterest are usually evidenced toward any major innovative proposal in which immediate and tangible benefits cannot be demonstrated.

THREE. The assumption that executive officials would themselves favor a predominately innovative orientation is by no means absolutely valid; not all executive bureaucratic officials are strongly committed to an innovative behavioral pattern. For many governmental administrators, the type of restrictions placed on their own bureaucratic operations by Congress maximize their own personal security, insure operating stability and continuity, and permit them to become, in J. Leiper Freeman's terms, the mid-level entrepreneurs of the public policy process.

FOUR. The short term of office of the President seriously restricts the extent to which major innovative efforts can be introduced into the public policy process. The odds being in favor of the incumbent President who seeks a second term, one can say that a President has eight years to carry out his programs. Now eight years may be viewed as a reasonable period to achieve certain tangible results, but in terms of current management planning concepts and data processing techniques, it does not represent an exceptionally long-term extension. And, actually, the President's "effective" term in office is somewhat less than eight years.

Consider, for instance, that the first year of nearly every new Administration is "wasted" in the sense that the new executive officials must learn to adjust their own administrative personalities to those of their colleagues, their subordinates, Congress, and the outside interest groups. There are exceptions, of course. McNamara introduced the PPBS concept into the Defense Department almost immediately, and by the end of the first Kennedy year in office, the Department had settled into a relatively smooth operating network. On the other hand, Kennedy was plagued well into his second year in office with the inability to get his foreign aid operation moving with any degree of effectiveness.

Realistically, the eighth, or last year of any President's two terms in office also has to be viewed as a "wasted" year. During this twelve-month period (if not even longer) the Administration takes on many of the characteristics of a caretaker operation. Key executive officials normally take an early departure in order to capitalize on the prestige gained from their executive positions, and the public policy machinery of the executive branch for the most part idles until the election returns are posted. Thus, to a very real extent, the President is faced with a six-year period in which his influence on public policy decisions can be maximized and effectively implemented. Under these circumstances, the President is almost forced to gear his entire program to immediate, or, at the most, short-range needs.

FIVE. The extent to which the President is able to develop innovative policies around projected future needs is further complicated by the normal attrition rate that can be expected among his top-level advisers. Innovative decisions stem from anticipated needs, and these determinations must be made by Cabinet Secretaries, policy planners, and other key Presidential advisers. The best plans of any Department head or policy planner will amount to very little if his resignation ushers in a successor whose vision may not extend as far. Bear in mind, for example, that at the beginning of 1968, Dean Rusk, Robert McNamara,[13] Orville Freeman, and Stewart Udall joined a rather select circle of approximately thirty former Cabinet officers who served in office seven years or longer. By public management standards, they must be considered real veterans; by private management standards, they would still be considered gradually maturing executives.

In summary, the lack of control, the lack of meaningful measurements of operating effectiveness, the lack of clear and precise operating standards or goal objectives, and the inability to discount the present for future benefits are four major reasons why executive bureaucracies are forced to adopt essentially different behavioral patterns than their nongovernmental counterparts. In practical terms, the consequences of each of these reasons within the federal executive structure simply tend to reaffirm and reinforce, in a cumulative sense, the commitment toward a consolidative-satisfying-bargaining attitude. This does not mean to imply that all private bureaucratic structures reveal innovative-optimizing-objective analysis orientations; it simply suggests that given the very real differences in the organizational characteristics of the two bureaucratic settings, innovative behavioral patterns are much more difficult to achieve in the one than in the other.

## The Future

As for the future of the world's largest and, in many respects, most successful governmental bureaucracy, one needs either wit and/or exceptional nerve to foresee Orwell's bureaucratic model becoming operative in the few years now remaining. However, one needs neither wit nor nerve to become legitimately concerned about the ability of the federal executive to meet many of the future needs of our society and, indeed, the

[13] McNamara resigned from his post as Secretary of Defense on November 29, 1967, although he did not leave his position until March 1, 1968.

world community. To repeat de Jouvenel's observation, "There is a continual dying of possible futures. And two mistakes are common: to be unaware of them while they are . . . alive, and to be unaware of their death when they have been killed off by the lack of discovery."[14]

In our federal governmental system the executive branch is now almost completely recognized as the prime initiator of public policy decisions. Given this virtually indisputable political fact of life, the manner in which this grave responsibility is carried out frequently suggests that all but a few of the vast army of executive bureaucrats become aware of our possible futures only after they have quietly expired due to the lack of discovery. The discovery of possible futures, and the systematic and rational development of programs to meet those futures have been defined here as innovation. When the futures become the present they are, in fact, already in the past. Organizational behavior associated with this phase of change has been referred to as consolidation. The challenge which faces the federal executive bureaucracy, if one may hazard such an opinion, is to shift its basic behavioral orientation more away from the latter in the direction of the former, i.e., innovation.

But even this prescription is troublesome. The French author Casamayor, quoted by Wilkinson, observed, "To make men rotten one must be a corrupter; to make societies rotten one must be an innovator."[15] The True Innovator, like The True Believer, one may conclude, is basically incapable of tolerating behavioral patterns which impair his progressive vision—or impede his visionary progress. For those who do not share his insights into the future, but, instead, focus their attention on the problems of the present (which are in many instances, the former futures killed by the lack of discovery) a Rousseauean solution is uneasily suggested.

[14] Quoted in Wilkinson, *op. cit.*, p. 18.    [15] *Ibid.*, p. 23.

As Wilkinson notes, the most successful innovations of the past have been those whose impacts have been effectively cushioned by the various social organisms in the society—the Law, the Church, the Military, *and the Bureaucracy*. However, having nearly reached the beginning of the fourth quarter of the twentieth century it seems reasonable to conclude that neither the Law, Church, nor Military is capable of providing the cushion to public policy innovations in the United States. And as public policy initiative has become the almost exclusive prerogative of the executive branch, it is hardly realistic to expect the innovators to also play the role of modifiers. Given the alternative, however, this may be the only reasonable course to follow.

Traditionally, in the United States, the basic alternative has rested in the legislative branch. Over the years of increased executive activity, the most effective check on innovative-designed change has been supplied by the Congress. Working in conjunction with the organized interests of our body politic, and the lower- and middle-level executive officials, Congress has generally been able to gear most innovative momentum down to manageable and tolerable proportions. For the most part, this has been accomplished by making public policy outcomes directly dependent upon the intricacies of the political bargaining process.

The experience that has accumulated from the politics of bargaining suggests two observations. First, in a positive sense, bargaining is a well-suited device by which stabilizing constraints can be built into innovative behavioral patterns to insure that policy decisions are implemented with a minimum degree of physical and/or psychological disruption and dislocation. Viewed in this fashion, an important function of Congress is to provide the stabilizing constraints that may minimize the direct impact of executive innovative decisions on the body politic. Second, in a negative sense, the bargaining process has, unfortunately, also served as a direct force against innovative change and, conversely, as a force to champion consolidative change and the maintenance of existing behavioral patterns. Given the basic organizational structure of the federal executive branch, it should be apparent that the politics of bargaining have been far more effective in influencing the outcome of public policy decisions in this second rather than in the first instance.

The role of political bargaining in resolving conflict and determining public policy decisions can, of course, prove to be extremely effective in instances where all participants share (1) similar values as to the efficacy of this technique, and (2) similar intellectual frames of reference as to the basic considerations involved in each particular policy decision. Insofar as this second proviso is concerned, it seems reasonably clear that one of the major dilemmas of our federal governmental system, beginning with the New Deal days, has been the gradual though steady divergence of the frames of reference, or public policy perspectives of top-level executive officials on the one hand, and key congressional members, on the other. To generalize in this regard is unfair in many respects, but the overall impression persists that the major public policy decisions made by the executive branch on the basis of national and international considerations are, for the most part, evaluated and adjusted by Congress on the basis of considerations that are intellectually rooted in an entirely different (i.e., subnational) frame of reference.

International perspectives are, of course, reflected in the legislative branch by various individual Congressmen, principally in the Senate, and national orientations are increasingly being evidenced even within the House. But, particularly within the House, subnational *attitudes* (not just interests) tend still to serve as the primary frame of reference for many Congressmen to judge the merits of executive policy decisions that, for the most part, have been made on a higher level of abstraction.

A politics of bargaining conducted in this context maximizes frustration in that two separate and distinct monologues frequently develop between legislative and executive discussants in lieu of a meaningful and mutually enlightening dialogue. To borrow Parsonian terminology, stabilizing constraints reflecting a particularistic, self-oriented, and ascriptive frame of reference can hardly be considered suitable cushions for innovative policies structured within an exactly opposite (universalistic, collectively oriented, and achievement oriented) frame of reference. Thus, one of the basic challenges facing both the executive and legislative branches of government, but especially the latter, is to achieve a common frame of reference that would allow the legislative participants to view innovative policy decisions within the same context in which they were formulated.

> It is possible here only to remind ourselves that the future is already the past in almost every event that acts to change the social order when effective constraints have not been introduced simultaneously and consciously with the innovation.[16]

A "little band of willful men" served as "effective constraints" on Wilson; civil rights legislation had been, for years, "effectively constrained" by Southern Democrats; the House Rules Committee represented an "effective constraint" to Kennedy; the constraint imposed by Otto Passman on the United States foreign aid program has been extremely "effective." And yet, in each of these instances, the constraints imposed were of a negative rather than a positive value; that is, they were primarily designed to inhibit change rather than to moderate or stabilize the environment in which change was to take place. A common public policy perspective does not mean the end of dissent; it does mean the beginning of a rational and responsible dissent which Congress is at the present time, politically, temperamentally, and structurally incapable of providing. Effective

[16] Wilkinson, *op. cit.*, p. 24.

constraints emerging from a dialogue of dissent need not be feared; grave concern should result, however, over constraints on innovative decisions that emerge from two monologues of dissent. That this mode of discourse between the executive and legislative branches of government can be altered in the immediate, foreseeable future is extremely doubtful; that it may ultimately be altered is a probable conjecture, although one suspects that the due date of this "futurible" has already become a past-due date.

As stated before, political bargaining can be utilized effectively to resolve conflict and to determine public policy decisions if all participants in the bargaining process (1) agree that this technique is the most efficacious, and (2) share a common frame of reference. Societal changes may ultimately close the gap that now separates legislative and executive public policy perspectives, but if and when that moment arrives it may represent a pyrrhic victory because another possible "futurible" is already starting to develop that—if it continues on its current course— may very well make the outcome of the challenge of convergent perspectives immaterial. Specifically it is felt that executive bureaucratic officials will find it increasingly to their advantage to shift from the techniques of political bargaining to the techniques of objective analysis as the choice decision-making and conflict-resolving mechanism. As a result of the initial experience with PPBS, for instance, the real decision-making "futurible" would seem to be a politics of analysis instead of a politics of bargaining.

Within the context of objective analysis, the responsibility of Congress as the intervening modifier between executive branch policy makers and the body politic looms all the more crucial. However, this consideration seems somewhat premature in that the basic problem in superseding a politics of bargaining with a politics of analysis is, once again, obtaining agreement from all participants in the public policy process that this technique is the most efficacious. McNamara, for one, demonstrated rather convincingly that some form of systematic internal analysis is—to reverse the order cited previously—operationally and economically feasible. What he was not able to demonstrate convincingly, particularly to many legislators, was that the Defense Department's system of objective analysis was politically desirable and/or desired.

The problem of demonstrating the political desirability of PPBS or some related alternative calls forth a mixed set of essentially normative responses. Many proponents of objective analysis have, unfortunately, stressed the value-free nature of their proposals, ignoring, of course, the normative bias which is built into the basic rationale of the scheme itself. The value-free claim needs to be viewed skeptically, although not necessarily with the same emotional intensity of some of the opponents of this approach who see only an horrendously computerized policy-making machine situated in Washington. Despite the strengths (of which there are many) of an objective analysis approach to the decision-making and conflict-resolving processes, the approach itself represents an innovation that has to be accepted before any of the other many innovative advantages may be realized. Executive branch advocates of the proposal must provide their own "cushion," so to speak, in order to minimize the impact of the change as it falls on Congress. However, the effects of change cannot be made tolerable if the inevitable normative questions that are being, and will continue to be, raised in connection with this new approach are ignored or dismissed cavalierly. The approach must, in other words, be made to appear not only operationally and economically feasible, but politically desirable as well.

For those executive branch officials who have discovered that public bureaucratic operations can, in fact, be systematically ordered and analyzed in terms of current as well as future needs, a lagging and skeptical legislative branch is bound to create frustration, antagonism, and alienation. The responsibility for insuring continued innovative progress in the formulation of public policy decisions *and* the responsibility for minimizing congressional ambiguity and potential antagonism rests solely with executive branch officials themselves. If the latter responsibility is ignored or partially discounted, then the former responsibility will never be effectively realized. A consolidative orientation, developed within a political bargaining framework, hardly seems to provide an adequate answer to any of our future governmental and societal challenges. An innovative orientation, developed within a political analysis framework, may be the answer. As usual, however, the burden of proof for change must rest on those who would propose the change; and, in connection with the change from bargaining to objective analysis, nothing appears more convincing than the belief that the future will most assuredly become the past if effective constraints are not introduced simultaneously and consciously with the innovation by executive branch officials themselves.

# Name Index

Aandahl, Fred, 62
Alexis, Marcus, 87, 90*n.*, 94, 97
Anderson, Adm. George W., 100
Anshen, Melvin, 232
Appleby, Paul H., 15*n.*
Argyris, Chris, 25*n.*, 32*n.*
Asbell, Bernard, 152*n.*

Baldwin, Hanson, 100
Banfield, Edward C., 193–94, 256
Barnard, Chester, 83
Bauer, Raymond, 113
Bennis, Warren G., 249–50
Blau, Peter, 32*n.*
Boulding, Elise, 26*n.*
Bowles, Chester, 216
Bruner, Jerome S., 113
Burdick, Eugene, 124
Busch, August, 49

Capron, William N., 230, 233–34, 248
Carroll, Holbert, 107
Casamayor, Louis, 261
Chamberlain, Lawrence, 190
Clay, Lucius D., 221
Cohen, Wilbur, 236
Cole, Albert M., 62
Conrath, David W., 92*n.*
Cotter, Cornelius, 164*n.*
Cyert, Richard M., 87–88

Dahl, Robert, 39, 66*n.*, 81*n.*
Dale, Ernest, 66
Davidson, Roger, 244*n.*
Dearborne, Dewitt, 113
Dechert, Charles, 245

DeGrazia, Alfred, 244*n.*
D'Ewart, Wesley, 62
Dexter, Lewis Anthony, 113
Dillon, Douglas, 157–58, 164
Dimock, Marshall and Gladys, 146*n.*
Driver, W. J., 236
Dulles, John Foster, 155
Dunkel, J. B., Jr., 61*n.*

Eisenhower, Dwight D., 108–9, 118, 126–28, 196, 251
Elder, Robert E., 206*n.*
Eldersveld, Samuel J., 78

Feldman, Julian, 55*n.*, 90*n.*
Fenno, Richard, 120
Freeman, J. Leiper, 66*n.*, 67*n.*, 79, 258
Freeman, Orville, 260
Friedrich, Carl J., 65, 244*n.*

Garceau, Oliver, 59
Gerth, Hans, 2*n.*
Giles, Robert, 236
Golembiewski, Robert, 32*n.*
Goodnow, Frank, 15*n.*
Gore, William J., 98–103, 123
Gronouski, John, 236
Guetzkow, Harold, 112, 113*n.*
Gulick, Luther, 28–29, 32*n.*

Halaby, N. E., 237
Harding, Warren G., 105
Hardy, Porter, Jr., 156–57
Harris, Seymour, 61, 62*n.*
Hays, Wayne, 205–6
Henderson, A. M., 2*n.*

Henry, Laurin, 60n.
Hitch, Charles, 231n.
Hoffman, Paul, 132, 222
Hollister, John B., 62, 155–56
Horwitz, Murray, 42n.
Hoover, J. Edgar, 115, 148–49
Hundley, William G., 115

Iacocca, Lee A., 61

Johnson, Lyndon B., 110, 126, 144n.,
    196, 204, 209, 220, 224–25, 227,
    230
Jones, James, 22
Jouvenel, Bertrand de, 261

Kahn, Robert L., 26n.
Kanter, Herschel E., 55n., 90n.
Katzenbach, Nicholas, 22–23
Kaufman, Herbert, 122
Kennedy, John F., 23, 118, 126, 144n.,
    164, 208–9, 216, 219, 221, 259, 264
Kennedy, Robert F., 23, 115–16, 160
Knight, Frances, 68, 150
Kramer, Robert, 164n.

Laux, Elgar F., 61
Lee, Richard, 151
Lindblom, Charles, 41n., 66n.
Long, Norton, 244n., 252
Lowi, Theodore, 181
Lundy, J. Edward, 61

Maass, Arthur A., 66n., 201, 202n.
Macy, John, Jr., 196, 197n.
Mailick, Sidney, 66n., 194n., 256n.
Mann, Dean E., 75n., 226
Marcuse, Herbert, 164n.
March, James G., 10n., 28, 32n., 33n.,
    44, 87–88, 90, 192–94
Marsh, Joseph F., Jr., 67n.
Martin, Norman, 199
Marx, Fritz Morstein, 15n.
Massie, John H., 28n., 31, 32n.
McCamy, James L., 211–12
McClellan, John, 160
McConnell, James J., 62
McIntosh, Dempster, 157–58

McKean, Roland N., 90n., 94
McNamara, Robert, 163–64, 167, 259–
    60, 266
Millet, John D., 146n.
Mills, C. Wright, 2n., 140
Mooney, James D., 31, 32n.

Neustadt, Richard E., 65, 73n., 117,
    129, 144, 189, 190n., 251, 253–54
Nigro, Felix A., 146n.
Novick, David, 231n., 232n., 233

Packard, Vance, 140
Parkinson, C. Northcote, 191–92, 194
Parsons, Talcott, 2n., 173, 178, 182,
    184
Passman, Otto, 264
Pfiffner, John, 146n.
Pool, Ithiel deSola, 113
Presthus, Robert, 4n., 26, 66n., 140,
    146n.

Reimer, Everett, 199
Ribicoff, Abraham, 216
Riddleberger, James, 205
Robinson, James, 212, 213n., 215
Roosevelt, Franklin D., 109–10, 117–
    18, 121, 128
Rusk, Dean, 149, 260
Russell, Richard, 164

Saccio, Leonard J., 160, 205–6
Sayre, Wallace, 146n.
Schick, Allen, 229
Schlesinger, Arthur, 110, 117, 118n.,
    121n.
Schwartz, Abba, 68, 150
Scott, Richard, 32n.
Shepard, Herbert A., 26n., 30, 31n., 34
Shils, Bud, 25n., 36n.
Simon, Herbert A., 6, 10n., 15n., 28,
    32n., 33n., 44, 82–83, 86, 88–101,
    113, 132n., 192–94, 210
Simpson, Maynard, 209
Smiddy, Harold, 39n.
Smithburg, Donald W., 15n.
Smithies, Arthur, 233
Sorenson, Theodore C., 126

Staats, Elmer, 209
Starbuck, William, 32$n$.
Stassen, Harold, 109, 159–64, 222–23
Stevenson, Robert, 61

Taylor, Donald W., 90$n$.
Taylor, Frederick W., 10$n$., 28, 32$n$.
Thompson, Stewart, 38$n$., 54$n$.
Thompson, Victor A., 15$n$.
Truman, Harry, 105, 127–28, 251

Udall, Stewart, 260
Urwick, Lyndall, 28, 32$n$.

Vance, Cyrus, 236
Van Ness, Edward H., 67$n$., 194$n$., 256$n$.
Vinceguerra, John, 237

Waldo, Dwight, 15$n$., 29$n$., 231–32
Wallace, George, 22–23
Warner, W. Lloyd, 146$n$., 199, 200$n$.
Warren, Earl, 144$n$.
Weber, Max, 2–5, 8–9, 12, 14$n$.
White, Leonard O., 15$n$.
Whittier, Sumner, 54
Whyte, William, 140
Wildavsky, Aaron, 169, 232–33, 257$n$.
Wilkinson, John, 243, 261–62, 264$n$.
Williamson, John C., 208$n$., 209
Willits, Perry E., 210
Willoughby, W. F., 15$n$.
Wilson, Charles Z., 87, 90$n$., 94, 97
Wilson, Woodrow, 15$n$., 264

Zalesnik, Abraham, 31$n$.

# Subject Index

Adaptation, 173–75, 177, 184
Administration, science of, 28–31
Anticipatory change, 178–81, 184, 242
    and innovation, 182–84
Anxieties, 123, 138–39, 147, 177, 192
Anxiety reward balance, 137–39
Authority
    and control, 37–39
    and decision making, 95
    delegation of, 21–23, 81, 109
    formal, 4, 29

Bargaining, 39, 66, 111
    in the executive branch, 70–81
    manipulated, 42, 44, 63
    in private organizations, 40, 46
    pure, 41–42, 44–46, 69–70, 78, 80,
        144
Bureau of the Budget, 129, 229, 233,
        235, 240
Bureaucracy
    advantages of, 7–10
    characteristics of, 2–7
    composite image of, 14
    and decision making, 15–19
    definition of, 1, 7
    differences between private and pub-
        lic organizations, 59
    disadvantages of, 10–19
    and efficiency, 30
    governmental and nongovernmental,
        differences between, 20
    limited resources of, 52
    and socialization, 9, 100
    and specialization, 8–9
        dysfunctions of, 23–26

Bureaucratic behavior
    and anxiety, 43, 100
    effects of anxiety on, 98–99
    informal, 43
    and subjective values, 128–29
Bureaucratic and nonbureaucratic
    structures, differences between,
        3, 9, 14, 18–19
Bureaucratic structures, difference be-
    tween private and public, 55

Career officials, 76–78
Conflict
    difference between private and pub-
        lic organizations, 53, 57–58, 63,
        69, 71
    in executive branch, 51–53
    causes of, 53–63
    inevitability of, 21–27
    reciprocal control of, 32–33
    unilateral control of, 43–44
Congress and annual review sessions,
        74–76
Congressional committees
    and career executive officials, 76–78
    and executive branch control, 71–77
    influence of, on executive subordi-
        nates, 123
    and middle level executive officials,
        75
Congressional expectations and ad-
    ministrative performance, 75
Congressional jurisdiction and execu-
    tive branch, 72
Congressional preference for admin-
    istrative details, 72–74

Consensus-building function, 221
Consolidation, 181–82, 184–85, 188
    basic component of, 181
    and the executive branch, 189–213
    and the executive departments, 207–
        12
    and executive reorganization, 207–
        11
    and the federal system, 200
    and the individual, 195–200
    and innovation, difference between,
        183
    and intradepartmental subunits,
        201–7
    model of, 187
    and pattern maintenance, 182
Consolidative behavior, 184, 186–87
Control
    and authority, 37–39
    and bargaining, 39–42
    conditions for effective, 52
    direct, 37–41, 43, 52, 72, 80, 111
        dysfunctions of, 64–65
        limitations of in executive branch,
            66
        and manipulated agreement, 44–
            46
        and manipulated persuasion, 35–
            37
        and objective analysis, 44–46
        of private organizations, 43
        and problem solving, 34
        and pure persuasion, 34–35
    techniques of, 80
        differences between private and
            public bureaucracies, 80–81
Corporation executives, tenure of, 59–
    61
Cost analysis and federal government,
    56–58

Decision making
    and access to information, 112, 165–
        67
    aspects of, 83–103
    and bureaucracy, 15–18
    as a composite process, 106–11
    and consensus, 110–11

differences between private and
    public bureaucracies, 111, 126
and direct control, 111
in the executive branch, limitations
    on, 111–18
and expertise, 15
and foreign policy, 106
and formal authority, 95–96
heuristic, 98–103
influence in by subordinate admin-
    istrators, 23
informal, 8–9
and the Kennedy administration,
    22–23
limitations of rational choice, 86–89
and manipulated persuasion, 111
nonprogrammed, 85, 88, 128
nonrational, 98–103, 123–24
and optimizing-satisfying, 89–95,
    124–26
and organizational values, 95
and primacy of political considera-
    tions, 57
programmed, 84
psychological aspects of, 113, 123–
    24
and rational choice, 84–85
and subjective rationality, 95–98,
    118–23
and subjective values, 9
and systems analysis, 228–38
and uncertainty, 92–94, 96, 125
Directions and forces of change, in-
    terrelationship between, 184–
    85
Directions of change, 178–84, 186
    choice between, 239–41
    and conflict resolution, 245–48
    and decision making, 242–45
    nonequal alternatives, 241–42

Economic Cooperation Administra-
    tion, 6–7, 132, 218, 222
Eisenhower administration, 54
Executive branch
    and annual review sessions, 74–76
    and congressional jurisdiction, 72–
        73

Executive branch (*cont.*)
  and cost analysis, 56–58
  and career officials, 76–78
  and decentralization, 49–51
  and manipulated agreement, 63–70
  and profit incentive, 55–58
Executive branch career officials
  formal structure of, 47–51
  and presidential control, 67–69
Executive branch conflict, causes of,
    53–63
Executive branch consolidation, 189–
    213
  and civil service system, 195–200
  and the individual, 195–200
  and intradepartmental subunits,
    201–7
Executive branch control, and the po-
    litical subsystem, 79–81
Executive branch decision making,
    105–30
  as a composite process, 106–11
  and foreign policy, 106–9
  irrevocable aspects of, 125–26
  nonrational, 123–24
  optimizing-satisfying, 124–26
  and subjective rationality, 118–23
  and withholding information, 112–
    17
Executive branch innovation, 214–38
Executive branch loyalty, 123–24, 142
  and conflicting demands, 149–50
  and defensive behavior, 165–70
  and external groups, 168–70
  influence of Congress on, 153–65
  limitations, 144–53
  and persuasion, 144
  and political conflict, 150–53
Executive branch subsystem, 66–69
Executive officials
  dependence of on subordinates, 16,
    23, 112
  tenure of, 59–61
Expertise, 8–9
  and decision making, 16
  dysfunctions of, 23–26
External groups, 78, 80–81, 149–50,
    152

and the executive branch, 70–81
influence of on decision making,
    123–24
influence of on executive branch
    foreign policy, 107–8
and private corporations, 70–71

Federal career service
  and executive branch consolidation,
    195–200
  and executive branch loyalty, 144–
    49
Forces of change, 172–78, 180–81,
    184–87
Forces and directions of change, inter-
    relationship between, 184–85
Foreign Operations Administration,
    159, 219
Frames-of-reference, 263–65

Goal attainment, 173, 184
Goals
  ambiguity of, 12
  and organization, 12

Heuristic decision making, 98–103

Information, consolidation of, 17
Innovation, 184–85, 188, 194, 261
  achieving, 215
  and creation of new operating units,
    217–19
  and decision making, 227–38
  encouraging, 224–38
  and the executive branch, 214–38
  and formal planning units, 215–17
  and goal attainment, 184
  and management development pro-
    grams, 224–27
  and operating efficiency, 180
  and Presidential Commissions, 220–
    24
  and systems analysis, 228–38
Innovative behavior, 182–84, 186–87,
    242–43
Innovative decisions and uncertainty,
    200

Integration, 173, 175–78, 184
Interest groups
    and congressional committees, 78–81
    and executive branch control, 78–81
International Cooperation Administration, 155, 205, 219

Loyalty of executive officials
    to external groups, 123–24
    to President, 123–24

Manipulated agreement, 63–70, 80, 245
Mutual Security Administration, 6–7, 219

Nationalization of political conflict, 244–45
Nonprogrammed activity, 211, 219

Objective analysis, 63, 245
Optimizing and decision making, 89–95, 242
Organization
    and formal authority, 4
    and informal behavior, 5
    continuity, 6
    growth, 3
    political aspects of, 33
    psychological aspects of, 33, 98–103
    sociological aspects of, 33
Organization conflict between experts and nonexperts, 25–26
Organizational behavior
    and anxiety, 138
    control of, 11–15
    restricting discretionary, 165–68
Organizational change
    and adaptation, 173–75
    anticipatory, 178–81
    and anxiety, 177
    and consolidation, 181–82
    and differences between private and public bureaucracies, 249–60
    directions of, 178–84
    forces of, 173–78

in executive branch, 259
and the future, 260–67
and goal attainment, 173
and innovation, 182–84
and integration, 173
and pattern maintenance, 173
responsive, 178–81
suggested relationships, 242–48
and systems analysis, 247
a theoretical model, 172–88
Organizational conflict, 177
Organizational continuity, 58–63, 65
    and tenure, 58–61
Organizational discontinuity, 58–63
Organizational effectiveness and the profit motive, 55–58
Organizational expertise, 8
    and decision making, 16
Organizational goals, 13, 34
    ambiguity of, 53–58
Organizational hostility, 42
Organizational innovation, 192
Organizational loyalty, 13, 131–71
    and anxiety-reward balance, 137
    and conflicting demands, 134–36, 140–42
    defined, 134–37
    development of, 137–40
    differences between private and public bureaucracies, 169–70
    in the executive branch, 142
    reciprocal, 150–53
Organizational resources, limitations of, 26–27
Organizational rewards, 27
Organizational theory
    and interpersonal behavior, 32–33
    and scientific management, 28–31
Organizational values, 10, 95, 97–98, 135, 195
    and decision making, 119, 123
Organizations, ambiguous goals of, 86

Pattern maintenance, 173, 182
Personnel management and the difference between private and public bureaucracies, 201

Persuasion, 39
  manipulated, 35–37, 44–45, 63, 66,
    69, 144
Policy-administration dichotomy, 15–
    18
Policy makers, and access to informa-
    tion, 4, 17–19
Policy making, influence of subordi-
    nate administrative officials on,
    16–19
Politics of analysis, 265–67
Politics of bargaining, 262–65
President and Cabinet, 120–21, 129
Presidential control
  of career officials, 67–69
  of executive branch, limitations on,
    64–70
  of independent regulatory commis-
    sions, 68
  span of, 65–66
Primary frame of reference, 140, 150
  and organizational loyalty, 136
Problem solving, 34, 39, 63
Programmed activity, 210, 219
Programmed decisions and consolida-
    tion, 213

Reciprocal loyalty in the executive
    branch, 150–53
Responsive change, 178–81, 184, 242–
    43
  and consolidation, 181–82

"Satisfying" and decision making, 89–
    95
Span of control, 65–66
Subjective rationality and decision
    making, 89–95

Uncertainties, 125
  and consolidation, 191
United States
  Corps of Engineers, 56, 66, 201–3
  Department of Defense, 56–57, 67,
    108, 120, 162, 240, 247, 266
  Federal Bureau of Investigation,
    67, 115, 122, 148
  Foreign Aid Program, 6, 56, 62, 131,
    155, 159, 204–7, 219, 221
  State Department, 49, 57, 68, 108,
    120, 155, 204, 211–12, 215–16

## DATE DUE

| | | | |
|---|---|---|---|
| MAR 19 '75 | MAR 10 '75 | | |
| DE 7 '83 | DEC 5 '83 | | |
| | | | |
| | | | |
| | | | |
| | | | |
| | | | |
| | | | |
| | | | |
| | | | |
| | | | |
| | | | |
| | | | |
| | | | |
| | | | |
| | | | |
| | | | |
| GAYLORD | | | PRINTED IN U.S.A. |